IMAGES
of America

PALISADES PARK

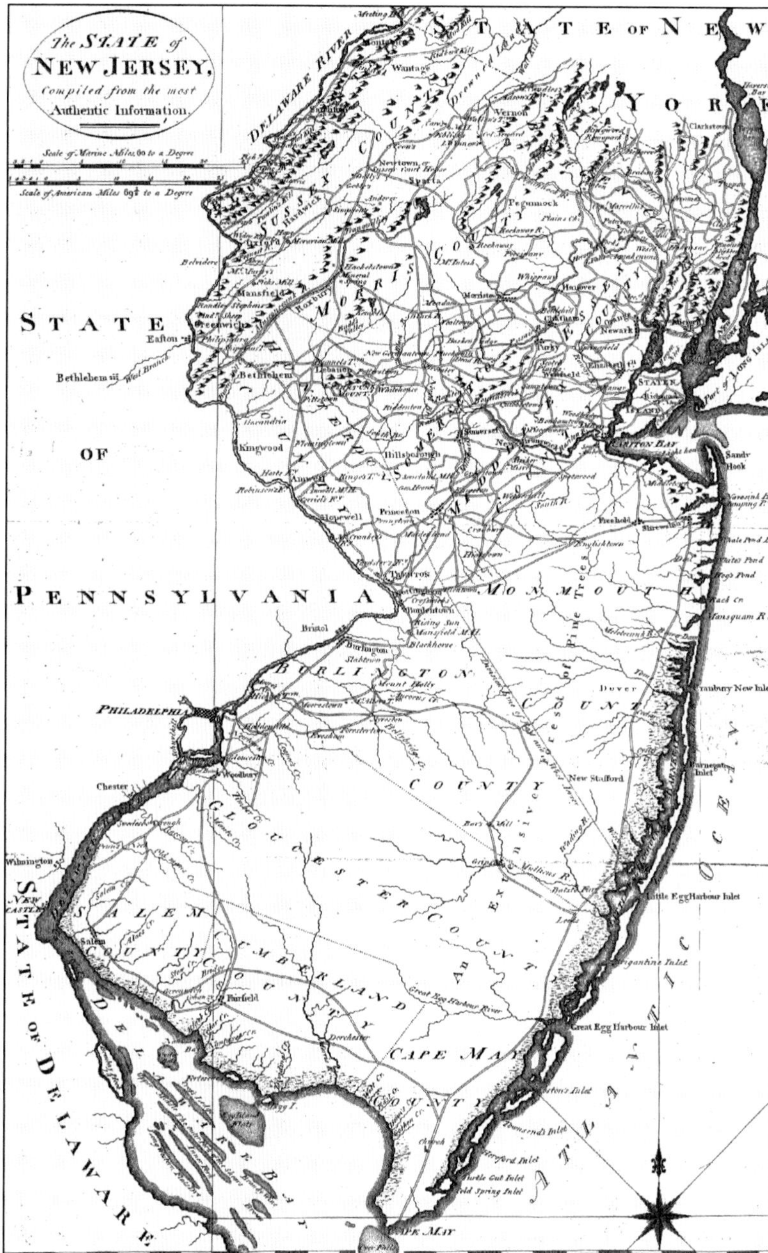

This 1795 map of the state of New Jersey depicts an area of land called English Neighborhood; a segment of this is now present-day Palisades Park. In 1871, parts of this English Neighborhood separated from Hackensack Township and organized into the Township of Ridgefield, which consisted of present-day Ridgefield, Ridgefield Park, Edgewater, Cliffside Park, Edgewater, Fort Lee, Leonia, and Palisades Park. The Borough Act of 1878 allowed areas among townships to split and incorporate. By the time Palisades Park formed on March 22, 1899, from portions of Ridgefield Township, all but Fort Lee were already swept in the "boroughitis" craze of the late 19th century.

On the cover: Please see page 118. (Courtesy of Leonard R. Cottrell.)

IMAGES
of America

PALISADES PARK

George M. Beck Jr.

ARCADIA
PUBLISHING

ISBN 978-0-7385-6543-9

Published by Arcadia Publishing
Charleston SC, Chicago IL, Portsmouth NH, San Francisco CA

Printed in the United States of America

Library of Congress Control Number: 2008941496

For all general information contact Arcadia Publishing at:
Telephone 843-853-2070
Fax 843-853-0044
E-mail sales@arcadiapublishing.com
For customer service and orders:
Toll-Free 1-888-313-2665

Visit us on the Internet at www.arcadiapublishing.com

To my parents, family, and Megan, who always encourage my ambitions. To them and all the residents, both past and present, who love Palisades Park, I dedicate this book.

Contents

Acknowledgments

First and foremost, I would like to thank the wonderful residents who contributed photographs, stories, and enthusiasm to complete this book. Special thanks to Evelyn Meier for the photographs and hours spent discussing local history and fond memories. Thanks to George J. Farrell and Arthur Anderson for the days spent over coffee, sharing memories and helping to record history accurately. Thanks to Carol Miraglia for the photographs and her sharp historical knowledge. Thanks to municipal historian Thomas Albanese and his wife Alice for their help securing images and historical information. Thank you to Leonia historian and author Carol Karels for her expert guidance. Thanks to the Palisades Park Public Library staff, especially Steven Cavallo, who painted two beautiful portraits for this book, and director Susan Kumar. Thanks to Harriet Burdock, Leonia Public Library archivist, and library director Deborah Bigelow. Thank you to former mayor Robert Pallotta for the photographs and information. Thanks to the Palisades Park High School, especially Maureen Tansey. Thanks to James Burns for all his help. Thanks to Andy Nam and Charlie Park for the photographs and the time spent discussing local history and Korean traditions. Thanks to Albino Matesic and Jason Mladjenovic from Talle Creative for assistance scanning and preserving images.

A special thanks to retired police captain Leonard R. Cottrell and retired police captain Robert Payton for the terrific photographs and historic police information. Thanks to retired chief of police Alan Lustman and retired police captain Remo Framarin for the photographs and the time spent discussing the history of the police department. Thank you to Chief Michael Vietri of the police department for the photographs and historical information. Thanks to Fire Chief Steven Killion for the photographs and information.

Thank you to all who have contributed photographs and/or information, especially George M. Beck Sr., Greggory K. Beck, Florence Moran, Pastor David Peng, Fr. Armando Palmieri, Fr James Reilly, Charles Martini, school principal Tony Bongrad, Peter Karadontes, Peter Sassano, James Benedetto, and Joseph Kurz. Recognition must also be given to the people who worked on the committees and contributed to the three Palisades Park history books: the 1949 *Golden Jubilee*, 1976 *Bicentennial Looking Back* edition, and the 1999 *Centennial Edition*. Their work is excellent.

Unless otherwise noted, all images appear courtesy of the author.

INTRODUCTION

Chapter 1 highlights the early years of Palisades Park. Well before Henry Hudson anchored his *Half Moon* in 1609, Chief Oratam (born 1577) of the Ashkineshacky Indians—a subgroup of the Unami, or Turtle Clan, of the Lenni-Lenape Indians—occupied the land with his tribe. There were about 1,000 Ashkineshacky Indians living in the area. They fished, farmed, and hunted peacefully. The Dutch originally settled on the Manhattan Island, which they called New Amsterdam. In 1630, independent Dutch immigrants began to expand and settle along the Hackensack River, erecting primitive log huts. Their relationship with the Native Americans was initially peaceful; however, as the Dutch began to expand their activities, irritations soon developed. The Dutch sold the Ashkineshacky Indians brandy, and quarrels became routine. The Ashkineshacky Indians were also plagued with intertribal difficulties, which reached a boiling point in 1643 when rampaging Native Americans went on a warpath, massacring or capturing nearly all white dwellers in the area. Due to the dangerous environment in the area, heavy settlement was discouraged until 1667, when peace was established after England forced out the Dutch.

In the early Colonial days, Palisades Park was part of the township of Hackensack, which encompassed almost all of present-day Bergen County. A segment of this land was known as English Neighborhood, a name given to the locality lying between the Hudson and Overpeck Creek. It encompassed present-day Fairview to Englewood. The land consisted mostly of farms, brooks, ponds, and springs. Most of the dwellings were set up along King's Highway, a crude and important roadway. In 1869, the state legislature renamed it Grand Avenue, and improvement began on the roadway. A year later in 1870, Broad Avenue was opened. In 1871, Palisades Park became part of Ridgefield Township and remained until March 22, 1899, when it was incorporated as a borough.

Chapter 2 traces the roots of Samuel Edsall. Much can be said about this pioneering family, which is among the oldest in Bergen County. The Palisade Park Edsalls are descendants of Samuel Edsall, a Hollander who emigrated from Reading, Berkshire, England, in 1649, during a period following the Siege of Reading, a part of the first English civil war. Samuel Edsall came to the colonies in the ship *Tryall*, which was mastered by Thomas Graves of Charlestown, Massachusetts. The *Tryall* set sail in May and arrived in July 1649. Between 1649 and 1655, little is known about Samuel Edsall; however, he was most probably engaged in trading furs with the Native Americans. During 1655, he married his first wife Jannetje Wessels in New Amsterdam. That same year he obtained a grant for a village plot in lower New Amsterdam from Gov. Peter Stuyvesant. Nearly opposite this lot on the shore was the weight house, which projected into the East River, the only wharf of the infant city. On this plot of land, Samuel Edsall erected a brick house modeled after the

Dutch pattern. In 1657, he was a "hoode-maker" or hatmaker, who prepared beaver skins for sale or export. Over the next few years, Edsall went on a trading expedition to Long Island, north on the Hudson River, and south of the Delaware River. He was proficient in Native American tongues and became a highly sought after translator from both the Dutch and English. In 1663, Edsall was appointed by Governor Stuyvesant as an ensign in the Esopus War of 1663. A year later he took the oath of allegiance to the English Crown, and shortly after he moved from New Amsterdam to Bergen. He was actively involved in politics and in 1668 became a member of Gov. Philip Carteret's council, a post he held for many years.

Edsall's roots in what is now Palisades Park came early in 1668 when he and Capt. Nicholas Verlett secured a grant for 1,820 acres at Bulls' Ferry, along the Hudson River, nearly to what is now Fort Lee, and stretching inland to Hackensack and Overpeck Creek. On this land he built farms, and his tenants tilled the land. The land later became the individual property of Samuel Edsall and his descendants, who included the borough of Palisades Park's first mayor, John S. Edsall.

Over the next 10 years, Edsall continued to reside in New Jersey; however, he spent the bulk of his time in New York and engaged in trading ventures in the Virginias, mostly for tobacco, while also serving as juror and arbitrator in New York and providing interpreting services between the governor and the Native Americans during important occasions at Fort James. He sometimes practiced in the courts, most notably in the case of Amigart Pappegoia, daughter of New Sweden's ex-governor Johan Printz, for whom he appeared in her first suit to recover Tinicum Island on the Delaware.

During Edsall's life, he married three or four times; however, the Edsalls of Palisades Park are descendants of Johannes, son from Samuel's first marriage to Jannetje Wessels. Johannes was baptized in New Amsterdam on September 12, 1660. He became an educated man, having received his tuition from Rev. Charles Wolley, chaplain of the fort in New York. Johannes married Charity Smith at Bergen on May 3, 1691. He preferred a more quiet, less political life, living on the estate in Bergen County he inherited from his father, known as English Neighborhood. Johannes died in 1714, leaving behind a son Samuel, who became Bergen's first sheriff in 1740. It was this Samuel who built one of the first dwellings in Palisades Park.

The first mayor, John S. Edsall, is a great-grandson of Samuel Edsall and Naomi Christinia Day. His grandfather was John Edsall, and his grandmother was Gertrude Lydecker. His father was Samuel, who married Isabella Christie. He grew up in Palisades Park on his father's farm, where he and his brother Samuel S. became skilled farmers. In 1894, he and his brother Samuel S. formed a partnership in a real estate firm named Edsall Brothers Real Estate. Throughout the real estate venture, both brothers maintain their farming interests.

Chapter 3 highlights Palisades Park's infancies. After the borough was incorporated, advancements in transportation and its small-town character attracted many New York City families to relocate to the beautiful undeveloped land, sparking massive growth. Residents gathered on Monday, April 24, 1899, to witness the installation of their newly elected mayor and council. Mayor John S. Edsall and councilmen-elect Michael Reid, Louis Schlumberger, Robert McDonald, and Henry Scholz were sworn into office by justice of the peace E. A. Gantert. The new council was two members short, as three of the remaining candidates each received 49 votes. Differences over a tiebreaking procedure developed, and it was not until several meetings later that John P. Davis and Daniel Kruger were finally sworn into the council, completing the new governing body.

Council meetings were held at the Goodwin Building on the corner of Central Boulevard and Grand Avenue until property could be secured to build a municipal building. Mayor John S. Edsall led the council to adopt its first ordinance on June 12, 1899, granting a franchise to the Hackensack Gas and Electric Company to construct and maintain service lines through the municipality. Ordinances were also adopted to regulate the use of carriages and other vehicles on municipal streets. Discussions began about the development of roads and sidewalks. The paving of Central Boulevard from Seventh Street to Anderson Avenue was the first major street improvement. A year later, in 1900, John S. Edsall's cousin John G. Edsall was sworn in as Palisades Park's second mayor. Under his leadership, the property on the southwest corner of Broad Avenue and Central Boulevard was purchased from Catherine Moran for $900.

In 1905, a two-story framed municipal building was erected. The building was also used as a classroom for local schoolchildren. Sadly, in June 1906, fire destroyed this new borough hall. Abram Cottrell, proprietor of the Heisenbuttle Hotel on West Central Boulevard near the Erie Railroad, offered the use of his hall for municipal matters. His offer was accepted. During this time, the borough's third mayor, Edward A. Gantert, presided over municipal issues and positive growth continued. Advancements in transportation, schools, streets, and sewage systems were either modernized or developed in some areas of the borough to accommodate the vastly growing population.

Chapter 4 highlights landscape and streetscape scenes. Emphasis on churches, halls, monuments, schools, and other scenes of freedom are detailed in this chapter. Religious freedom has been the hallmark of Palisades Park and many other communities across country since the birth of this wonderful nation. Residents from different faiths have settled, built houses of worship, and lived among others with different religious beliefs without fear of persecution. The education of the children has long been a top priority. Well-built and modernized schools were constructed throughout the years to handle the growing school-aged population. From the days of a single schoolhouse on Grand Avenue west of Harwood Terrace built in 1802 to the recently built Early Childhood Learning Center, the commitment to educate the youth has remained true.

Moving ahead into chapter 5, a candid view into the life and spirit of the community presents itself. Palisades Park has a long-celebrated history of volunteerism, service, and community togetherness. Throughout the years, Palisades Park has become the loving home for many people from diverse ethnicities. Over the last 400 years, Palisades Park has welcomed large groups of Dutch, English, Italian, Polish, Japanese, Croatian, Korean, Hispanic, and other dwellers. Each of these groups brought a unique piece of their heritage to the land in the spirit of freedom and the principals for which this country was founded. Athletics and leisure have contributed to the spirit of Palisades Park. Semiprofessional, municipal, and school-organized ball clubs have enjoyed much success over the years. This chapter is a glimpse into the people and their service, heritage, and enthusiasm.

In chapter 6, the history of the police department is presented. Over 20 years after the Borough of Palisades Park was organized, Mayor Robert Todd and councilman/police commissioner Albert King instituted the Palisades Park Police Department on December 14, 1920. For many years prior, policing was operating with either a constable or marshal, who was appointed by the mayor and council. However, the growth of the borough and the rapid influx of new residents required the need for an organized police department with sworn police officers patrolling the streets and protecting the community. The first sworn police officer was Joseph J. Shokoff, who previously served as a marshal/constable for several years. He was appointed with William R. Romaine, who resigned 17 days later, and David J. W. Bell was appointed to fill the vacancy. A small front room in the borough hall was used as police headquarters, and large telephone bells were affixed to the outside of the building. The department was usually unattended, and these bells were used to summon the patrolman. During this time, all calls were answered on foot. The appointment of patrolman Robert E. MacDonald in 1922 expanded policing services, allowing for an officer to be on active duty 24 hours daily. As development in the eastern half of the borough rapidly increased, the need for a vehicle to respond quickly up the hillside landscape was apparent. In 1924, a Model T Ford was purchased and an officer was assigned to motor vehicle patrol. Throughout the years the Palisades Park Police Department has grown from a two-patrolman operation into a professional and efficient department bravely serving and protecting the community.

Along the same vein of service and heroism, chapter 7 highlights the brave firefighters. The volunteer fire department was organized on September 24, 1894, when local men gathered to develop a fire protection unit. Their fire apparatus consisted of a chemical engine, hook and ladder, and hose reel purchased in January 1895. The first fire apparatus was pulled by the men throughout the borough to fight house and brush fires. On January 11, 1898, the fire department received its first out-of-town assistance call when 11 men and their apparatus responded to Leonia. The membership of the fire department began to expand, and on October 24, 1904, the original fire company was taken over by the borough. This new municipal unit became Hose Company No. 1, and nearly three months later was officially organized as the borough fire department with Albert Soderlund becoming the first chief.

The rapid growth of the infant borough required additional fire protection. This led to the formation of the hook and ladder company in October 1909, with a nonmotorized hook and ladder apparatus being purchased. Due to the steep hillside in the borough, and the difficulty of pulling the apparatus up the primitive terrain, on November 10, 1910, men who lived at the top of the hill came together to form Hose Company No. 2, a private unit that on September 20, 1911, was officially accepted as a municipal unit. The borough presented the new company with a chemical hand-drawn, hose reel, and hose.

In 1927, the borough erected a firehouse, bringing the three companies together in one centrally located building. Throughout the years, the fire department has grown from a small group of brave men fighting fires with hand-drawn apparatus to a fully functional professional unit with modernized equipment and professionally trained firefighters and officers, who maintain the brotherhood of their founding fathers, providing exceptional and heroic service, risking their lives for the betterment of others and the community they love.

Palisades Park closes with the tradition of services to the community, accenting the ambulance volunteers who have given generously and cared much for the residents. The Palisades Park Ambulance Corps was formed in 1938. The American Legion, Edward Parkyn Post No. 48, presented the members their first ambulance that same year, which they housed on Henry Avenue. The corps began to grow, and fund-raising events were headed by Major John J. Dickerson, honorary chairman; Dr. Ross B. English, chairman; George Stevens; Verner Cottrell; and Fred Zweil. Eventually the corps received a new ambulance and a garage located on Belleview Place. The corps later moved to its present home at 410 Second Street, where by 1976 it had answered more than 30,000 calls. The corps continues to professionally handle a large volume of calls, serving the residents of Palisades Park as well as neighboring communities through a mutual-aid agreement.

In closing, *Palisades Park* has provided a unique view of the community and the people who have settled and enjoyed this beautiful sloped land west of the Hudson River. Palisades Park continues to grow and progress into the 21st century, priding itself on its culture, diversity, and advancement.

One

The Early Years

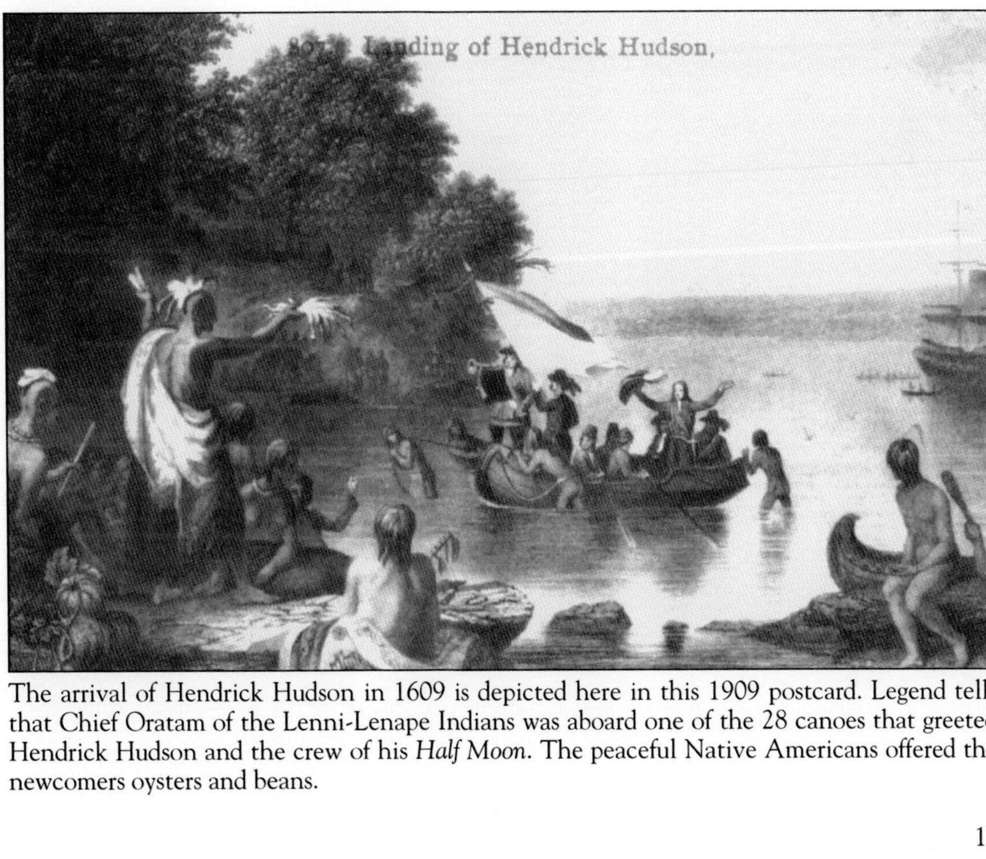

The arrival of Hendrick Hudson in 1609 is depicted here in this 1909 postcard. Legend tells that Chief Oratam of the Lenni-Lenape Indians was aboard one of the 28 canoes that greeted Hendrick Hudson and the crew of his *Half Moon*. The peaceful Native Americans offered the newcomers oysters and beans.

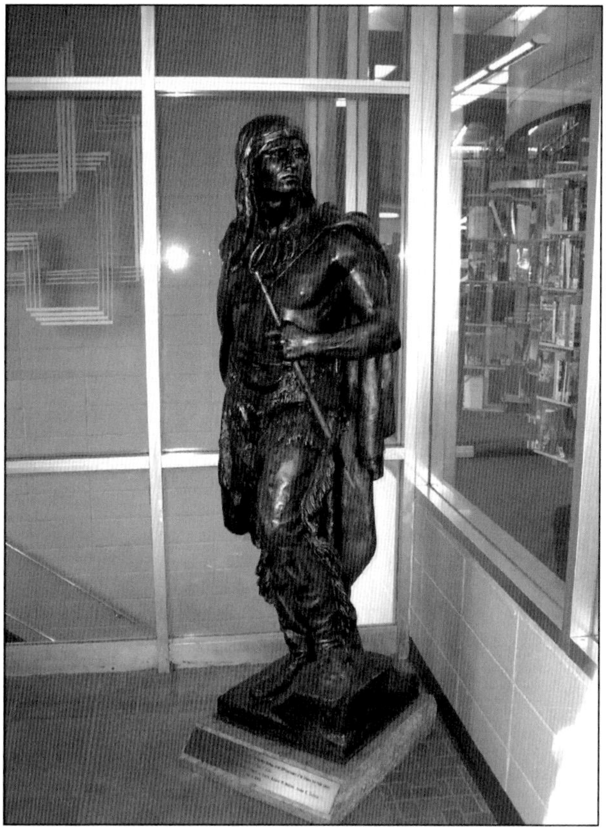

The statue of Chief Oratam is proudly presented in the foyer at the Johnson Library of Hackensack. Oratam's castle was located within Palisades Park in the area of Castle Hill Road (present-day Roff Avenue and East Harwood Terrace). The grant of 1668 to Samuel Edsall and Nicholas Varlett included Oratam's castle in it. Edsall and Varlett obtained this grant a year after Oratam's death.

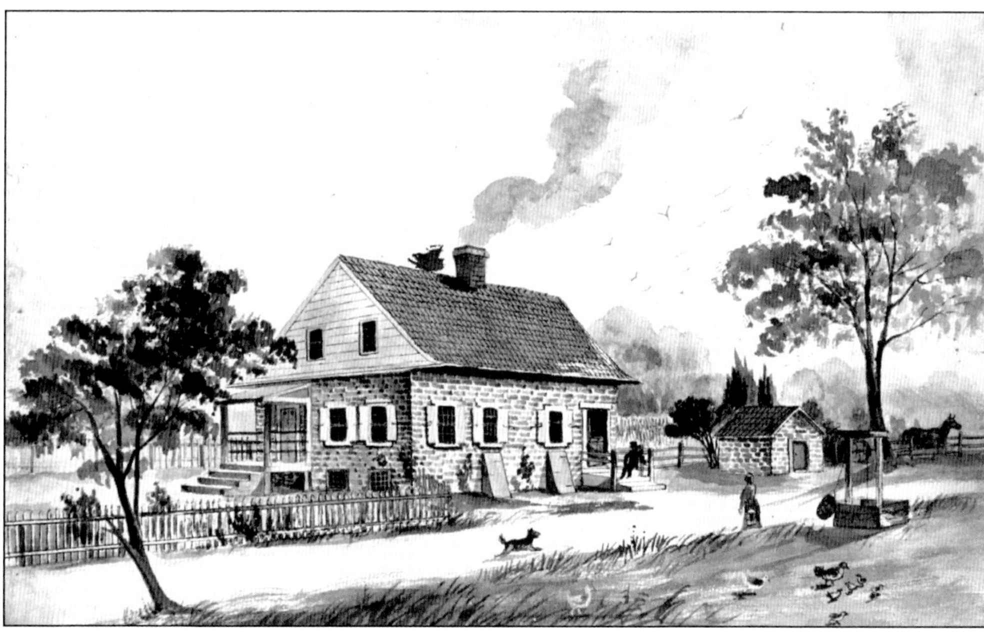

This 18th-century painting shows the old Edsall house located on Grand Avenue, which is perhaps one of the earliest homes in the community. (Courtesy of *Golden Jubilee of 1949*.)

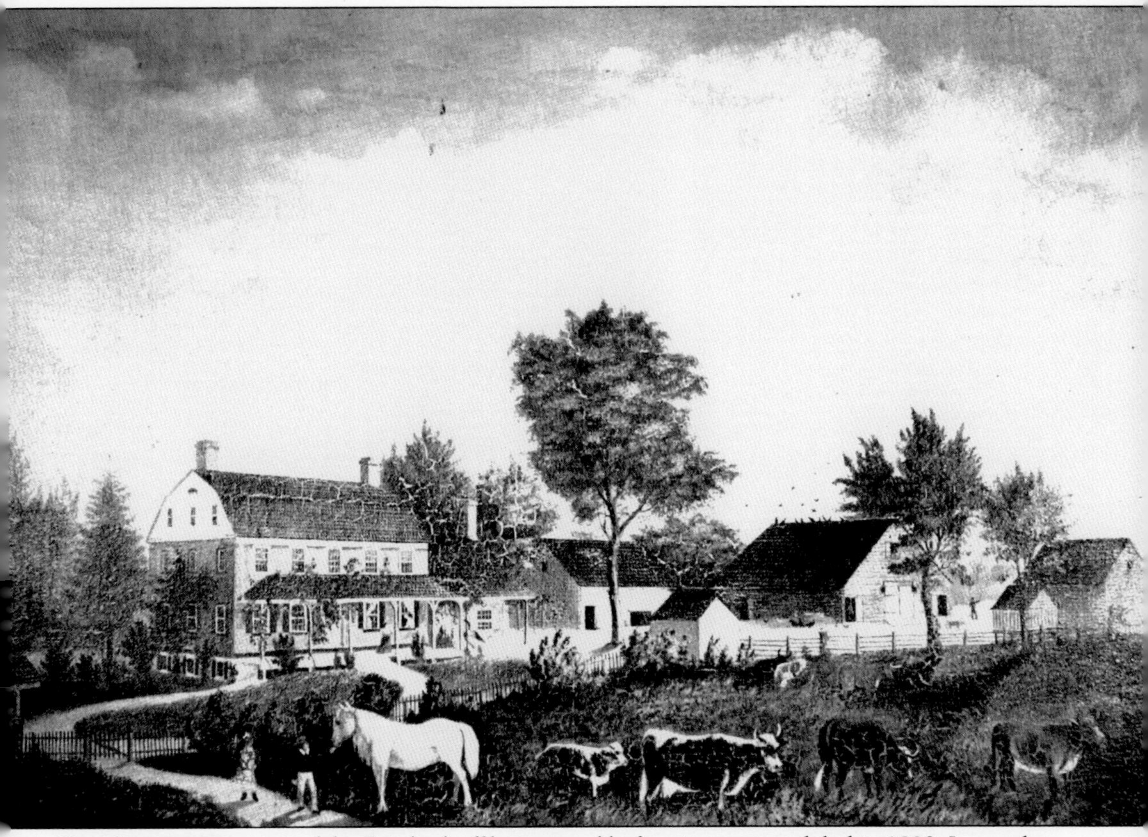

Seen here is a painting of the Brinkerhoff homestead before it was remodeled in 1893. It was the second Brinkerhoff homestead in the borough and was built in 1838 by Henry J. Brinkerhoff. It was torn down in 1925 to allow for the construction of Henry Avenue from Broad Avenue to Grand Avenue. The original Brinkerhoff homestead was built in 1758 by John Brinkerhoff. Members of the Brinkerhoff family of Palisades Park are descendants of Joris Derickson Brinkerhoff of Denthe Province, Holland, who settled at Flushing, Long Island, in 1638. In 1685, his son Hendrick Brinkerhoff purchased 200 acres of land, which is now present-day Ridgefield Park, Bogota, and Teaneck. (Courtesy of *Golden Jubilee of 1949*.)

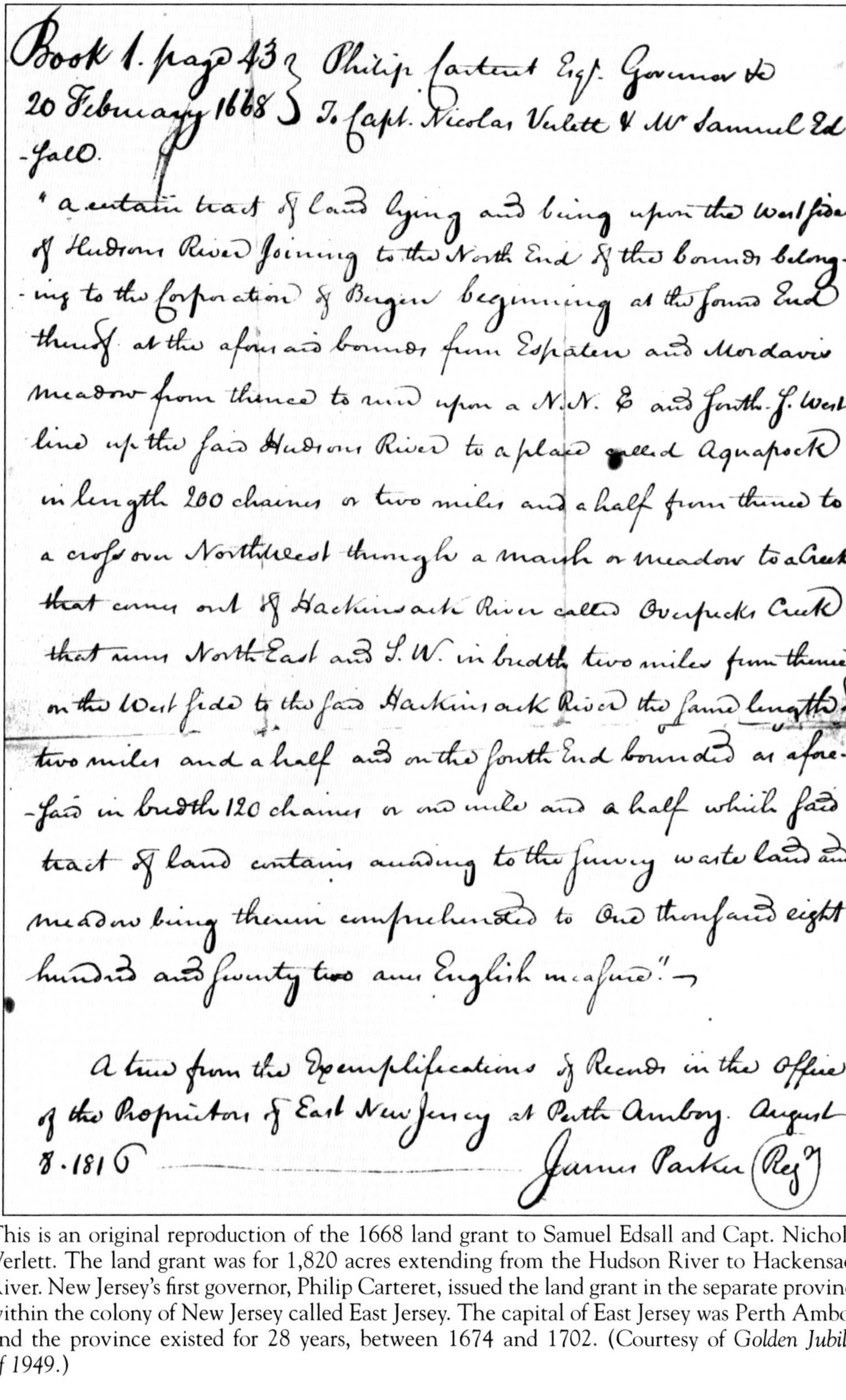
Book 1. page 43 } Philip Carteret Esq. Governor &c
20 February 1668 } To Capt. Nicolas Verlett & Mr Samuel Ed-
-sall.

"a certain tract of land lying and being upon the West side of Hudsons River Joining to the North End of the bounds belong-
-ing to the Corporation of Bergen beginning at the South End thereof at the aforesaid bounds from Espaten and Mordavis meadow from thence to run upon a N.N.E and South S. West line up the said Hudsons River to a place called Aquapock in length 200 chaines or two miles and a half from thence to a cross over Northwest through a marsh or meadow to a Creek that comes out of Hackinsack River called Overpecks Creek that runs North East and S.W. in bredth two miles from thence on the West side to the said Hackinsack River the same length of two miles and a half and on the South End bounded as afore-
-said in bredth 120 chaines or one mile and a half which said tract of land contains according to the survey waste land and meadow being therein comprehended to One thousand eight hundred and twenty two acres English measure."

A true from the Exemplifications of Records in the Office of the Proprietors of East New Jersey at Perth Amboy. August 8. 1816

James Parker (Regr)

This is an original reproduction of the 1668 land grant to Samuel Edsall and Capt. Nicholas Verlett. The land grant was for 1,820 acres extending from the Hudson River to Hackensack River. New Jersey's first governor, Philip Carteret, issued the land grant in the separate province within the colony of New Jersey called East Jersey. The capital of East Jersey was Perth Amboy, and the province existed for 28 years, between 1674 and 1702. (Courtesy of *Golden Jubilee of 1949*.)

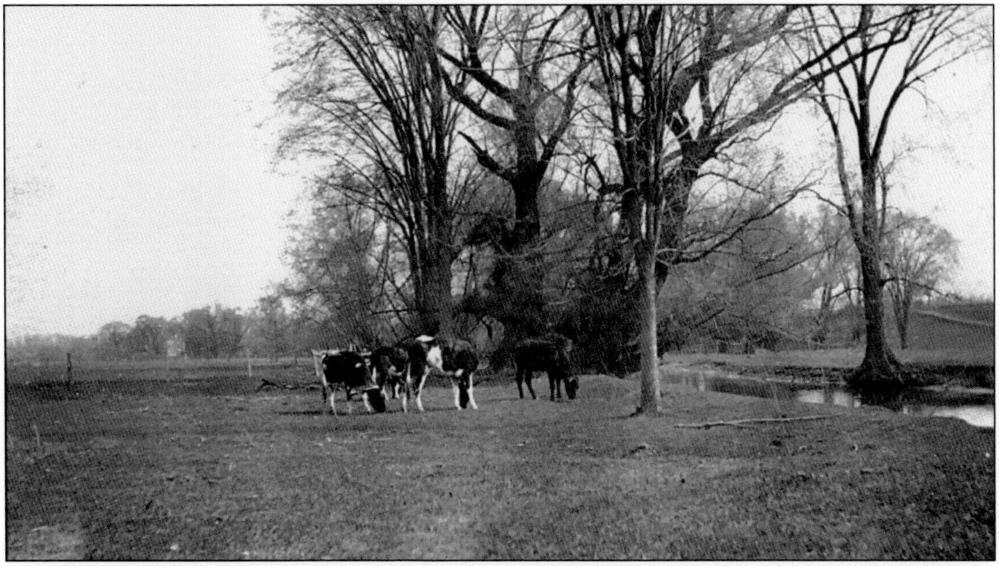

Cows graze on the Edsall farms around 1895. This vast farmland pictured was between present-day Oakdene Avenue and West Edsall Boulevard, looking east toward Broad Avenue. The brook traveled west, emptying into the Overpeck Creek. North of this photograph was the Moore Farms of Leonia. Throughout the years, the Edsall and Moore families intermarried, merging these two pioneering families. (Courtesy of Leonia Public Library.)

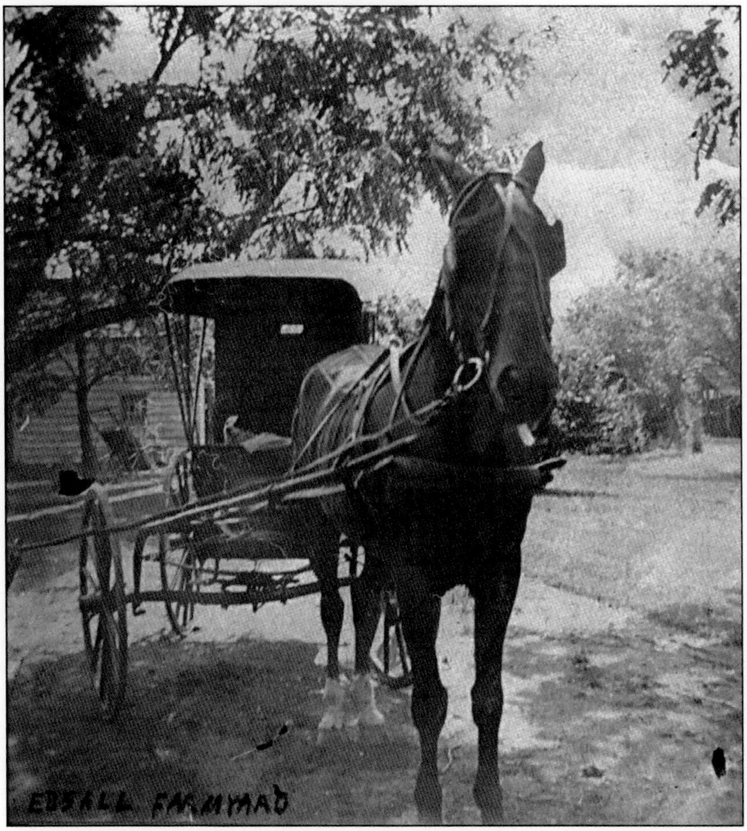

A horse and carriage on the Edsall farmyard are pictured here around 1895. During this period, much of Palisades Park consisted of farmland, scant trails, and wooded areas. Most dwellings were located along Grand Avenue and in proximity. (Courtesy of Leonia Public Library.)

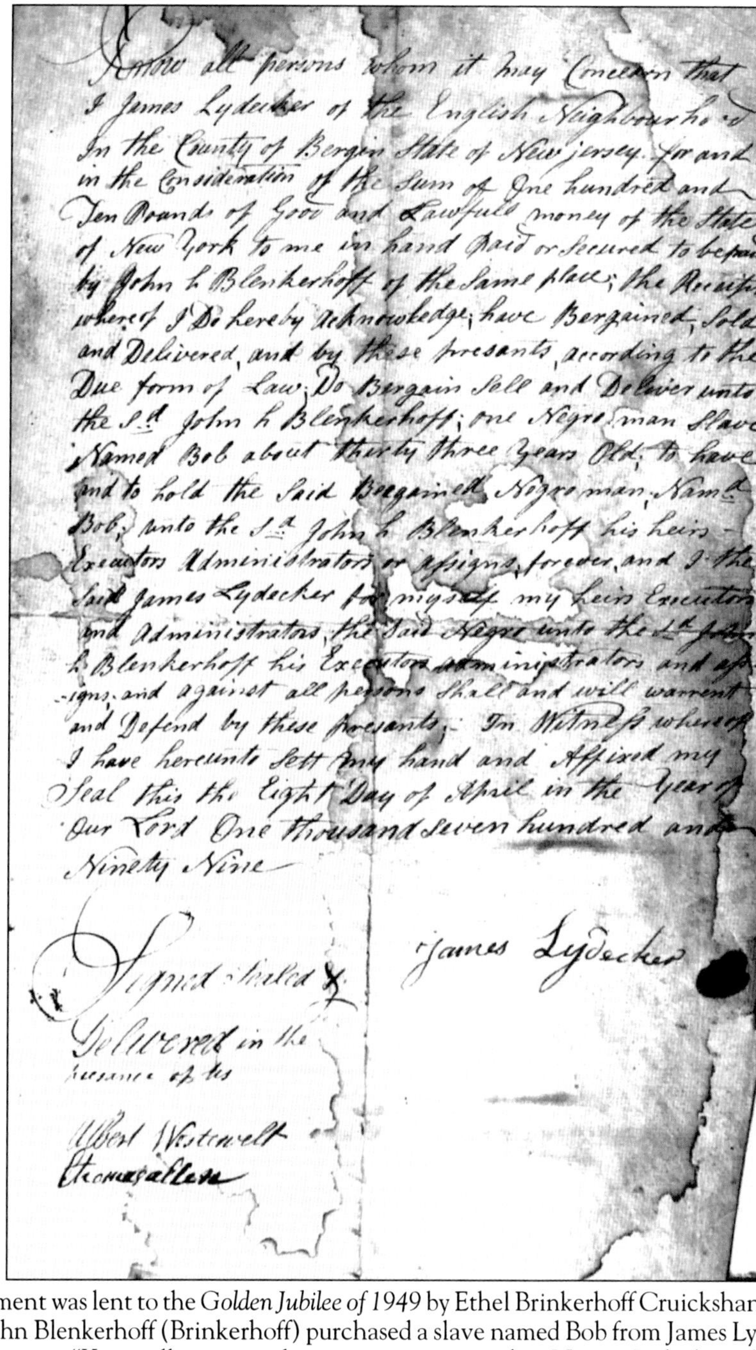
Know all persons whom it may Concern that
I James Lydecker of the English Neighbourhood
In the County of Bergen State of New jersey. for and
in the Consideration of the Sum of One hundred and
Ten Pounds of Good and Lawfull money of the State
of New York to me in hand Paid or Secured to be paid
by John L Blenkerhoff of the Same place; the Receipt
whereof I Do hereby acknowledge; have Bergained, Sold,
and Delivered, and by these presants, according to the
Due form of Law; Do Bergain Sell and Deliver unto
the Sd John L Blenkerhoff; one Negro man Slave
Named Bob about thirty three Years Old; to have
and to hold the Said Bergained Negro man, Namd
Bob, unto the Sd John L Blenkerhoff his heirs -
Executors Administrators or assigns, forever, and I the
Said James Lydecker for myself my heirs Executors
and Administrators, the Said Negro unto the Sd John
L Blenkerhoff his Executors administrators and as-
-signs, and against all persons Shall and will warrent
and Defend by these presants. In Witness whereof
I have hereunto Sett my hand and Affixed my
Seal this the Eight Day of April in the Year of
Our Lord One thousand seven hundred and
Ninety Nine

Signed Sealed & Delivered in the presence of us

James Lydecker

Albert Westervelt
[illegible]

This document was lent to the *Golden Jubilee of 1949* by Ethel Brinkerhoff Cruickshank. On April 8, 1799, John Blenkerhoff (Brinkerhoff) purchased a slave named Bob from James Lydecker. The document states, "Know all persons whom it may concern that I James Lydecker of the English Neighborhood in the County of Bergen State of New Jersey, for and in the consideration of the sum of one hundred and ten pounds of good and lawful money of the State of New York to me in hand paid or secure to be paid by John Blenkerhoff [Brinkerhoff] of the same place, the receipt where of I do hereby acknowledge; have bargained, sold, and delivered, and by these foresants according to the due form of law . . . one negro man slave named Bob about thirty three years old." (Courtesy of *Golden Jubilee of 1949*.)

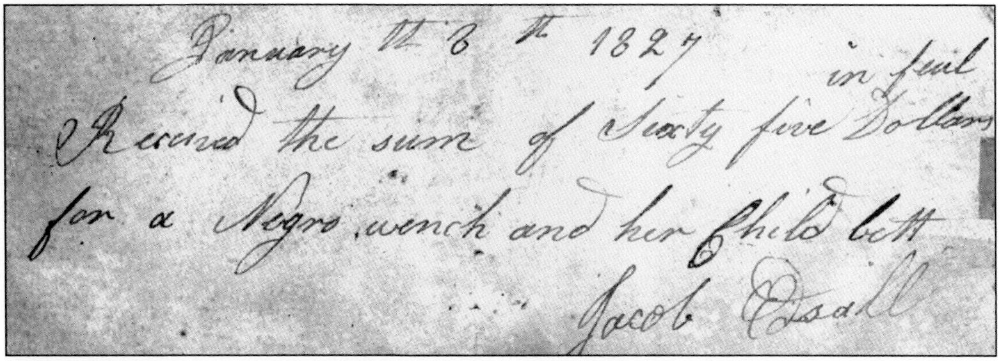

January the 8th 1827 in full
Received the sum of Sixty five Dollars
for a Negro wench and her Child bett
Jacob Edsall

This receipt, dated January 8, 1827, was given by Jacob Edsall for $65 for a "Negro wench and her Child bett." As a matter of history, landowners in the English Neighborhood bought and sold slaves. (Courtesy of *Golden Jubilee of 1949*.)

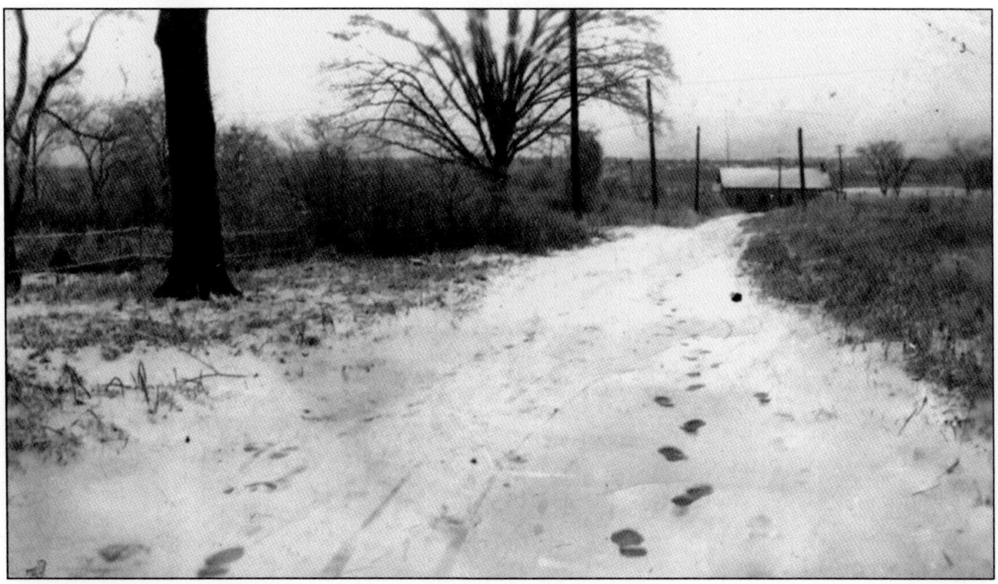

Snow covered a trail slightly south of present-day West Oakdene Avenue on the property of the Edsall family around 1900. This trail led to Grand Avenue at the Civil War drill hall. On the north side of this photograph are the Moore Farms of Leonia. (Courtesy of Leonia Public Library.)

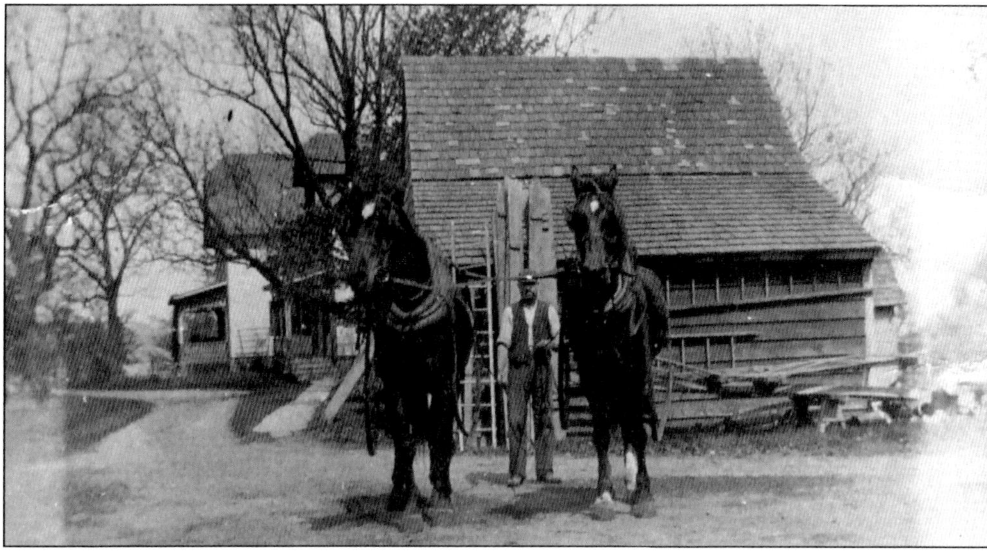

Pictured here about 1899 are the Edsall workhorses with hired hand Cornie. A valuable asset to the Edsall family, these strong horses had many jobs, which included pulling the produce wagon from the Edsall farms to markets in Jersey City and New York City. (Courtesy of Leonia Public Library.)

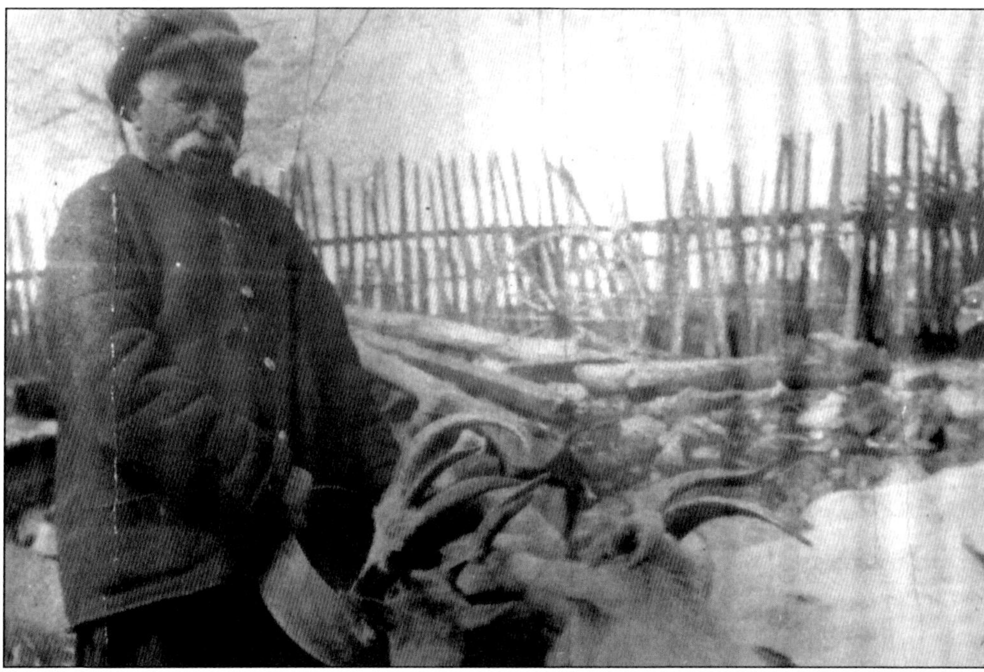

Mr. Brescia feeds his goats in 1895. He had a hilltop farm on what was referred to as Nanny Goat Hill. This steep-sloped rocky land encompassed present-day Sixteenth Street to Seventh Street and was stretched wide from East Edsall Boulevard to East Brinkerhoff Avenue. The goats roamed the hillside and provided milk for drinking purposes and making ricotta cheese. Around 1900, residents of this land were mostly of Italian descent, with many families remaining throughout the generations. Between Ninth and Eleventh Streets, Patsy Pirraglia had 50 goats grazing the land. (Courtesy of Palisades Park Public Library.)

Two

The Edsall Family

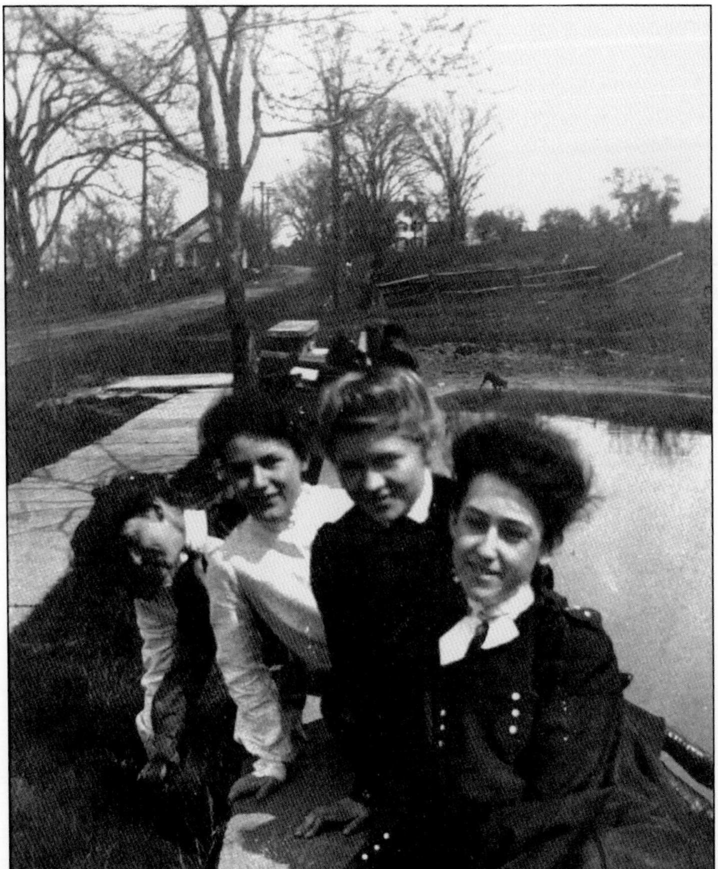

Members of the Edsall family are seen here around 1895, sitting alongside the Edsall pond, which was located at the northeast corner of Grand Avenue and West Edsall Boulevard. The pond had a beautiful waterfall that fell over a wall and under Grand Avenue to the Overpeck Creek. A sand pit was on the southeast corner of West Edsall Boulevard at Grand Avenue. In the distance in the photograph are the Civil War drill hall and the home of the Moore family of Leonia. (Courtesy of Thomas J. Albanese.)

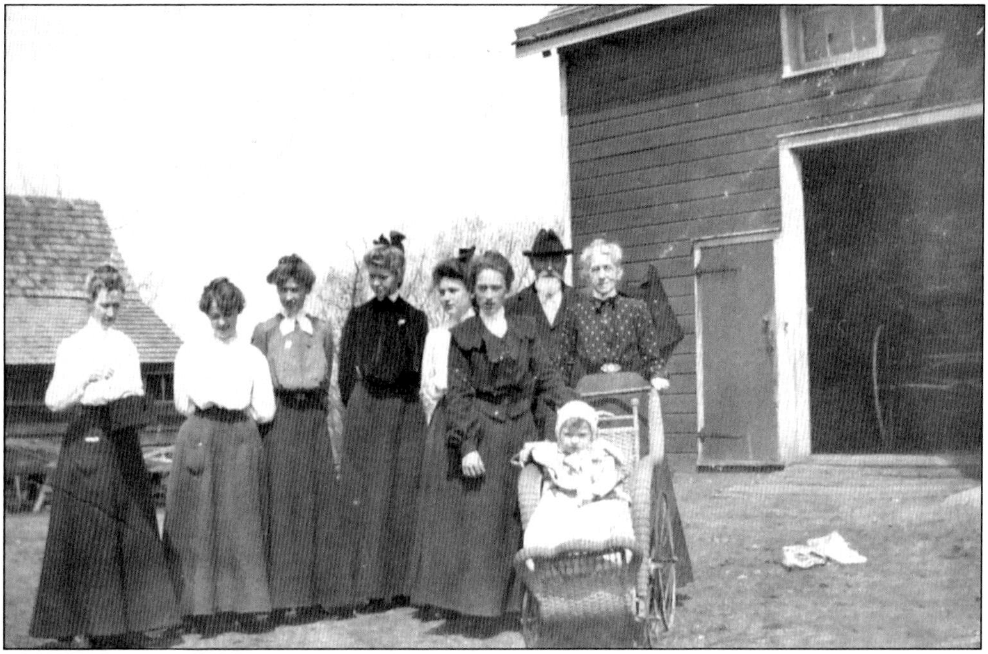

Members of the Edsall family pose for a photograph outside their barn around 1899. The man standing in the photograph is Mayor John S. Edsall, who on February 25, 1858, married Lydia Banta, daughter of Garrett S. Banta. They had eight children: Belle Lena, Mary Agnes, Gertrude, Sarah B., Charles, Garrett, Agnes Naomi, and Lily May. (Courtesy of Leonia Public Library.)

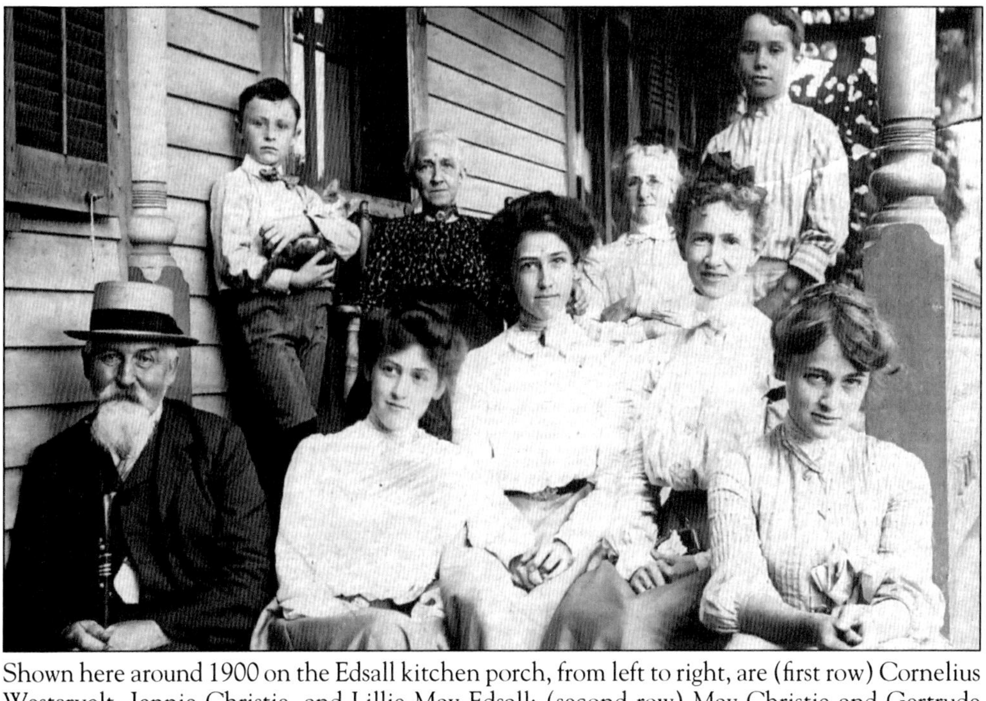

Shown here around 1900 on the Edsall kitchen porch, from left to right, are (first row) Cornelius Westervelt, Jennie Christie, and Lillie May Edsall; (second row) May Christie and Gertrude Edsall; (third row) John Edsall Jr., Lydia Edsall, Sarah Westervelt, and Chas Weber. (Courtesy of Thomas J. Albanese.)

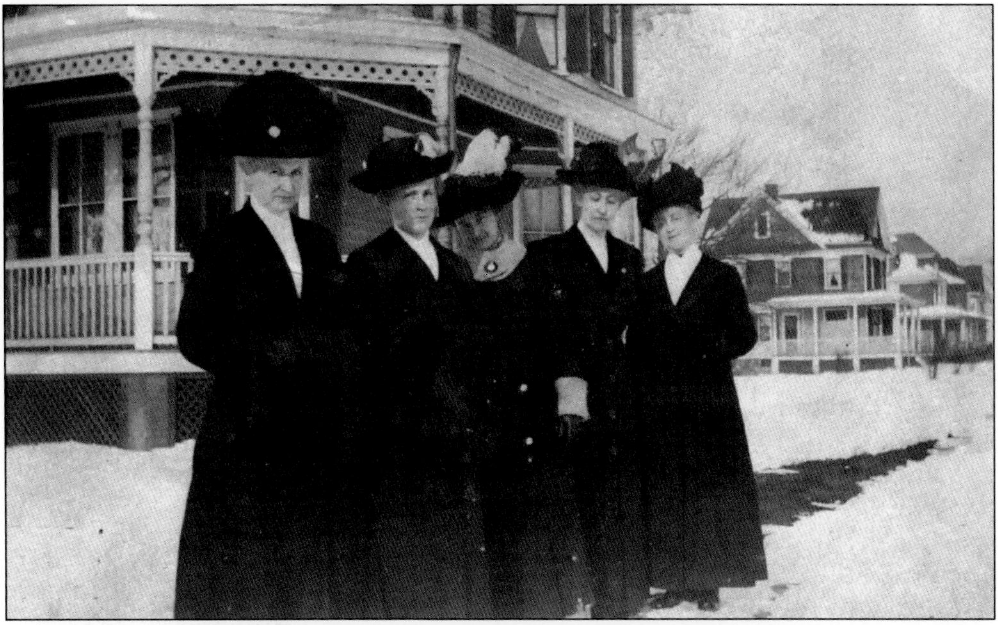

Ladies of the Edsall family, dressed in Victorian fashion, are seen in this *c*. 1905 photograph outside their Grand Avenue homestead on a cold and snowy day. (Courtesy of Leonia Public Library.)

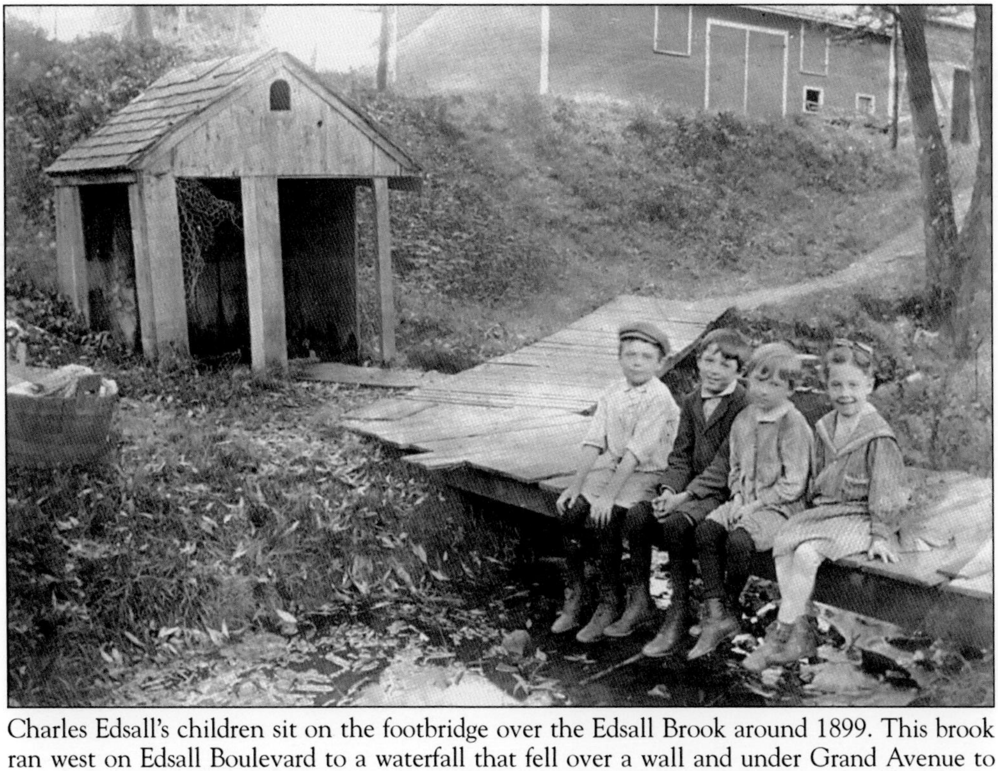

Charles Edsall's children sit on the footbridge over the Edsall Brook around 1899. This brook ran west on Edsall Boulevard to a waterfall that fell over a wall and under Grand Avenue to Overpeck Creek. The Edsall springhouse and barn are in the background. Charles Edsall was the son of John S. Edsall. (Courtesy of Leonia Public Library.)

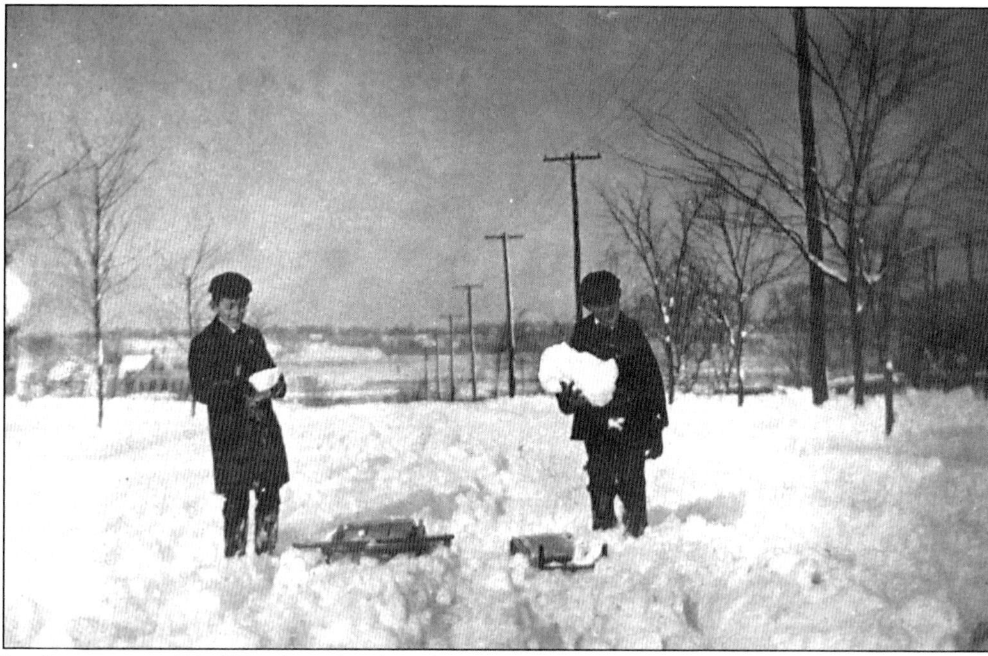

Looking west on Edsall Boulevard, John Edsall Jr. and Harry Moore play in the snow around 1900. During the winter months, the children of Palisades Park enjoyed ice-skating and sleigh riding. Klauser's pond on East Palisades Boulevard or the Fifth Street pond near East Homestead Avenue attracted ice-skating enthusiasts. Sleigh riding was from East Central Boulevard at Twelfth Street to the Erie Railroad tracks. Someone would be stationed at Broad Avenue and Grand Avenue to stop traffic, mostly farmers heading to market. (Courtesy of Thomas J. Albanese.)

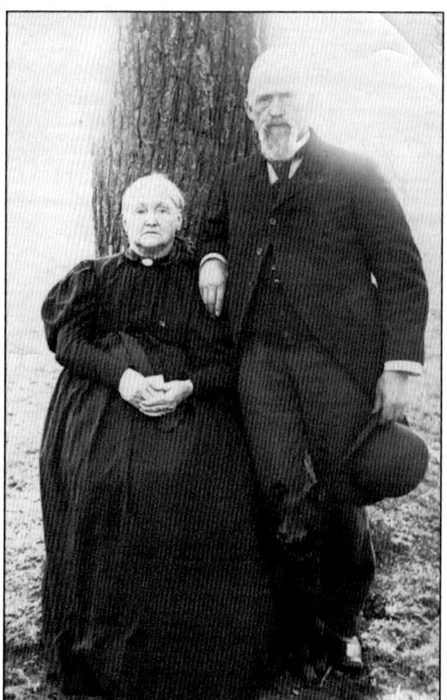

John S. Edsall and his mother Isabella pose on the Edsall lawn around 1902. Mother Isabella, a Christie from Leonia, was born on June 3, 1818. On December 24, 1835, she married Samuel Edsall, merging the two families. (Courtesy of Thomas J. Albanese.)

Pictured in this *c.* 1866 photograph are twins Mary Agnes and Gertrude Geneva, daughters of John S. and Lydia Edsall. They were born on June 16, 1863. (Courtesy of Thomas J. Albanese.)

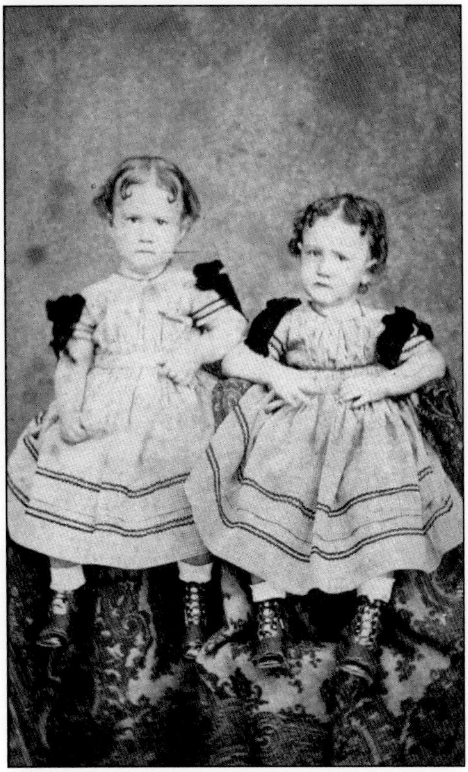

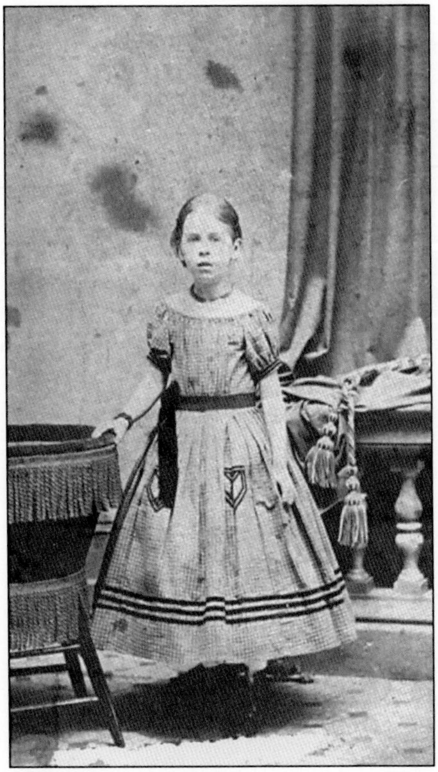

Belle Lena Edsall, the first child of John S. and Lydia Edsall, was born on December 6, 1858. She married Abram Christie on October 27, 1880. After their marriage, they made their residence in Englewood, then New York, before returning home to Palisades Park in 1894. They had two daughters, Jennie De Ronde Christie and Mary A. Christie. Abram Christie was a charter member of Fire Company No. 1. (Courtesy of Leonia Public Library.)

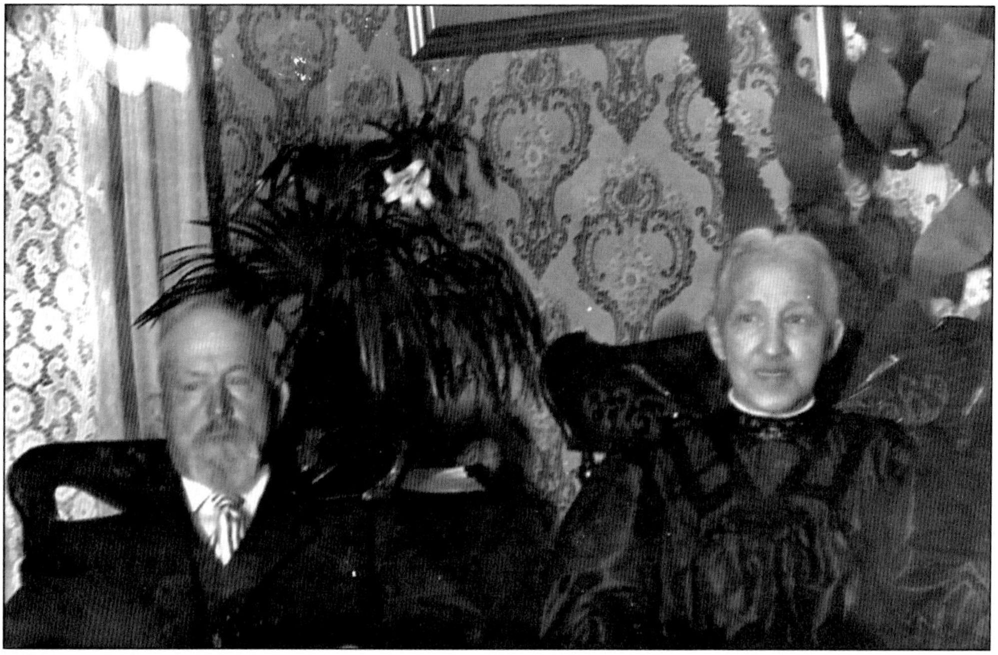

John S. and Lydia Edsall celebrated their 50th wedding anniversary on a Tuesday evening on February 25, 1908, at their Grand Avenue home. Over 100 friends and relatives gathered to celebrate. The Edsall rooms were decorated with yellow ribbon. Dancing began at 8:30 and went until 11:00 at night, with a light meal being served at 9:00. The couple received beautiful gifts consisting of gold spoons, cut glass, pictures, and much more. (Courtesy of Thomas J. Albanese.)

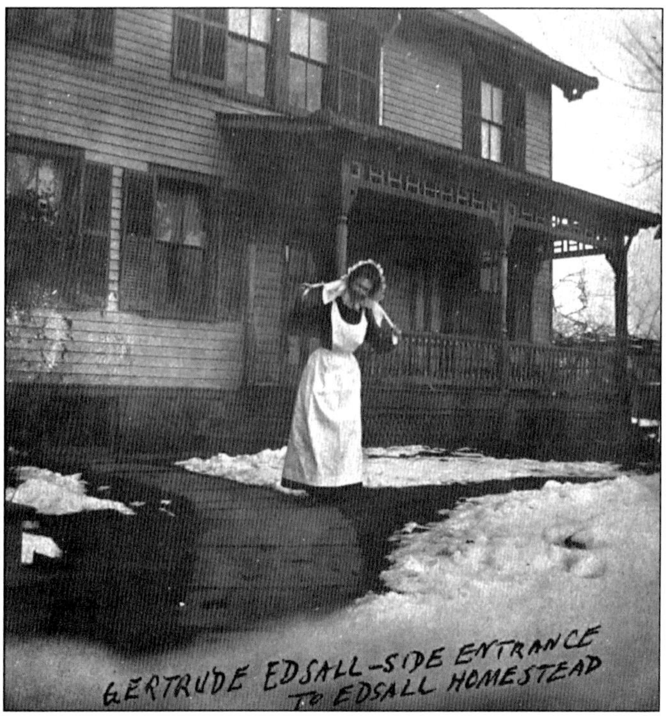

Gertrude Edsall models her apron outside the side entrance to the Edsall homestead on Grand Avenue in 1904. She was a charter member of the First Presbyterian Church of Palisades Park and an active member of its Ladies Aid Society. Gertrude was also active in the auxiliary of the Christian Orphanage, Fort Lee, for many years. (Courtesy of Leonia Public Library.)

Members of the Edsall family are seen pumping water from the well in this *c.* 1904 photograph. Standing in the rear of the photograph are Jennie Christie and Lillie May Edsall. The woman at the pump and the child are unknown. (Courtesy of Leonia Public Library.)

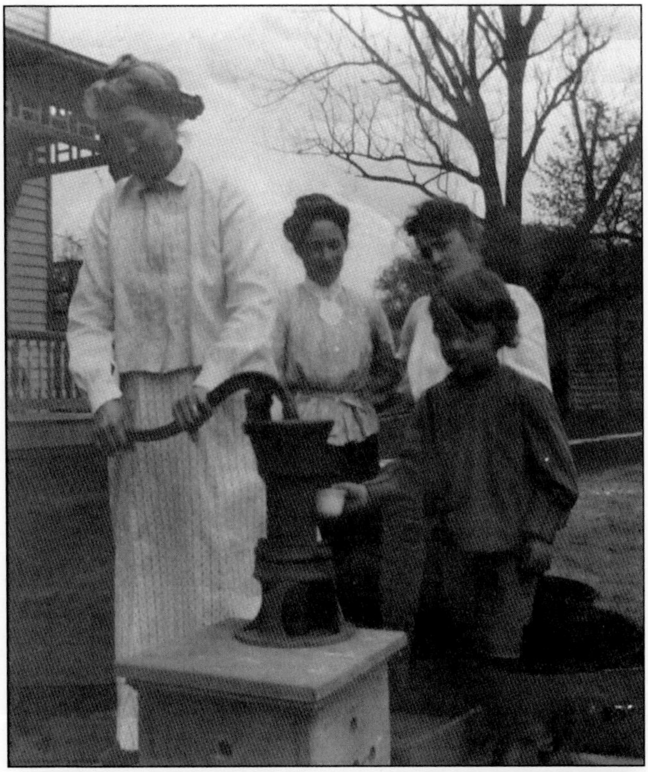

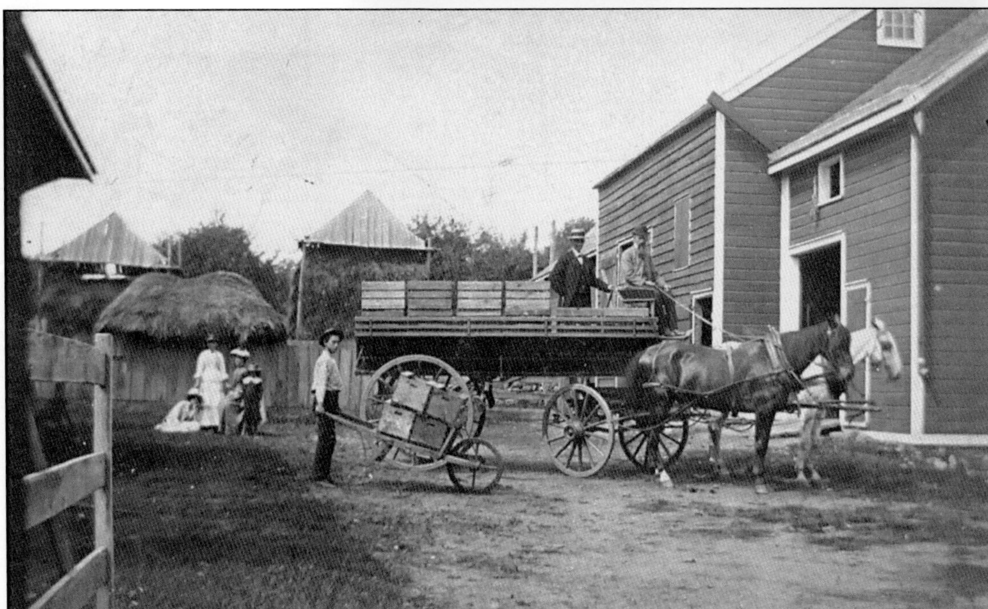

Seen here is a *c.* 1908 tintype of the Edsall barns and farmyard. Operating the horse-drawn produce carriage is John S. Edsall, with his brother Samuel S. standing behind him. In the rear of this tintype are tall stockpiles of hay. Although both brothers were actively involved in real estate ventures, they remained active in their farming pursuits, a family tradition for over 200 years. (Courtesy of Thomas J. Albanese.)

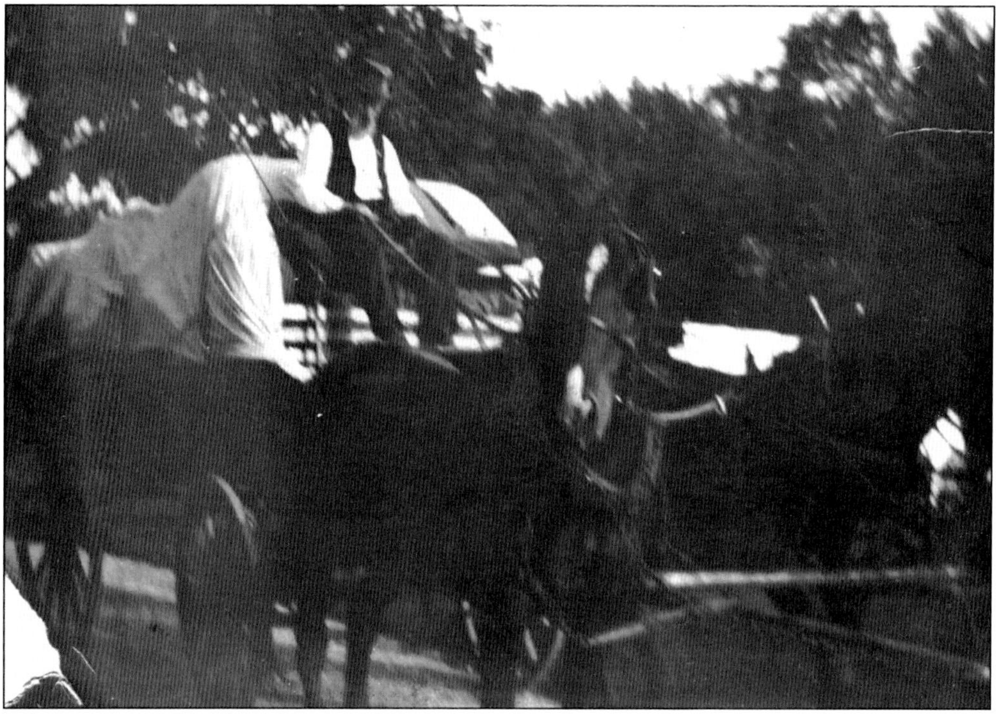

John S. Edsall (above) hauls produce in 1910. Samuel S. Edsall (below) is at work on the farm, also in 1910. Both brothers grew up on the farm of their father, Samuel, and became skilled farmers. Produce was hauled south along Grand Avenue to markets in Jersey City and New York City. In 1892, Samuel S. Edsall became the postmaster of Palisades Park. (Courtesy of Thomas J. Albanese.)

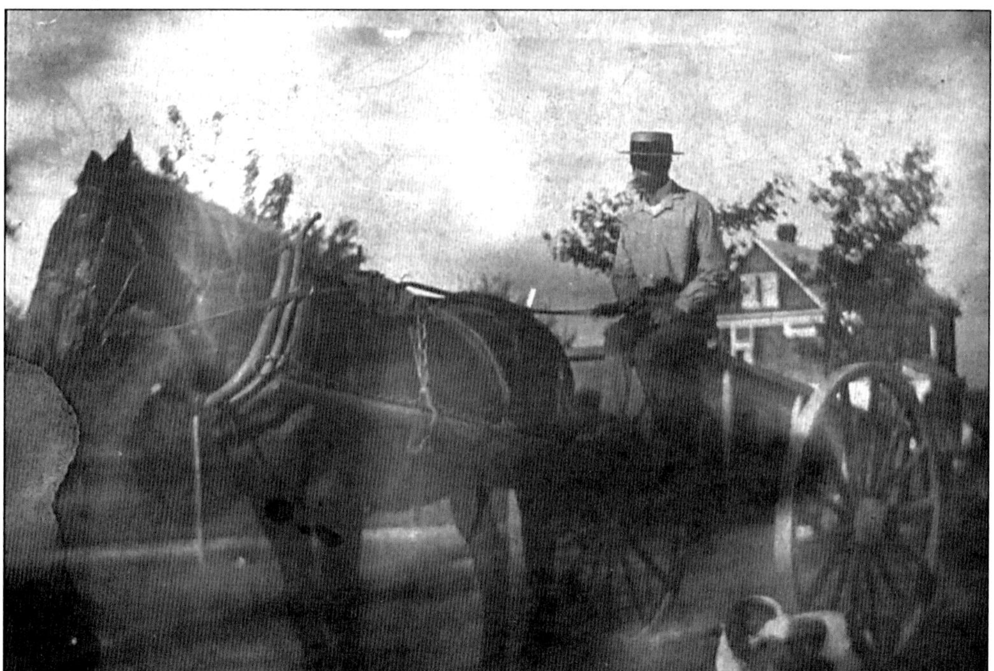

A member of the Edsall family (right) feeds three piglets and a chicken in the Edsall barnyard around 1908. Members of the Edsall family (below) gather around the pigpen. John S. Edsall is standing in the rear against the barn. The Edsall family had many animals on their farm, which included many different breeds of dogs they kept for pets. (Right, courtesy of Thomas J. Albanese; below, courtesy of Leonia Public Library.)

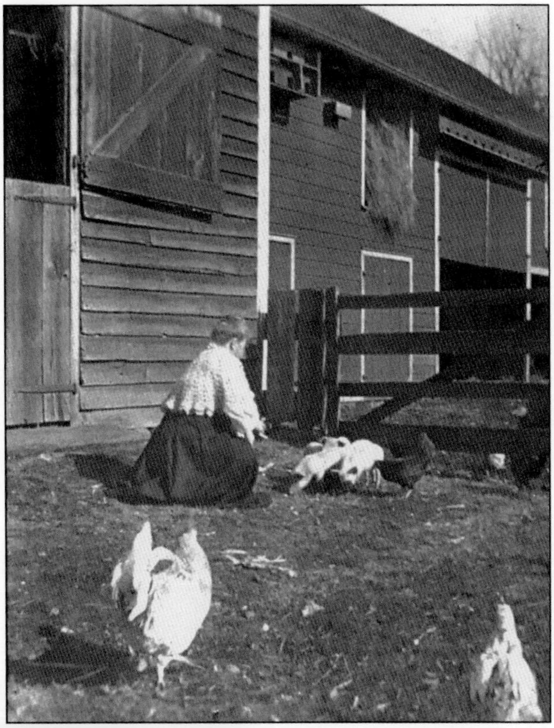

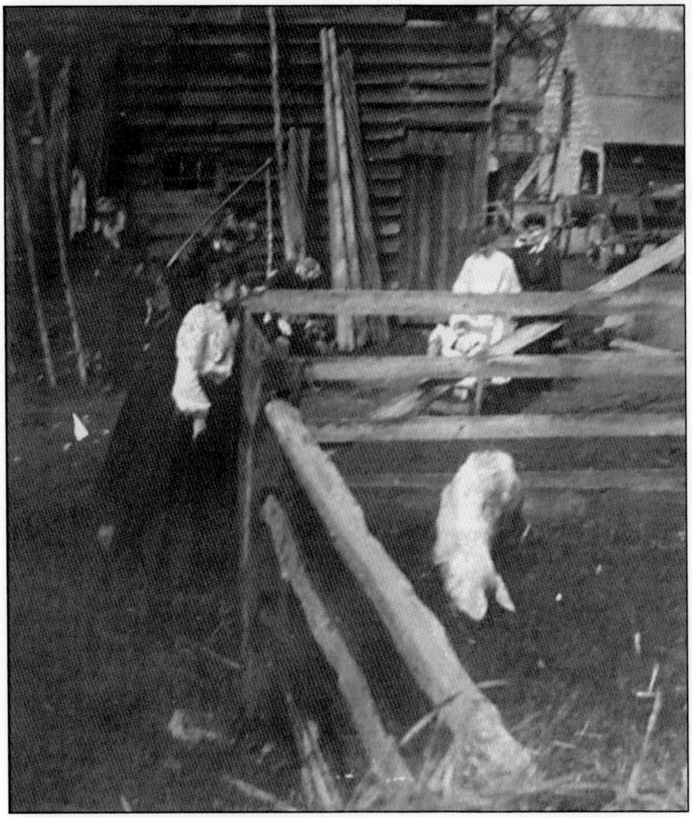

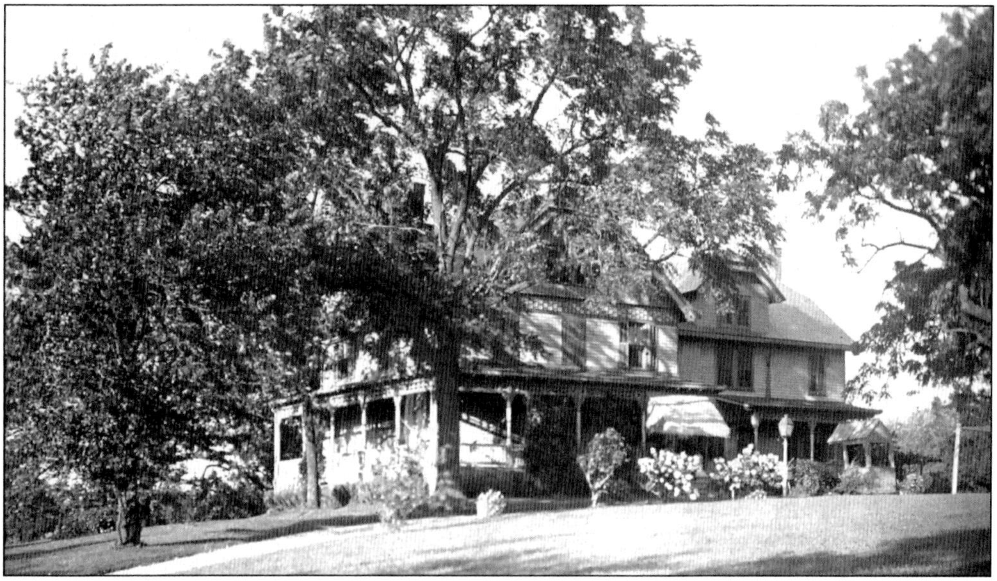

Seen here is a 1900 photograph of the Edsall house. This was the home of first mayor John S. Edsall. It was well-constructed and beautifully maintained. A board of health officer quarantined this house for a mild case of scarlet fever and arrested John S. Edsall twice because he would not observe the ban, although he occupied a part of this house remote from the secluded patient. (Courtesy of Thomas J. Albanese.)

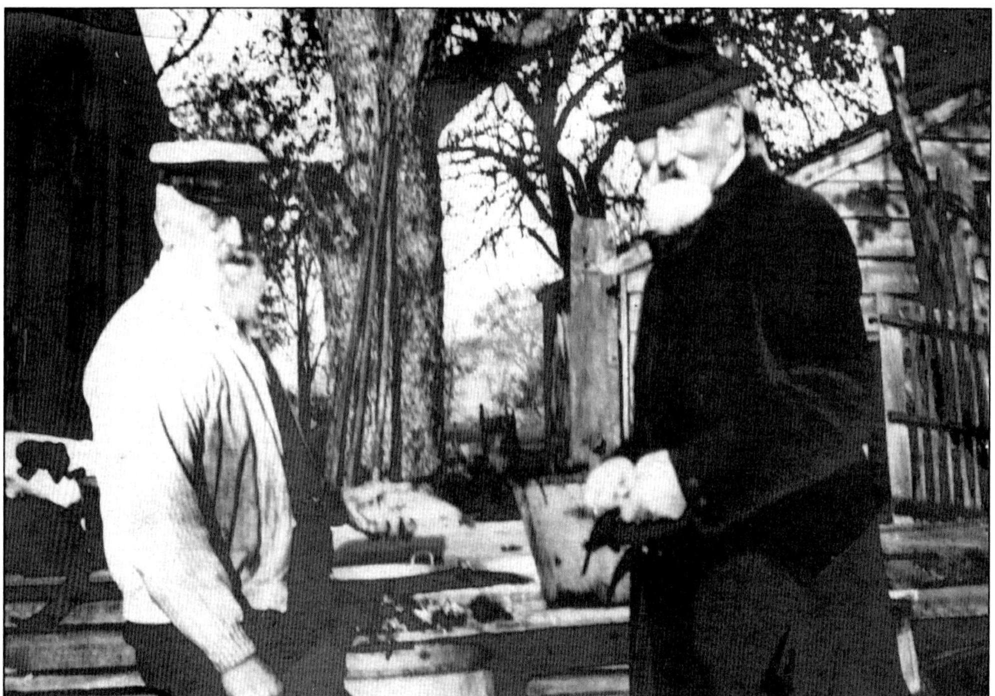

John S. Edsall and Cornelius Westervelt are pictured here on the Edsall farm. They became brothers-in-law on September 20, 1860, when Cornelius Westervelt married John S. Edsall's sister Sarah Ann Edsall. (Courtesy of Thomas J. Albanese.)

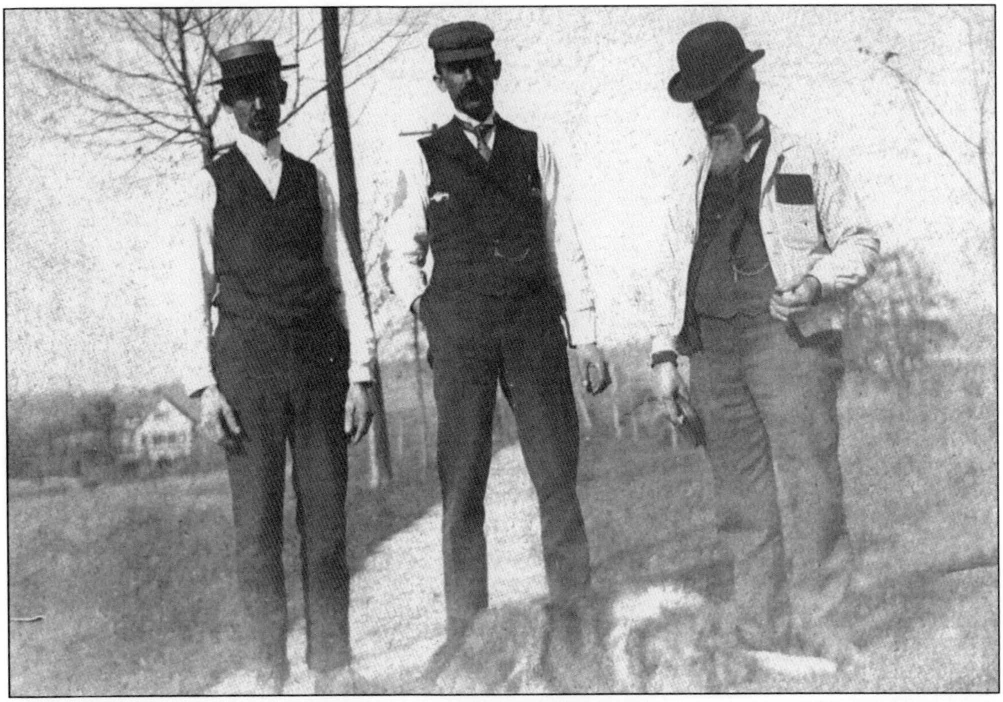

Samuel Edsall (left), Abram Christie (center), and John S. Edsall (right) stand for a photograph with their collie around 1910. Abram Christie was married to John S. Edsall's daughter Belle Lena. Notice the few homes pictured in the landscape. (Courtesy of Thomas J. Albanese.)

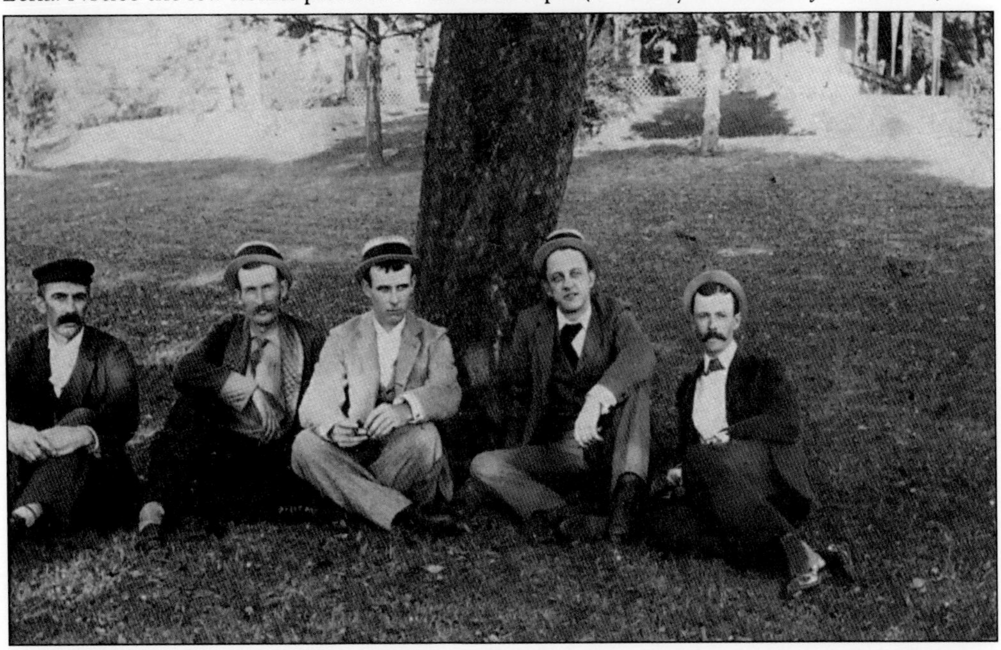

Men gather on the lawn of the Edsall homestead on Grand Avenue. From left to right are Abram Christie, James V. Moore, Frank Barrett, unidentified, and Samuel Edsall. James V. Moore became the son-in-law of John S. Edsall when he married John's daughter Sarah B. on September 10, 1890. (Courtesy of Leonia Public Library.)

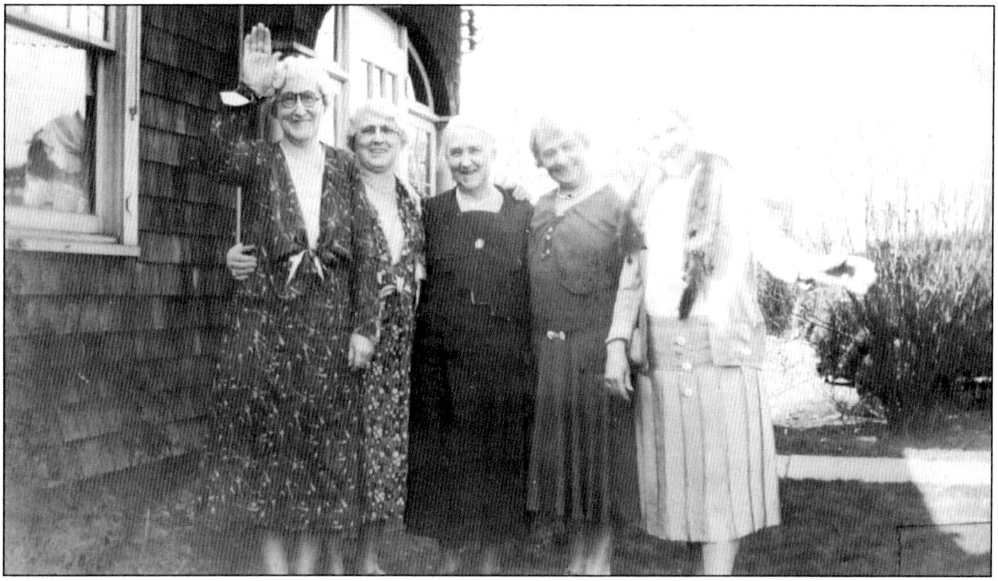

Pictured here on April 16, 1931, are the Edsall sisters, from left to right, Sarah B, Agnes Naomi, Belle Lena, Lillie May, and Gertrude Geneva. (Courtesy of Leonia Public Library.)

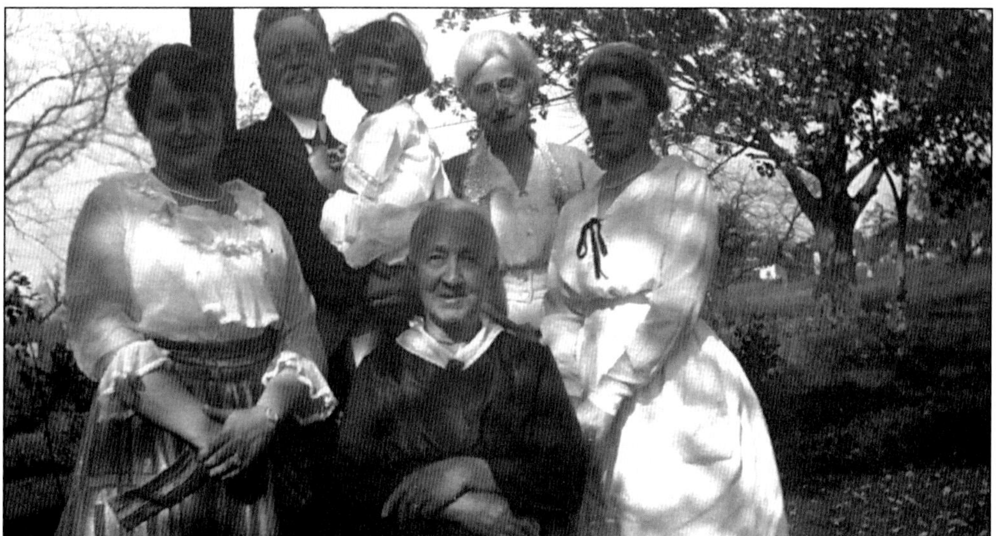

Shown here with Grandma Edsall (seated) in this *c.* 1916 photograph are, from left to right, Lillie May Star, Dr. Joseph Huger, unidentified child, Sara Westervelt, and Agnes Naomi Edsall. Dr. Joseph Huger was a well-known local physician. One morning, while making his rounds, he narrowly escaped a deadly accident. While approaching the southbound Whiteman Street trolley crossing in Fort Lee, another automobile struck his, causing a substantial amount of damage. The doctor fortunately escaped injury at the dangerous intersection, where several others have had serious accidents. Dr. Huger's office was located at Backstrom's store near the train depot. Office visits were 50¢ and home visits an even $1. (Courtesy of Leonia Public Library.)

Three

Formation of the Borough

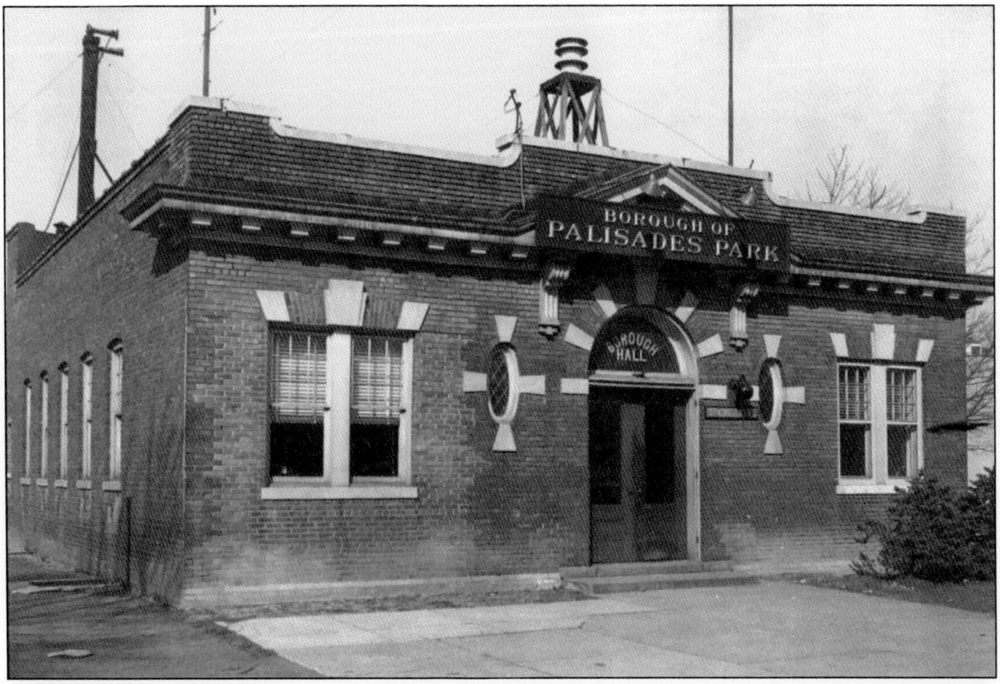

Pictured here is the second borough hall of Palisades Park. After fire destroyed the original borough hall in June 1906, officials of Palisades Park did not want to incur a large debt, so after considerable discussions, they finally decided that a one-story fireproof structure would be erected with the money received on adjustments of fire insurance. Groundbreaking began on October 23, 1907. The Steenland Brothers Company erected the building and completed it in May 1908. (Courtesy of *Golden Jubilee of 1949*.)

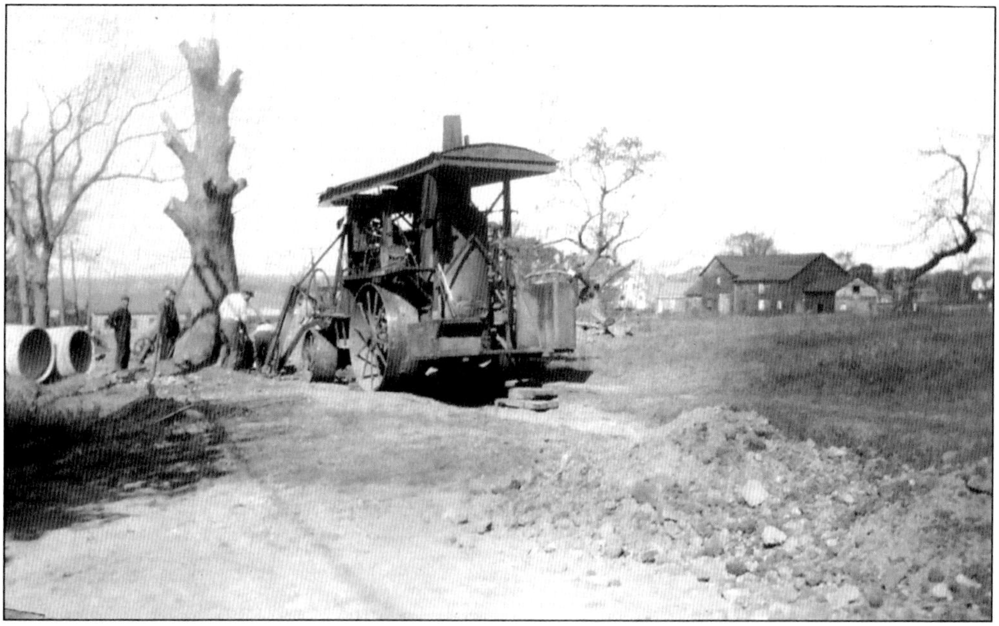

Men are seen using a steam traction engine to remove an old tree to allow for the underground sewer pipes on West Oakdene Avenue around 1915. In the distance is the Civil War drill hall. (Courtesy of Leonia Public Library.)

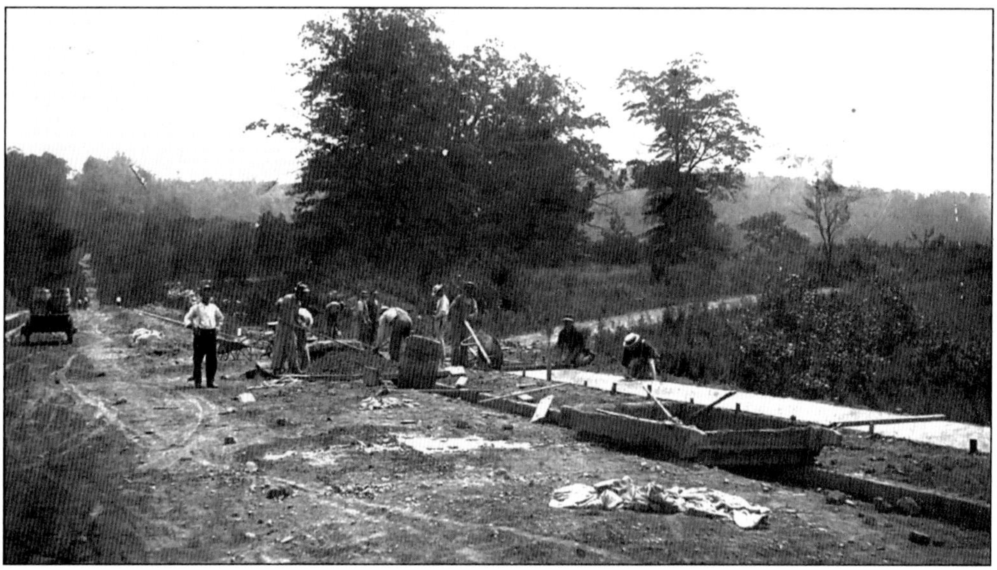

Sidewalks are being installed on East Central Boulevard in this *c.* 1903 photograph. Before this project began, there were board sidewalks from the Erie Railroad to Seventh Street and only on Central Boulevard. On July 10, 1899, the first major street pavement was authorized by the borough to pave Central Boulevard from Seventh Street to Anderson Avenue. S. Lewandowski oversaw the project. During the late 1800s and into the early 1900s, there was a sizeable Polish community in Palisades Park. In November 1891, Dr. H. P. Lewandowski with Father Klaswiter purchased an option in a tract of land at Castle Hill from H. A. Freeman, a land developer. Father Klaswiter had unofficially named this area of land New Czestochowa. (Courtesy of Thomas J. Albanese.)

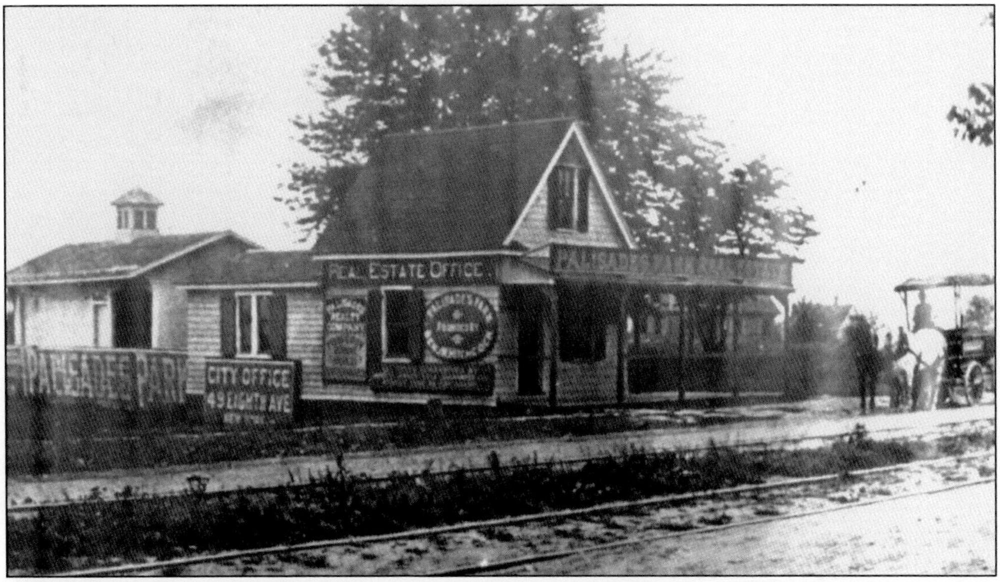

Benjamin Hitchcock's Palisades Real Estate Office, seen here in 1887, was located along the Erie Railroad. Trains began to run through Palisades Park in 1859 but did not stop until 1887 when Hitchcock built this new station. (Courtesy of Palisades Park Public Library.)

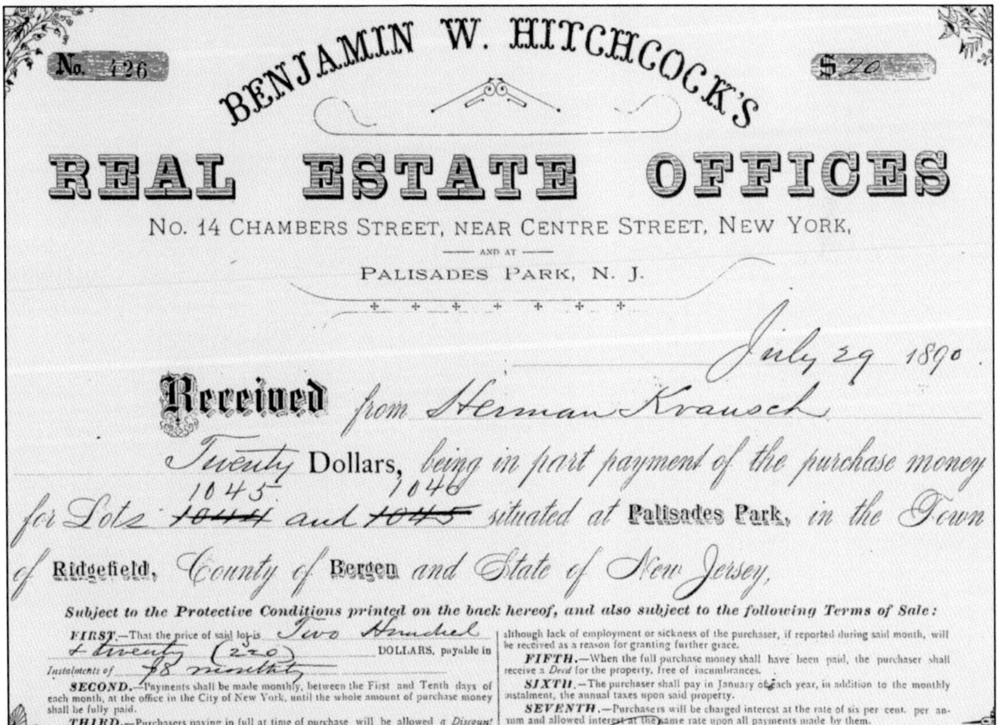

No. 426 $20

BENJAMIN W. HITCHCOCK'S

REAL ESTATE OFFICES

No. 14 CHAMBERS STREET, NEAR CENTRE STREET, NEW YORK,

AND AT

PALISADES PARK, N. J.

July 29 1890.

Received from Herman Krausch

Twenty Dollars, being in part payment of the purchase money for Lots ~~1044~~ 1045 and ~~1045~~ 1046 situated at Palisades Park, in the Town of Ridgefield, County of Bergen and State of New Jersey,

Subject to the Protective Conditions printed on the back hereof, and also subject to the following Terms of Sale:

FIRST.—That the price of said lot is Two Hundred & twenty (220) DOLLARS, payable in *Instalments of* $8 monthly

SECOND.—Payments shall be made monthly, between the First and Tenth days of each month, at the office in the City of New York, until the whole amount of purchase money shall be fully paid.

THIRD.—Purchasers paying in full at time of purchase will be allowed *a Discount* and receive Deeds at once. Those who shall fully pay within six months after purchase, shall receive their Deeds, and a remission of Interest,

although lack of employment or sickness of the purchaser, if reported during said month, will be received as a reason for granting further grace.

FIFTH.—When the full purchase money shall have been paid, the purchaser shall receive a *Deed* for the property, free of incumbrances.

SIXTH.—The purchaser shall pay in January of each year, in addition to the monthly instalment, the annual taxes upon said property.

SEVENTH.—Purchasers will be charged interest at the rate of six per cent. per annum and allowed interest at the same rate upon all payments made by them.

Pictured here is a deed dated July 29, 1890, for two lots situated at Palisades Park in the township of Ridgefield (present-day Palisades Park). The cost to buyer Herman Krausch was $220 for both lots. Benjamin Hitchcock was a successful real estate entrepreneur who bought bulk parcels of land in the borough and divided them into individual lots. (Courtesy of Thomas J. Albanese.)

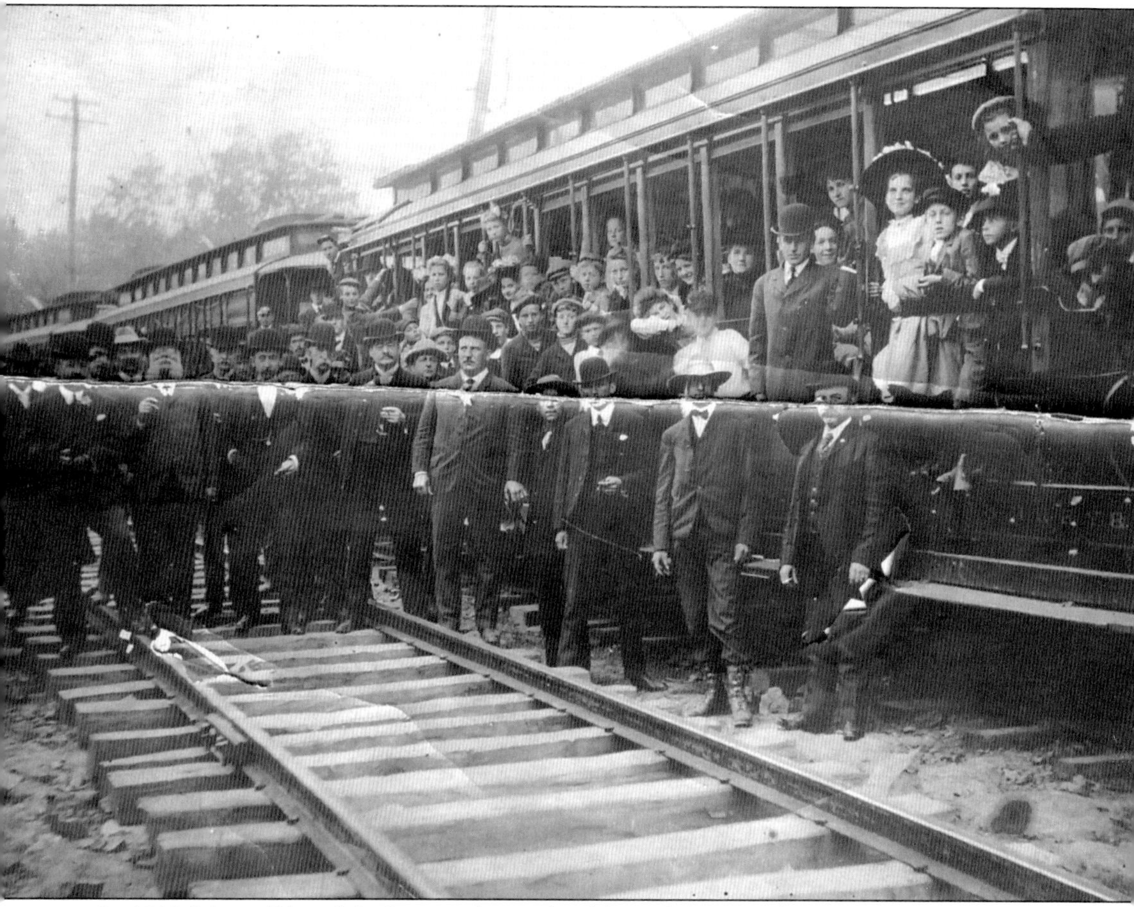

In 1907, Mayor Edward A. Gantert (center) celebrated the arrival of the first trolley car. Mayor Gantert was Palisades Park's third mayor, serving from 1904 to 1907. The tracks were laid by Ford, Bacon, and Dairs, engineers for the New York and New Jersey Railway and Ferry Company. The trolley company invited Mayor Gantert and the residents to ride along the line, where they were taken to the Palisades Amusement Park to enjoy refreshments the company provided. Ten trolley cars were used for this purpose. The trolley was part of the Hudson River line, which extended from Edgewater, through Palisades Park, to Paterson. Initially the tracks were laid along the curb of Broad Avenue, but when the roadway was improved in the 1920s, the tracks were moved into the middle of the street. Residents commuting to Manhattan would board the trolley on Broad Avenue and travel to Edgewater, where a ferry would take them across the Hudson River. (Courtesy of Leonia Public Library.)

In 1894, John S. and Samuel S. Edsall formed this real estate firm, selling remaining portions of the land they inherited from their father, Samuel, after his death on March 17, 1882, at the age of 70. They divided the land into individual lots, and while this real estate venture was successful, they both continued to maintain their farming interests in the borough. (Courtesy of Leonia Public Library.)

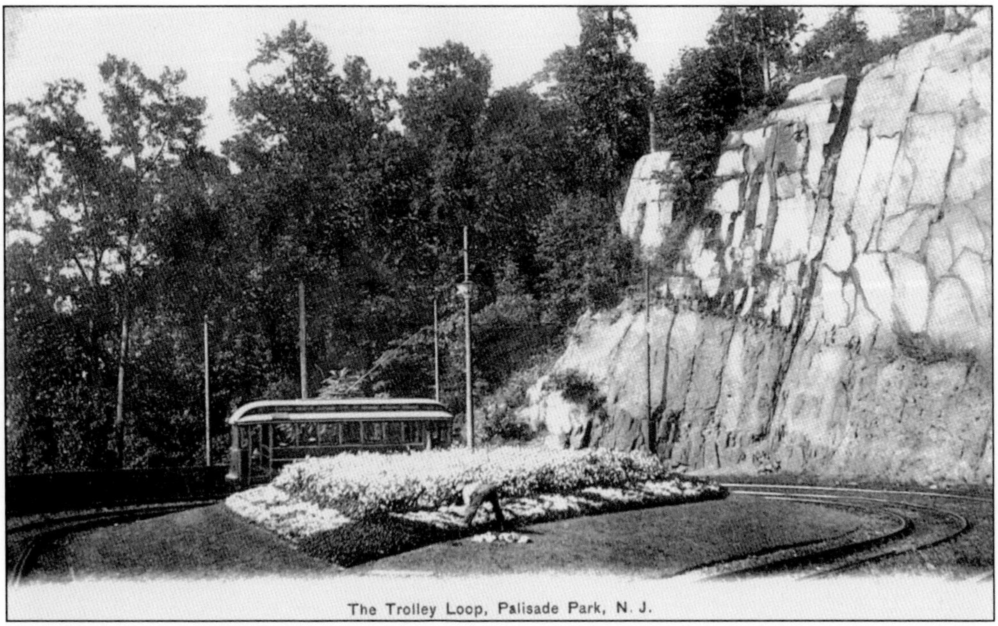

This 1906 postcard shows the trolley loop that led to the Palisades Amusement Park. Little is known about where the name Palisades Park originated from, although some say it was from developer Benjamin Hitchcock. Several movements were led to change the name of Palisades Park, to avoid confusion between Palisades Interstate Park and Palisades Amusement Park, both in proximity. In 1914, the name Oakdene was selected and placed on the election ballot. It was defeated by a vote of 138 to 125. In 1923, another name change was considered, this time the name Morsemere was chosen. The residents voted 624 to 280 against the name change.

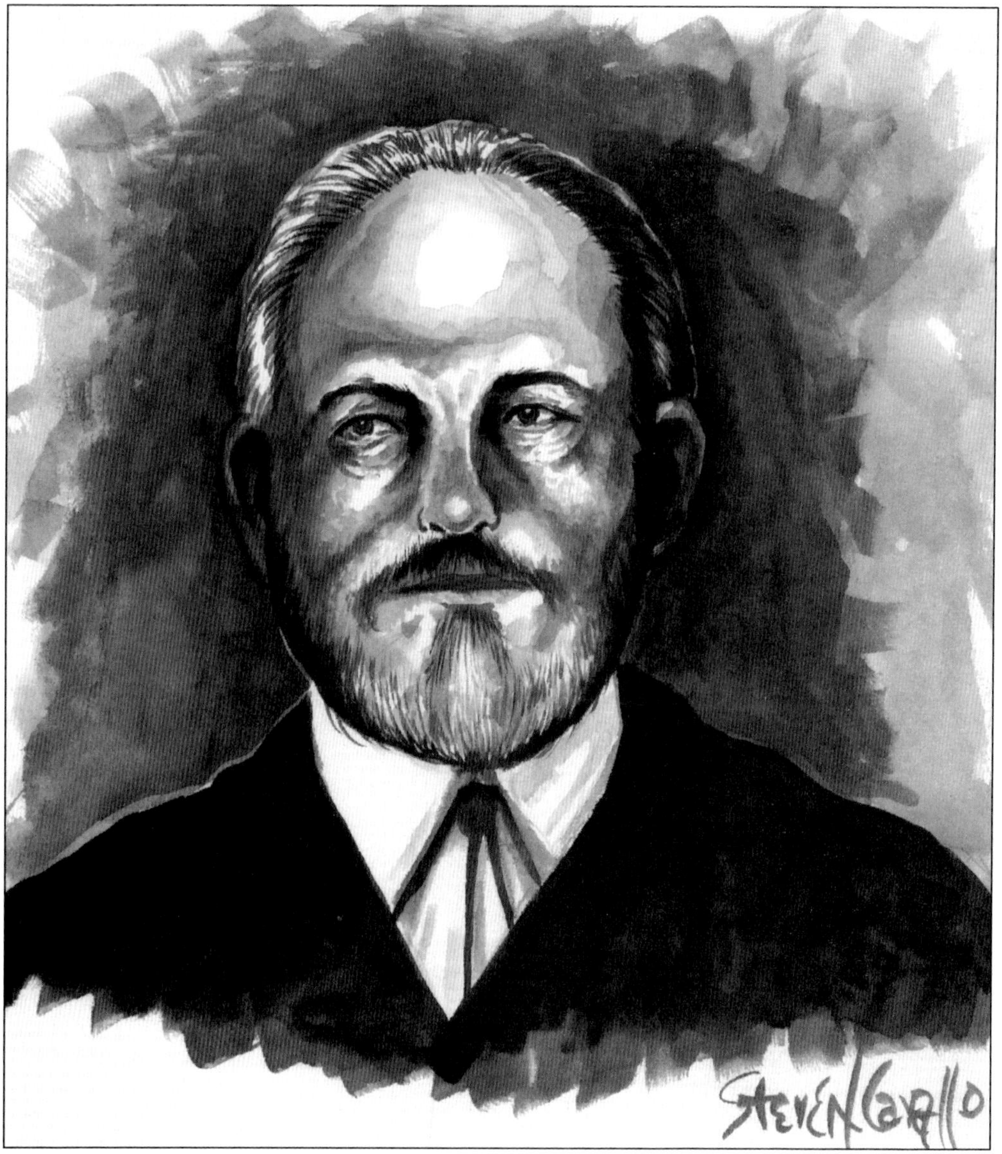

John S. Edsall was born on December 14, 1837. He grew up on his parents' farm, and his farming ventures were successful. He served in the military, becoming a charter member of the 2nd Battalion, or Bergen Brigade, "Jersey Blues," which was organized on May 7, 1861. He served throughout the Civil War, and when he returned home he stayed active in military affairs, holding different ranks until he was made captain of the Leonia Company of the National Guard on October 16, 1888. With the assistance of Leonia's Col. Stephen H. V. Moore, and other patriotic neighbors, he assisted in the construction of the armory on Grand Avenue, which later became Company L's official headquarters. After Palisades Park became a borough, he was elected and sworn into office on April 24, 1899, as the borough's first mayor. Mayor Edsall is considered one of the greatest pioneers of Palisades Park and throughout his life did much for the advancement of the borough and the quality of life for its residents. (Courtesy of Steven Cavallo.)

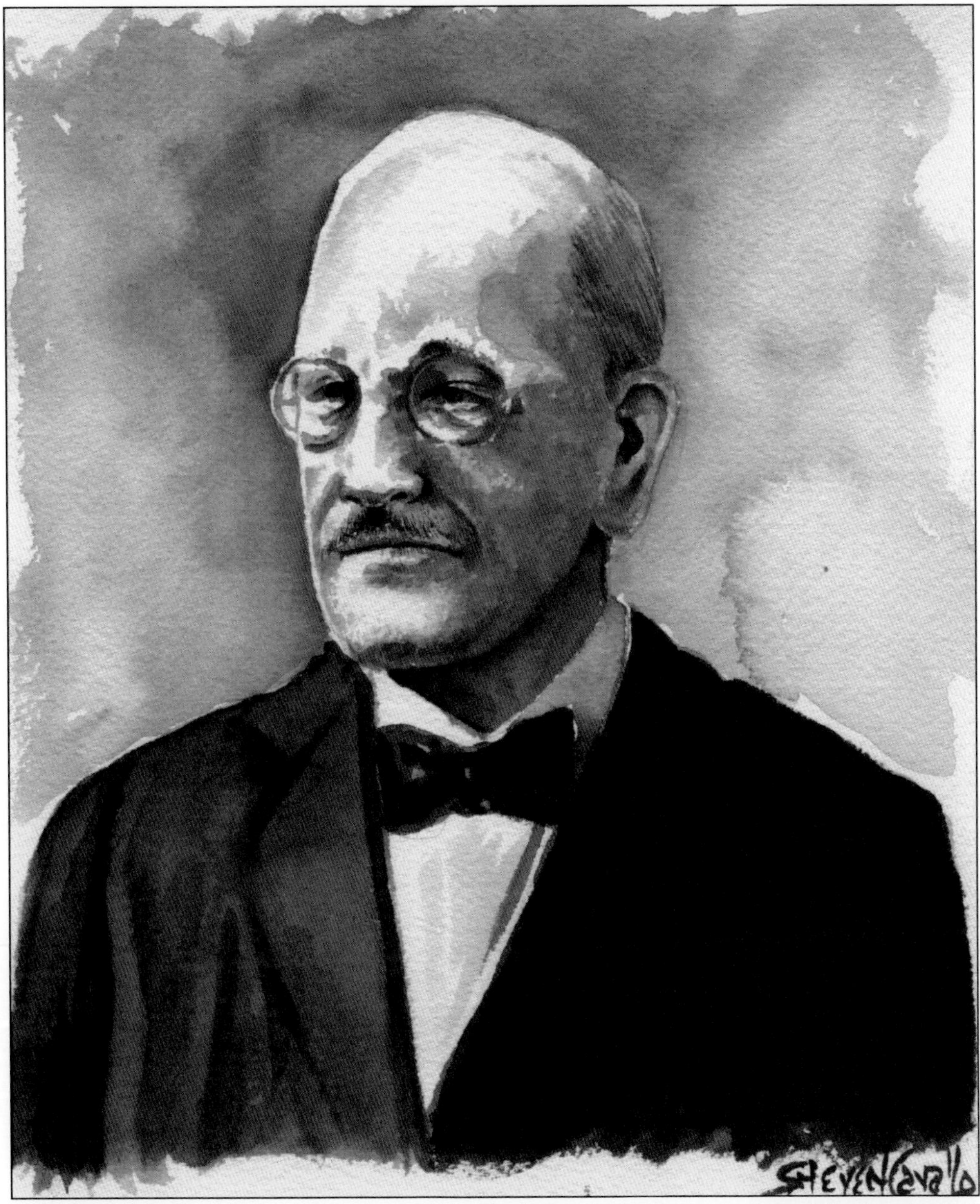

John Brinkerhoff, a direct descendant of Hendrick Brinkerhoff, is seen here. The Brinkerhoff family owned a large tract of land within the borough. This land extended from the Hudson River to the Overpeck Creek. Throughout the years the farm was consolidated to an area between West Homestead Avenue and Cleveland Place. John Brinkerhoff was a skilled farmer who plowed the land with his horses. The farm also consisted of a slew of apple trees. John Brinkerhoff was actively involved in borough affairs, becoming the first tax collector, first postmaster, and first custodian of school funds. Throughout his life, he was committed to serving the people of the borough. He was a charter member of the first volunteer fire department and remained actively involved in the borough until his death on January 16, 1934. John Brinkerhoff's efforts helped the residents of Palisades Park to enjoy life in the infant borough. (Courtesy of Steven Cavallo.)

Palisades Park

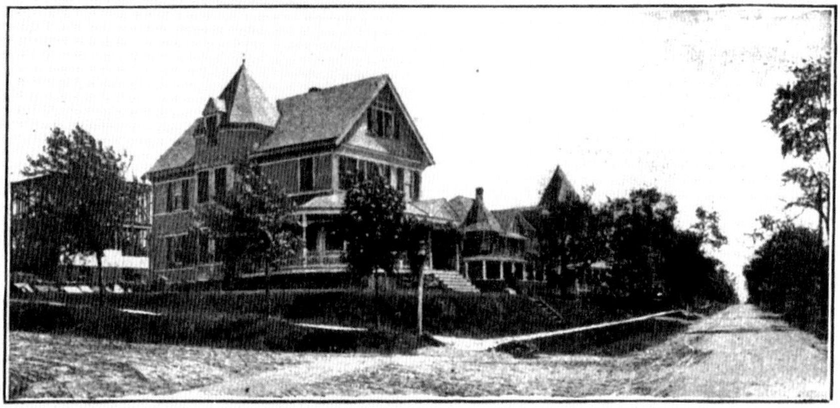

COR. CENTRAL BOULEVARD AND GRAND AVENUE, PALISADES PARK, LOOKING SOUTH TOWARD JERSEY CITY.

THE TOP SHELF OF NEW YORK, 300 feet higher than the Hudson River, directly opposite Grant's Mausoleum at 125th Street. May be reached by a number of different routes (see below), from all points of the city.

PALISADES PARK is not merely a "section" or "subdivision," but a wide expanse of beautiful rolling land, a park offering the freedom and the pure air of the ideal suburban residence locality, macadamized streets, stone sidewalks, water, gas, electricity, a perfect sewerage system, shade trees in abundance, and good transportation facilities, which later will present even a greater degree of perfection when the tunnels now building under the Hudson River are completed. As the bird flies it is less than a mile and a half from one of the highest priced residential sections in America—Riverside Drive.

Stupendous Profits UPON THE COMPLETION OF THE HUDSON RIVER TUNNELS

await all who avail themselves of our special offer and secure building lots at present low prices for cash or on small monthly payments of $10 in this superb locality—the coming **Suburban Residence District.** Adjoining property is being rapidly bought up, by syndicates of wealthy and far sighted men who will not offer one lot for sale until the tunnels are completed. Over **One Hundred** residences have already been erected, and are occupied by their owners, thrifty, discriminating people who enjoy at their very door every home convenience; churches of different denominations, good public schools, and stores and markets that are first class.

$10.00 DOWN AND $10.00 A MONTH

BUYS A BUILDING LOT IN PALISADES PARK.

In a park where property is absolutely sure of an enormous increase in value. When the Tunnels are completed, Palisades Park will grow faster than Brooklyn ever did.

The greatest investment ever offered in desirable real estate. **Titles Guaranteed** by the North Jersey Title Guarantee Company. Reached via the Erie Railroad, only 24 minutes from Jersey City; or from Franklin St., and also from 42d Street, New York, land at West Shore Ferry, Weehawken, thence by trolley crossing property. Can also be reached by Barclay or 14th Street Ferries to Hoboken, thence by trolley. Commutation on the Erie, including ferries, only 9 cents, insuring comfortable seats in commodious cars, no crowding, no transferring; station at **Palisades Park.** We have recently sold to a large Construction Company 61 lots, upon which 23 additional houses will be erected at once, and as orders are in hand for more than this number, negotiations are now pending for the construction of double this amount.

Lots in Palisades Park, Choice Locations May Now Be Had for less than at any other suburban locality. Terms made to accommodate circumstances. Advance in price of many hundred per cent. unquestionably assured. Send for Illustrated Descriptive Booklet, Our Special Offer, Map and Free Tickets via Erie Railroad. The greatest opportunity to share in the New York Real Estate Boom—now on. Address

Palisades Park Co., **100 BROADWAY or 244 West 23rd Street, NEW YORK**

This advertisement, from 1902, appeared in *Harper's Bazaar* magazine. For only $10 down and $10 a month, a building lot could be purchased. The photograph in the picture was the old Maple House located on the corner of Central Boulevard and Grand Avenue.

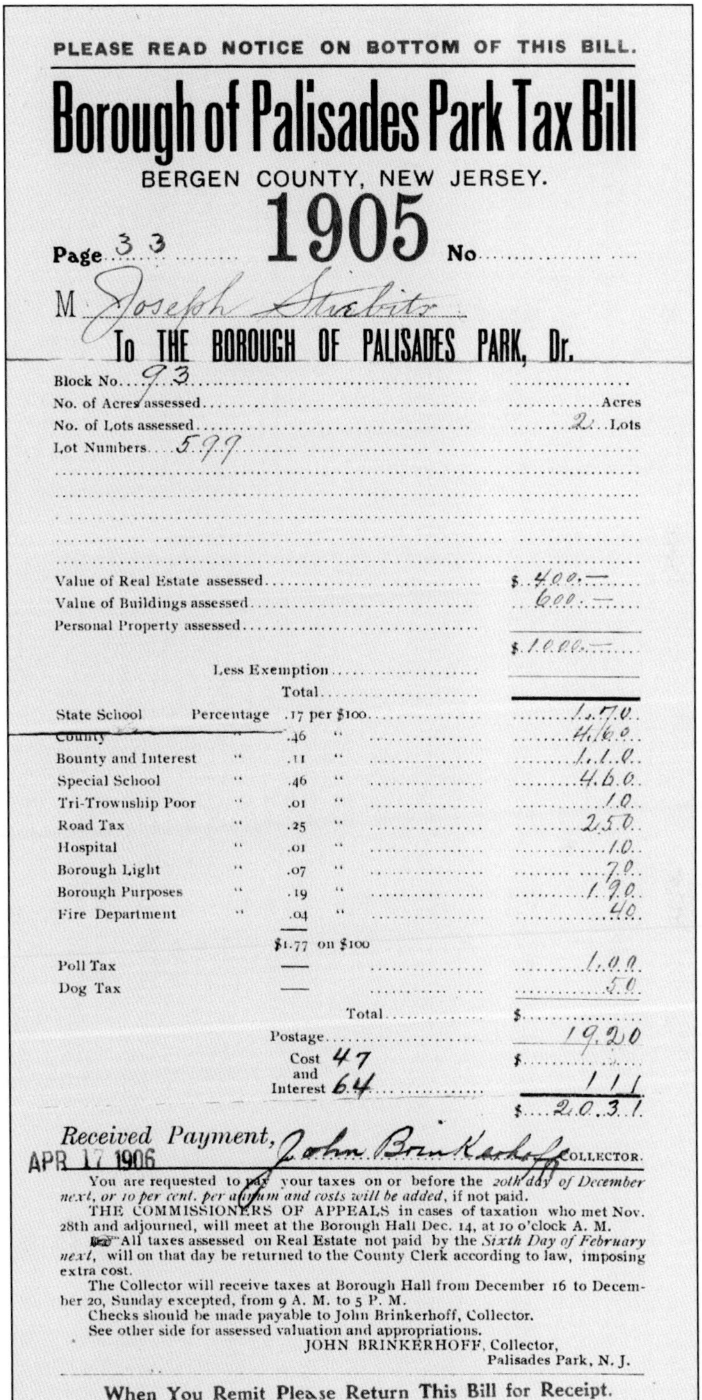

PLEASE READ NOTICE ON BOTTOM OF THIS BILL.

Borough of Palisades Park Tax Bill

BERGEN COUNTY, NEW JERSEY.

1905

Page 33 No

M Joseph Strebitz

To THE BOROUGH OF PALISADES PARK, Dr.

Block No. 93	
No. of Acres assessed	Acres
No. of Lots assessed	2 Lots
Lot Numbers 599	
Value of Real Estate assessed	$ 400.—
Value of Buildings assessed	600.—
Personal Property assessed	
	$ 1000.—
Less Exemption	
Total	

State School	Percentage	.17 per $100	1.70
County	"	.46 "	4.60
Bounty and Interest	"	.11 "	1.10
Special School	"	.46 "	4.60
Tri-Township Poor	"	.01 "	10
Road Tax	"	.25 "	2.50
Hospital	"	.01 "	10
Borough Light	"	.07 "	70
Borough Purposes	"	.19 "	1.90
Fire Department	"	.04 "	40
		$1.77 on $100	
Poll Tax		—	1.00
Dog Tax		—	50
		Total	$
		Postage	19.20
		Cost 47	$
		and Interest 64	111
			$ 20.31

Received Payment, John Brinkerhoff COLLECTOR.

APR 17 1906

You are requested to pay your taxes on or before the *20th day of December next, or 10 per cent. per annum and costs will be added*, if not paid.

THE COMMISSIONERS OF APPEALS in cases of taxation who met Nov. 28th and adjourned, will meet at the Borough Hall Dec. 14, at 10 o'clock A. M.

All taxes assessed on Real Estate not paid by the *Sixth Day of February next*, will on that day be returned to the County Clerk according to law, imposing extra cost.

The Collector will receive taxes at Borough Hall from December 16 to December 20, Sunday excepted, from 9 A. M. to 5 P. M.

Checks should be made payable to John Brinkerhoff, Collector.

See other side for assessed valuation and appropriations.

JOHN BRINKERHOFF, Collector,
Palisades Park, N. J.

When You Remit Please Return This Bill for Receipt.

Seen here is an original 1905 tax bill for two lots paid to the borough's first tax collector, John Brinkerhoff. The value of the real estate was $400, and the building was valued and assessed at $600. The total value of the building and both lots was $1,000. The total amount paid by the taxpayer was $20.31. (Courtesy of Thomas J. Albanese.)

THE GROWTH OF NEW YORK IS MARVELLOUS!!

If you are at a distance and want to invest in this Suburb, directly opposite the centre of New York City, you can remit $10 and we will select the best unsold lot and mail you a contract for it. Then you can each month remit $10 per lot until paid for, when we will forward a free and clear deed with guarantee of title without further expense to you.

Palisades Park

ON THE TOP SHELF OF NEW YORK, 300 feet higher than the Hudson River, directly opposite Grant's Mausoleum at 125th street. May be reached by a number of different routes (see below) from all points of the city. PALISADES PARK is not merely a "section" or "sub-division," but a wide expanse of beautiful rolling land. A PARK offering the freedom and the pure air of the ideal suburban residence locality, improved with all the advantages of the city; macadamized streets, stone sidewalks, water, gas, electricity, a perfect sewerage system, shade trees in abundance and good transportation facilities, which latter will present even a greater degree of perfection when the tunnels now building under the Hudson River are completed.

STUPENDOUS PROFITS

UPON THE COMPLETION OF THE

HUDSON RIVER TUNNELS

await all who avail themselves of our special offer and secure building lots for cash or on small monthly payments of $10 in this superb locality — the coming RESIDENCE DISTRICT on the Jersey side. Over ONE HUNDRED residences have already been erected, and occupied by their owners, a most desirable class of thrifty, discriminating people who enjoy at their very doors every home convenience, churches of different denominations, good public schools, and stores and markets that are first class.

$300 BUYS A BUILDING LOT

FOR CASH, OR

$10 Down and $10 a Month

IDEAL HOME SITES

Here is the ideal spot to buy or erect a home and here may also be found the greatest investment ever offered in desirable real estate. TITLES GUARANTEED BY THE NORTH JERSEY TITLE GUARANTEE CO. But you cannot appreciate the unparalleled inducements herein described without personally visiting the property, which may be reached via the Erie Railroad or from Franklin street and also 42d street, New York, landing at West Shore Ferry, Weehawken, thence by trolley crossing property. Can also be reached by Barclay, or 14th street ferries to Hoboken, thence by trolley. Commutation on the Erie, including ferries, only 9 cents, insuring comfortable seats in commodious cars, no crowding, no transferring, station at PALISADES PARK. BUILDING LOTS IN PALISADES PARK, CHOICE LOCATIONS, MAY NOW BE HAD FOR $300. Terms made to accommodate purchasers. Advance in price of many hundred per cent unquestionably assured. Call at any time at our office on the property. Take 1:20 train from foot of Chambers street, or West 23d street to Erie Depot at Jersey City. Send for Illustrated Descriptive Booklet, Map, Free Tickets on the Erie Railroad, the greatest opportunity to share in the Real Estate Boom — now on. Call or address

PALISADES PARK COMPANY

100 Broadway, New York, or 244 and 246 West 23d Street, New York

22

This original advertisement from *New England Magazine* of August 1902 describes Palisades Park as "offering the freedom and pure air of the ideal suburban residence locality, improved with all the advantages of the city; macadamized streets, stone sidewalks, water, gas, electricity, a perfect sewage system. Shade trees in abundance and good transportation facilities, which later will present even a greater degree of perfection when the tunnels now building under the Hudson River are complete."

Palisades Park, N.J. July 22 1913

M Captain Edsall

Bought of JOHN BACKSTROM

GROCERIES, WINES, LIQUORS AND CIGARS

CENTRAL BOULEVARD, near Depot.

Telephone Connections

This is a receipt given to Capt. John S. Edsall on July 22, 1913. This general store was opened in March 1893 by John Backstrom and Albert Soderlund. It was located on West Central Boulevard, between Grand Avenue and the Erie Railroad. At one time, the store served as a post office. (Courtesy of Leonia Public Library.)

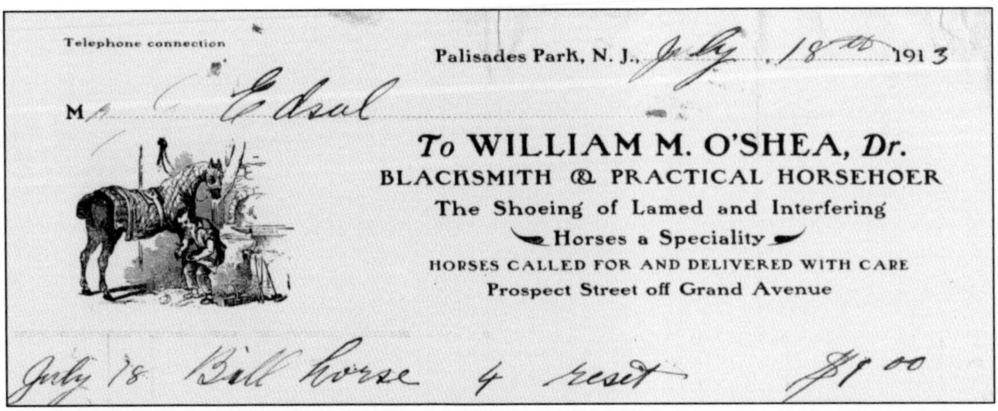
Telephone connection

Palisades Park, N. J., July 18th 1913

M Edsal

To WILLIAM M. O'SHEA, Dr.

BLACKSMITH & PRACTICAL HORSEHOER

The Shoeing of Lamed and Interfering

Horses a Speciality

HORSES CALLED FOR AND DELIVERED WITH CARE

Prospect Street off Grand Avenue

July 18 Bill horse 4 reset $1.00

This invoice was given to Capt. John S. Edsall on July 18, 1913. After the incorporation of Palisades Park, the population began to grow rapidly and more horses, carriages, and wagons were used, and a demand for blacksmiths and horseshoeing developed. This receipt is from William O'Shea's shop, located on Prospect Street off Grand Avenue. Also in the same area was the shop of Cy Sransky. Roman Busch had a shop on Sixth Street north of Palisades Boulevard. In 1912, Michael O'Shea established another blacksmith shop on Glen Avenue and Central Boulevard. (Courtesy of Leonia Public Library.)

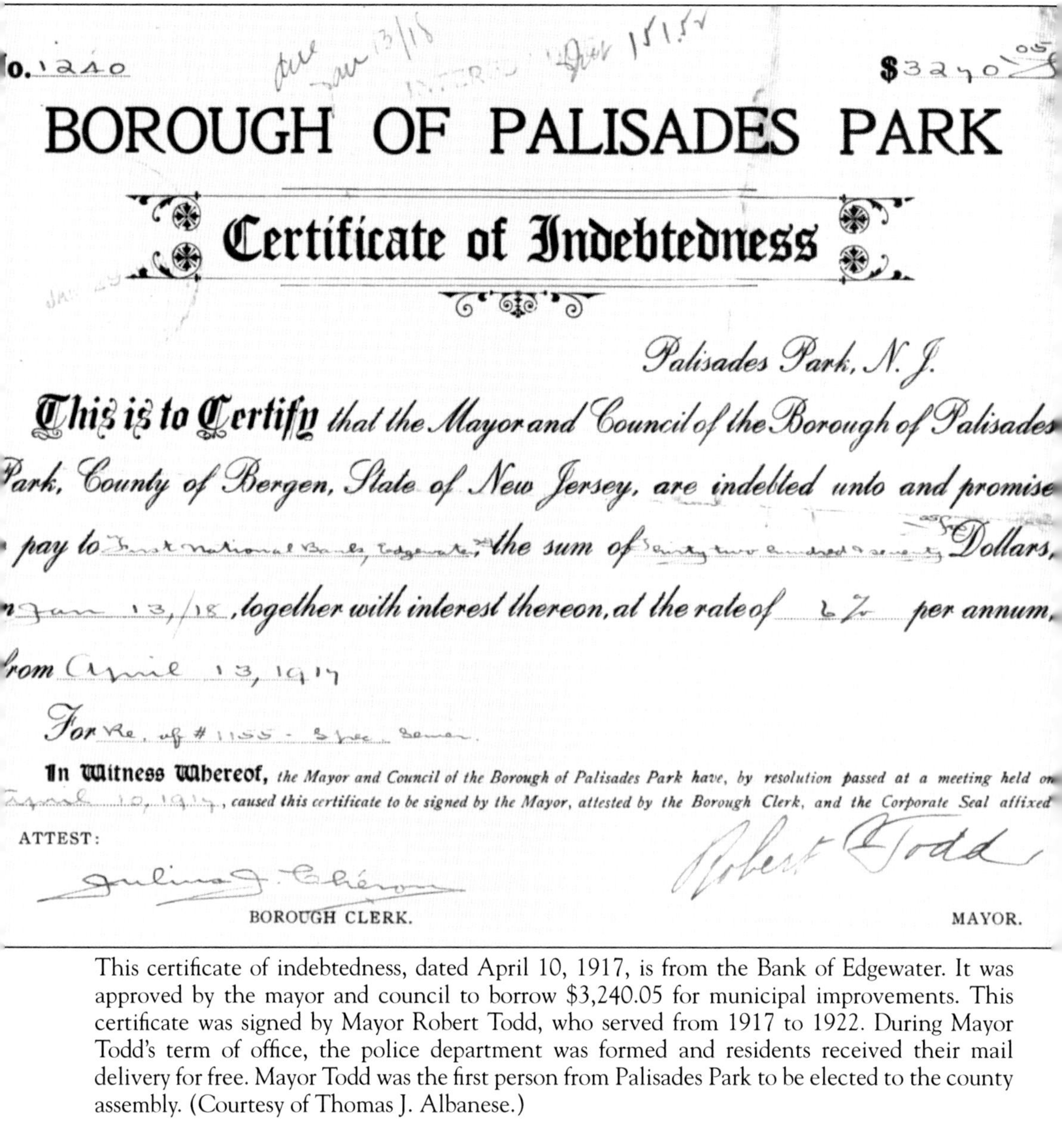

No. 1210 $3240.05

BOROUGH OF PALISADES PARK

Certificate of Indebtedness

Palisades Park, N. J.

This is to Certify that the Mayor and Council of the Borough of Palisades Park, County of Bergen, State of New Jersey, are indebted unto and promise to pay to First National Bank, Edgewater, the sum of [illegible] Dollars, on Jan 13/18, together with interest thereon, at the rate of 6% per annum, from April 13, 1917

For Re. of # 1155 - [illegible]

In Witness Whereof, the Mayor and Council of the Borough of Palisades Park have, by resolution passed at a meeting held on April 10, 1917, caused this certificate to be signed by the Mayor, attested by the Borough Clerk, and the Corporate Seal affixed

ATTEST:

BOROUGH CLERK.

Robert Todd

MAYOR.

This certificate of indebtedness, dated April 10, 1917, is from the Bank of Edgewater. It was approved by the mayor and council to borrow $3,240.05 for municipal improvements. This certificate was signed by Mayor Robert Todd, who served from 1917 to 1922. During Mayor Todd's term of office, the police department was formed and residents received their mail delivery for free. Mayor Todd was the first person from Palisades Park to be elected to the county assembly. (Courtesy of Thomas J. Albanese.)

Four

LANDSCAPES AND STREETSCAPES

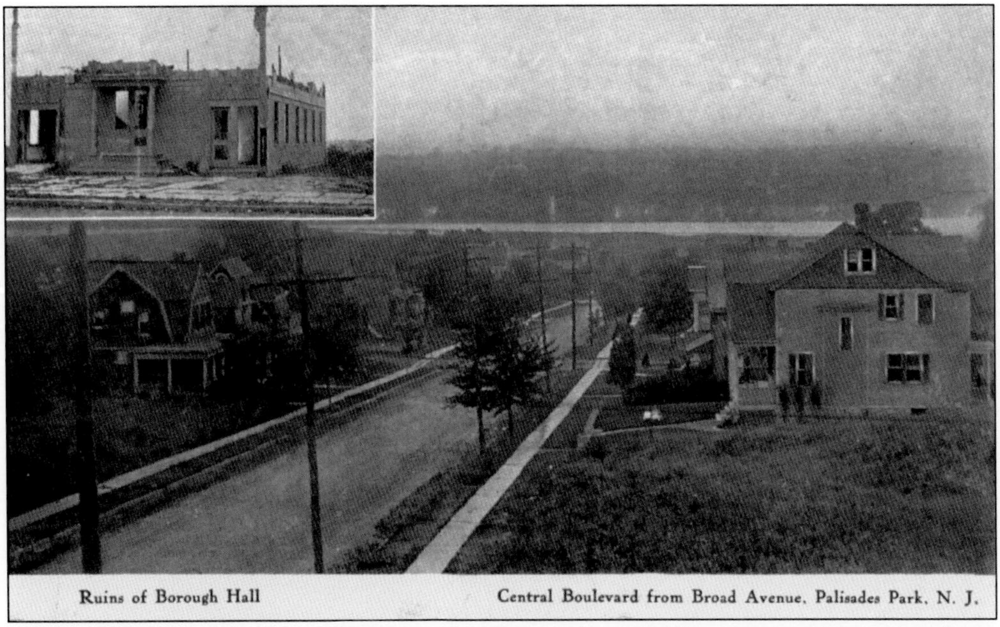

Ruins of Borough Hall Central Boulevard from Broad Avenue, Palisades Park, N. J.

This is a 1907 view of Central Boulevard from Broad Avenue. The insert in the top left shows the ruins of the first borough hall, a two-story framed building opened on March 13, 1905. The building was also used for social events and classrooms. In June 1906, fire destroyed the building. Municipal meetings, matters, and events were temporarily held at Abram Cottrell's Heisenbuttle Hotel, located on West Central Boulevard near the Erie Railroad, until May 1908, when a new fireproof building was built. (Courtesy of Evelyn P. Meier.)

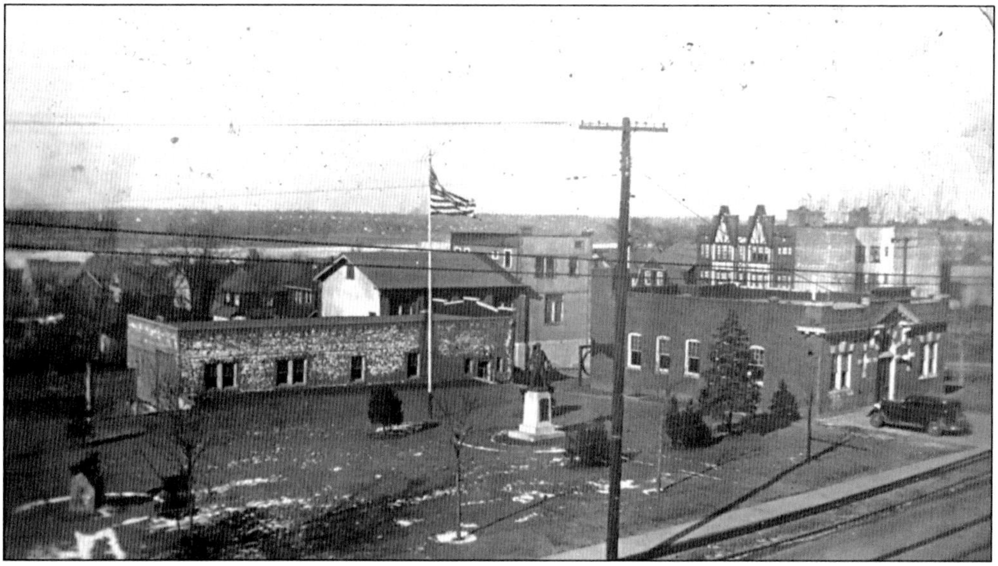

This photograph from January 16, 1935, shows the American flag flying proudly in the park adjacent to the borough hall. The property was purchased in 1904 from Catherine Moran for $900. In 1961, the World War I soldier monument was moved to allow for the construction of the current municipal building. (Courtesy of Leonard R. Cottrell.)

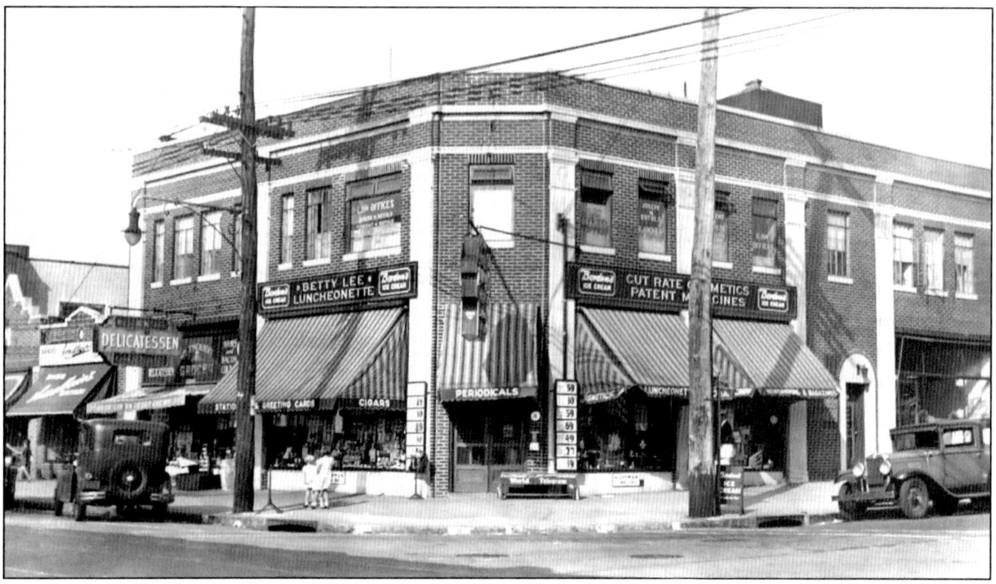

The Betty Lee Luncheonette, seen here around 1929, was located on the northeast corner of Broad Avenue at East Central Boulevard. One store north was Rinckhoff's Grocery and Butcher Shop, where customers purchased fresh hams and bacon. Occupying the second floor of the building were the law offices of Joseph M. Rotolo, who also served as municipal court judge from 1938 through 1955. His grandson Joseph J. Rotolo was appointed municipal court judge in January 2008 and currently presides over the municipal court. (Courtesy of Evelyn P. Meier.)

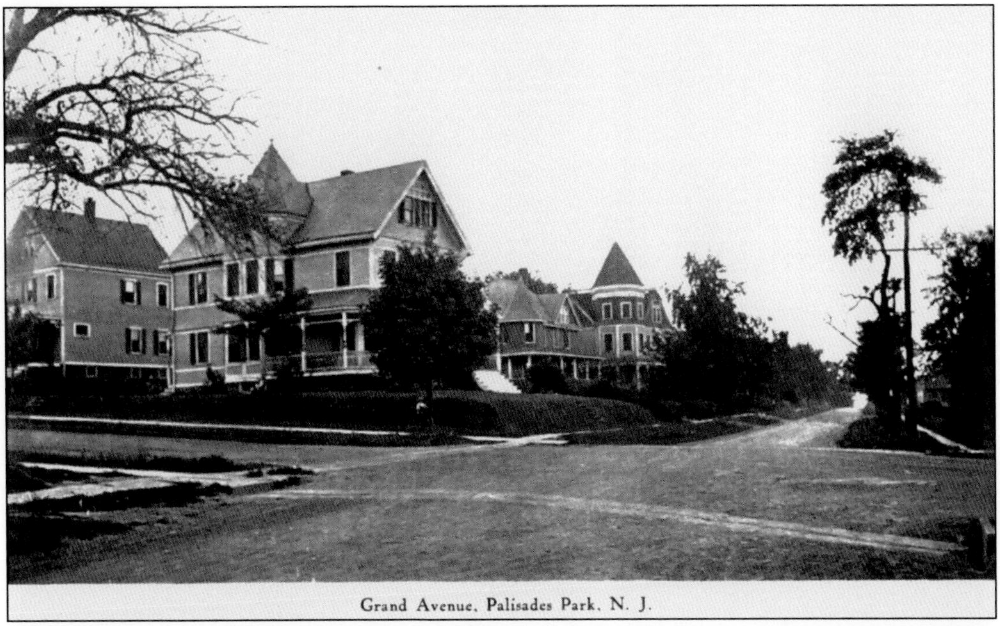

This postcard is postmarked October 12, 1908. Pictured is the intersection of Grand Avenue and Central Boulevard.

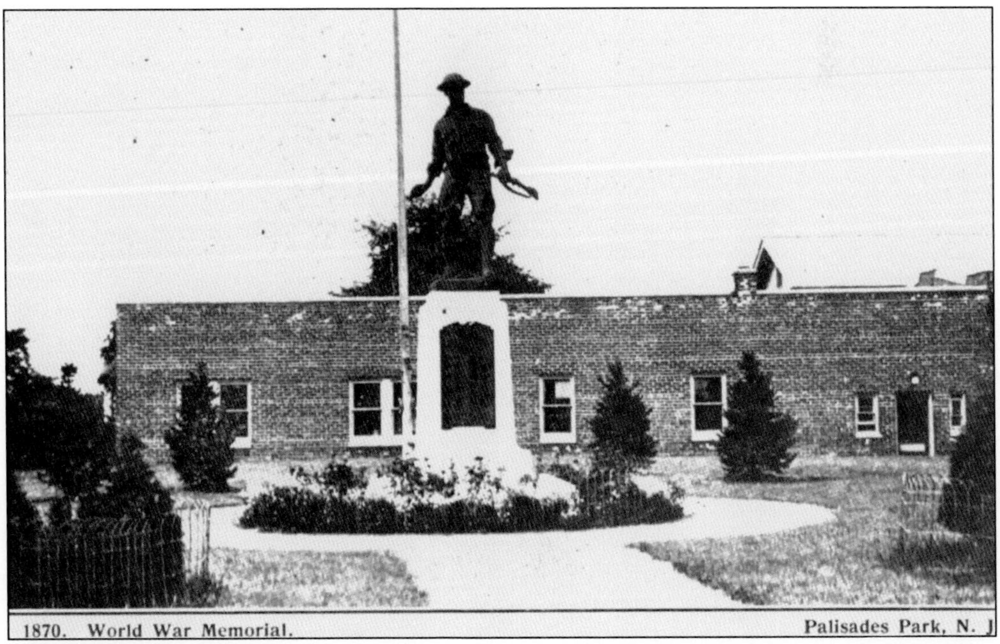

This 1937 postcard features a minuteman statute, a World War I monument in the park at borough hall.

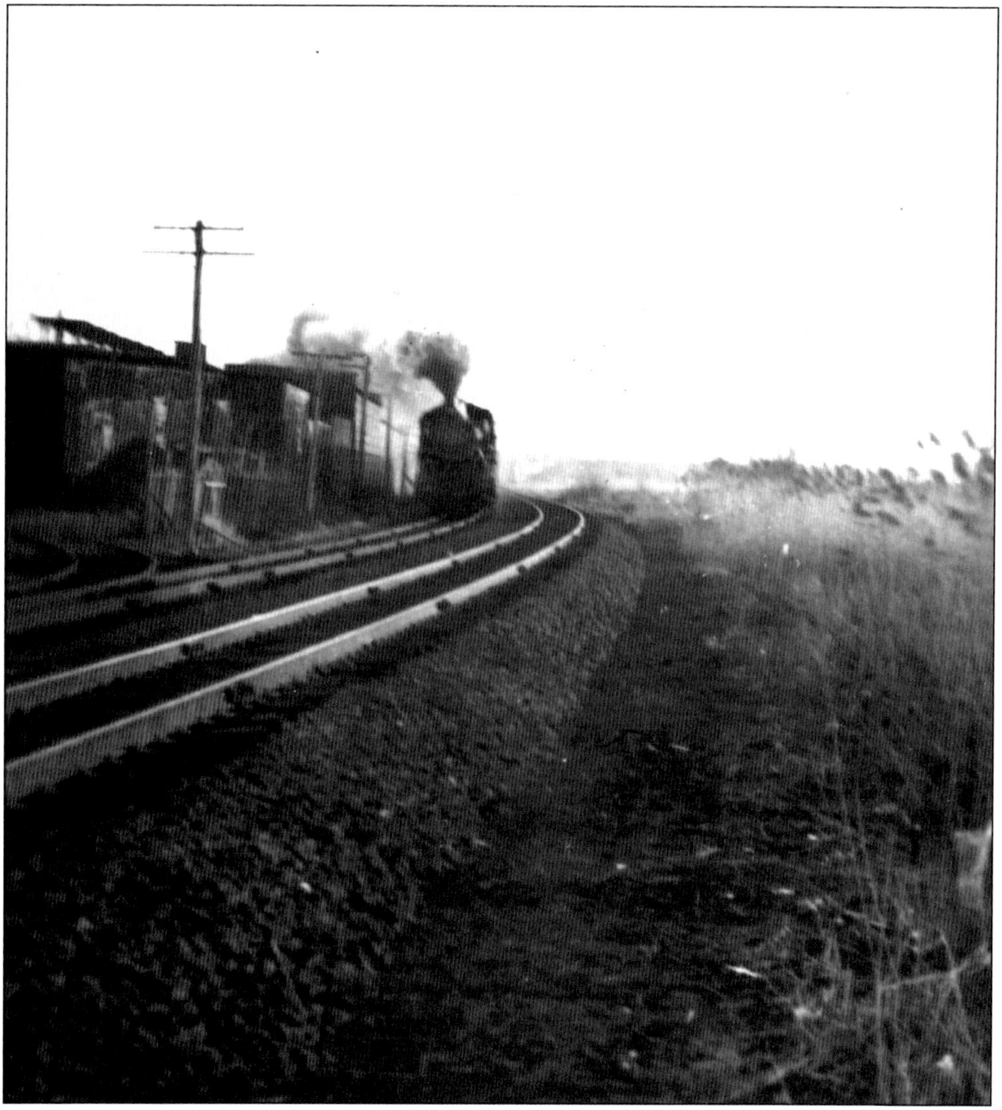

Seen here around 1930, an Erie Railroad train travels north. In April 1893, tragedy struck along the tracks. Four New York City youths schemed to run away from home to see the world's fair in Chicago. They had 42¢ between them and set out on Monday, April 17 at 7:00 p.m. The boys were Thomas Eugene Ralston, 15 years old; James M. Connors, 12 years old; and two others named McLaughlin and McCarthy. Early along the way, McLaughlin and McCarthy were frightened and headed back home. Young Ralston and Connors continued on their journey, sleeping that night in a wagon at a ferry house in Jersey City. They set out at 5:00 a.m. on Tuesday, and at 8:00 that night, the boys slept on a platform at Palisades Park. At about 10:00 p.m., young Connors awoke and Ralston was missing, so he went looking for him. It was then he discovered that his friend Ralston was struck and run over by the train. Young Connors later told authorities he believed Ralston must have walked onto the tracks in his sleep. (Courtesy of Arthur Anderson.)

The railway express mail building and the Palisades Park railroad station are seen here around 1930. This railroad station replaced the original building that was destroyed by fire in 1892. A victim of nonuse and vandalism, this building was knocked down sometime in the 1950s. The post office used this building to store the mail, which came in and out by train. (Courtesy of Arthur Anderson.)

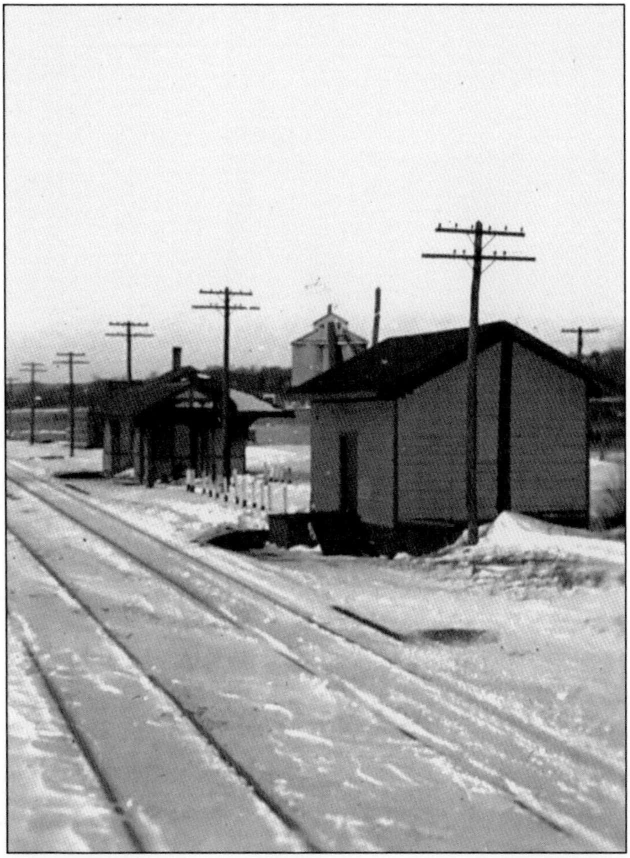

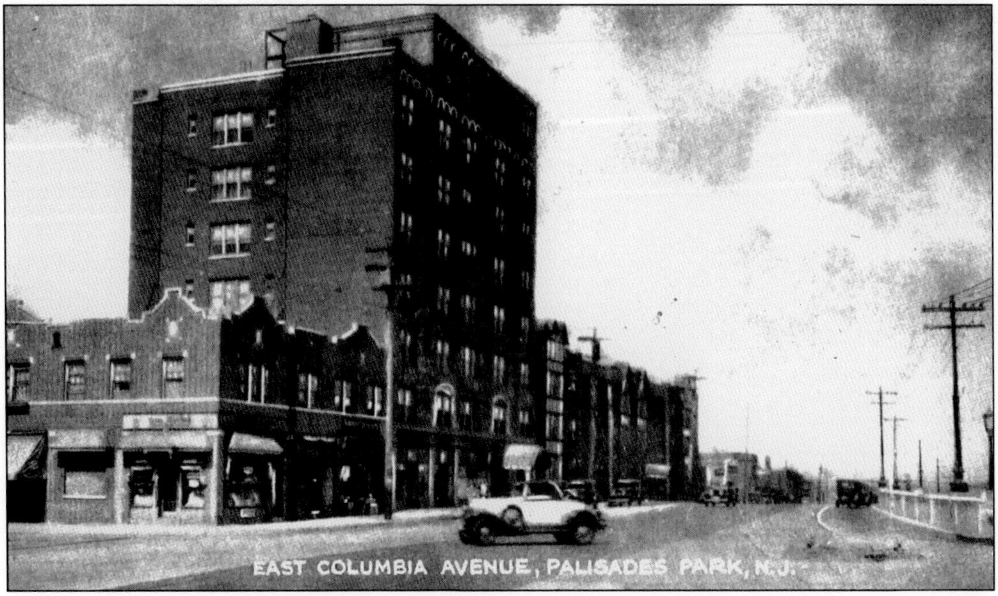

This c. 1940 vintage view shows East Columbia Avenue at the intersection of Roff Avenue. The tall building is at 40 East Columbia.

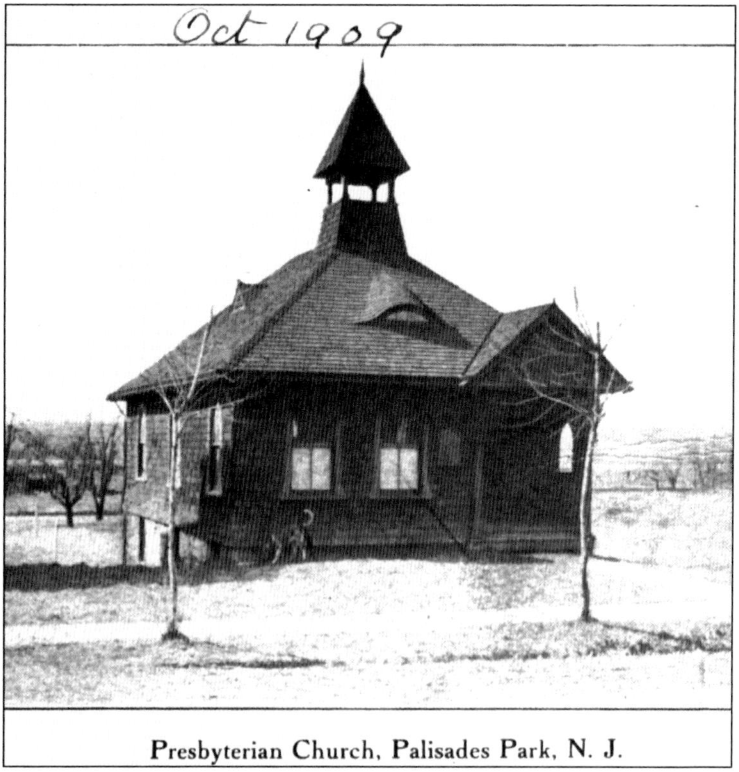

This Presbyterian church was originally called Union Chapel of Palisades Park. In 1897, John and Henry Brinkerhoff donated the land, now 219 Grand Avenue, to build this chapel, pictured here in October 1909. The cornerstone was laid on November 28, 1897, and dedication with first services were celebrated on March 6, 1898. Prior to February 19, 1909, when the Union Chapel became a Presbyterian church, it was undenominational. (Courtesy of Pastor David Peng.)

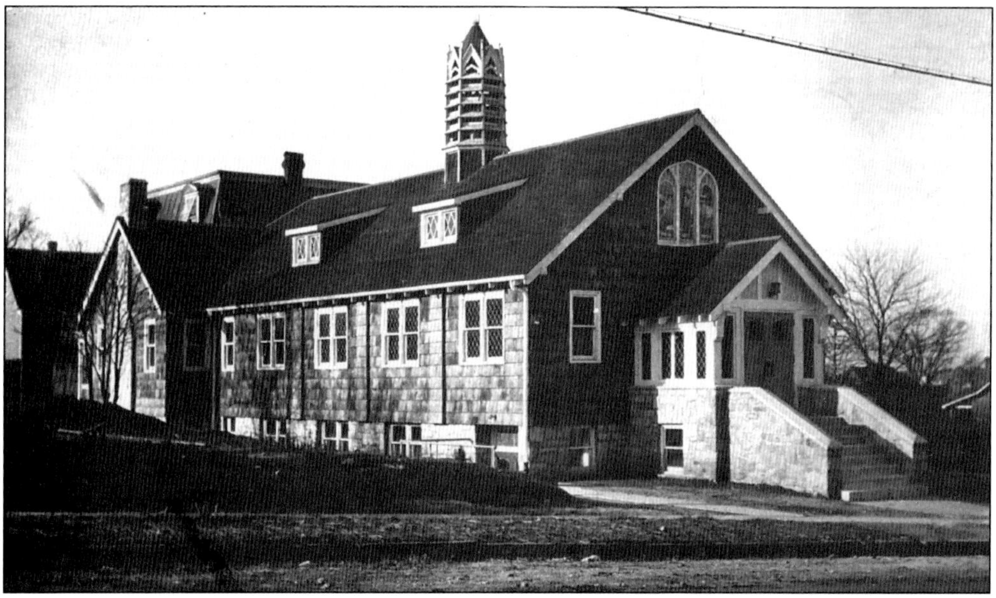

This *c*. 1920 photograph shows the First Presbyterian Church located on West Palisades Boulevard at Hillside Avenue. This church was dedicated on July 9, 1916, and still serves the community today. Some of Palisades Park's most notable families, such as the Edsalls and Brinkerhoffs, were founding members. The Edsall family believed strongly in their faith and their church, and Samuel and John S. Edsall left large donations in their wills. (Courtesy of Pastor David Peng.)

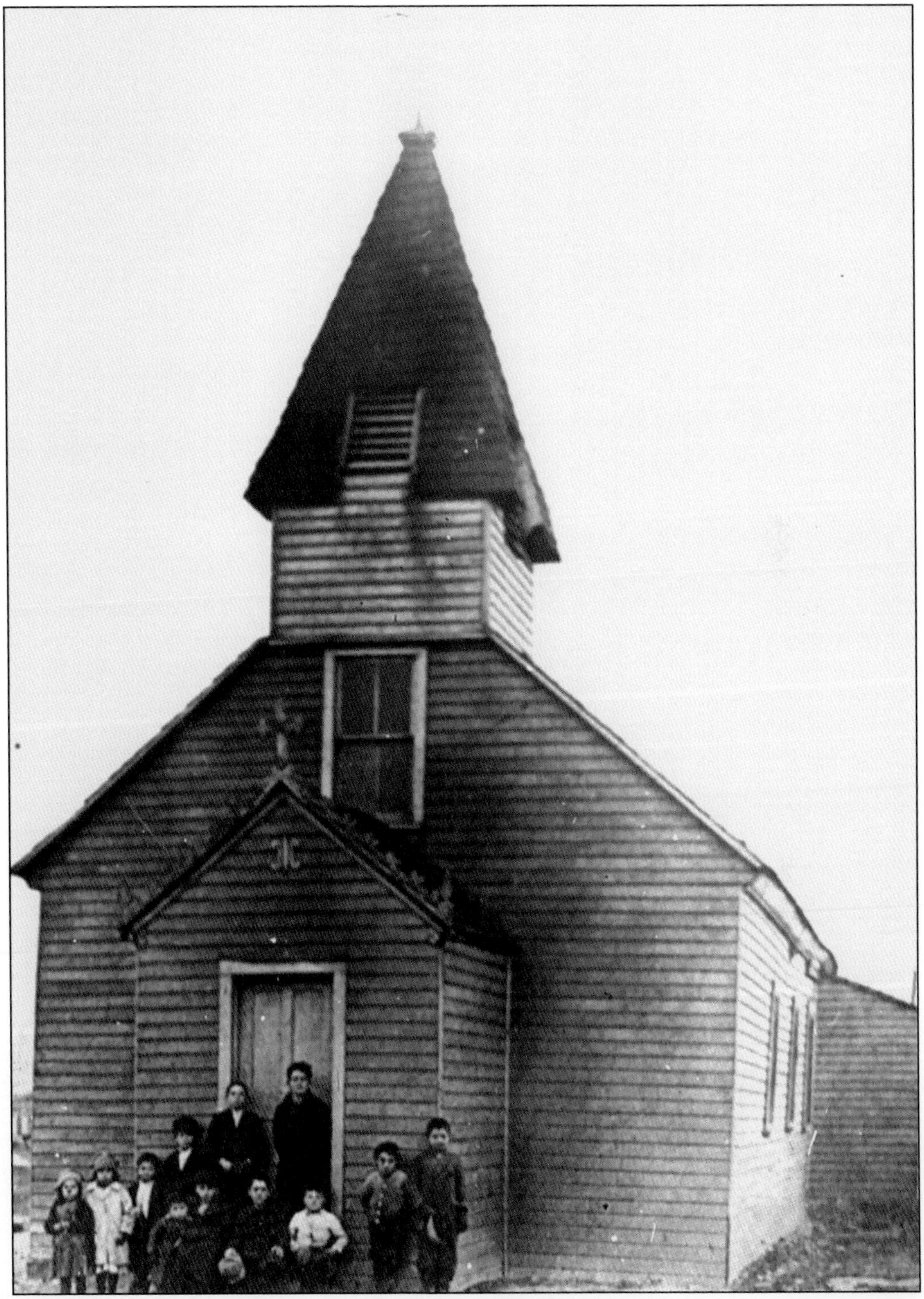

Children gather at the front door of St. Nicholas Church in 1923. In 1893, a small concentration of Italians settled on the hill of Palisades Park, often referred to as Nanny Goat Hill. The Italians resided among a sizable Polish community that occupied the heavily wooded area, building a wood-framed church they called Our Lady of Czetochowa. Polish priests were having difficulty keeping the church open to parishioners because no priest could conveniently reside there due to many hardships. Eventually in 1923, a rectory was built with the help of the parishioners, and on March 12, 1923, the church became legally established as St. Nicholas Italian Roman Catholic Church. (Courtesy of Charles Martini.)

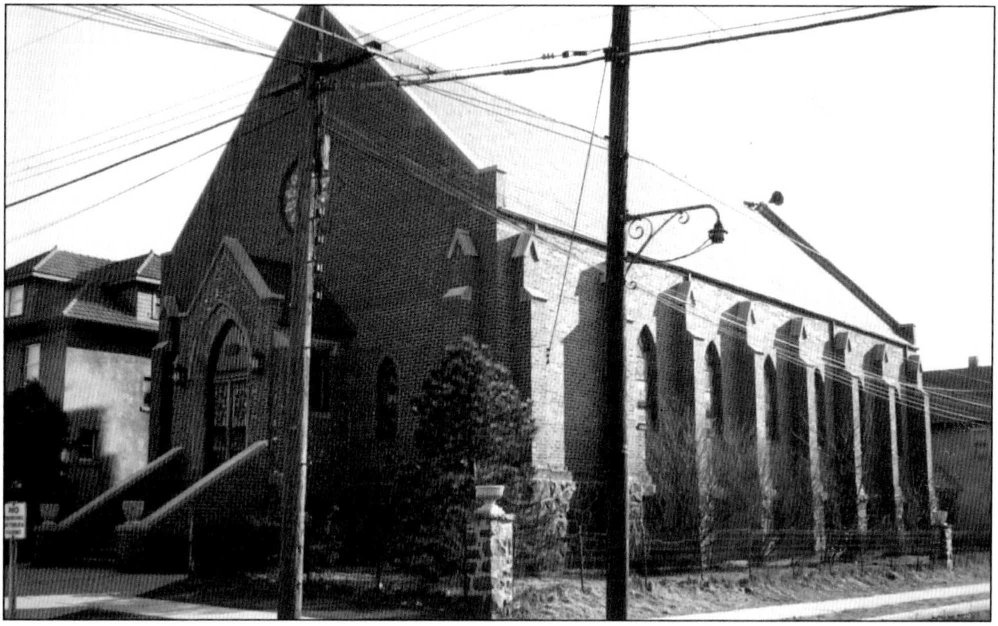

Rev. Ferdinand Anzalone was appointed pastor of St. Nicholas on June 29, 1927, and began securing funds for a new church. In October 1929, construction began, and on May 4, 1930, parishioners were delighted to welcome their new church (seen above) with a dedication from Archbishop Thomas J. Walsh. In 1948, a convent was built and housed the Filippini Sisters. During 1958, a rectory and school were completed. Later in 1962, the old icehouse was purchased at auction to provide a parking facility for parishioners. (Courtesy of *Golden Jubilee of 1949*.)

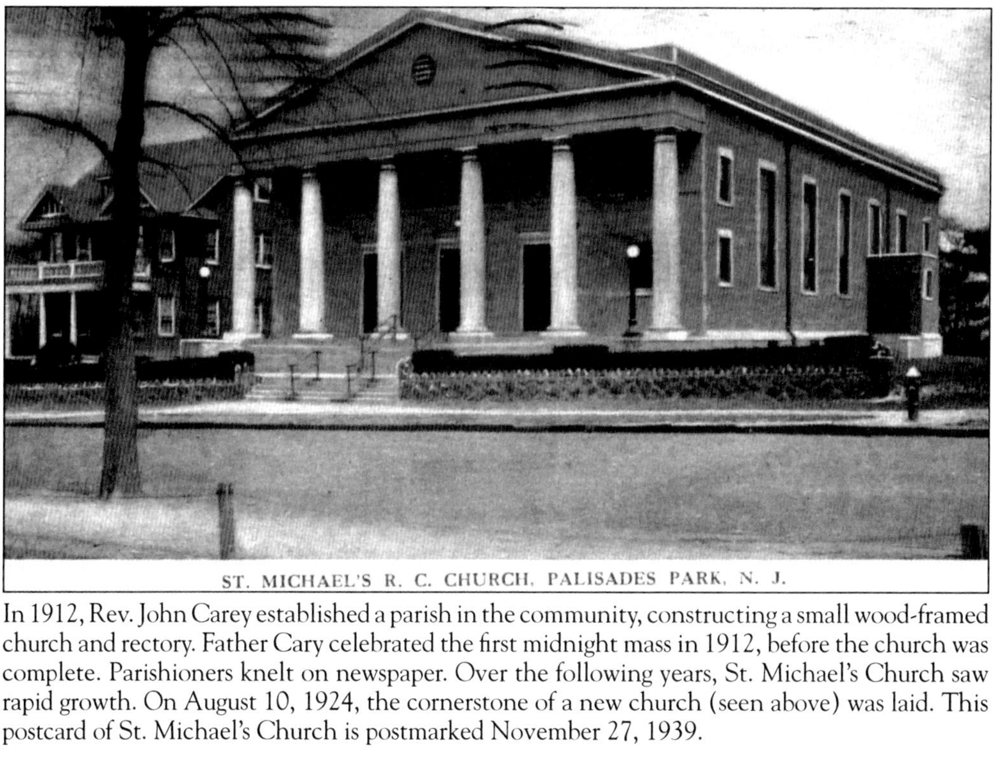

ST. MICHAEL'S R. C. CHURCH, PALISADES PARK, N. J.

In 1912, Rev. John Carey established a parish in the community, constructing a small wood-framed church and rectory. Father Cary celebrated the first midnight mass in 1912, before the church was complete. Parishioners knelt on newspaper. Over the following years, St. Michael's Church saw rapid growth. On August 10, 1924, the cornerstone of a new church (seen above) was laid. This postcard of St. Michael's Church is postmarked November 27, 1939.

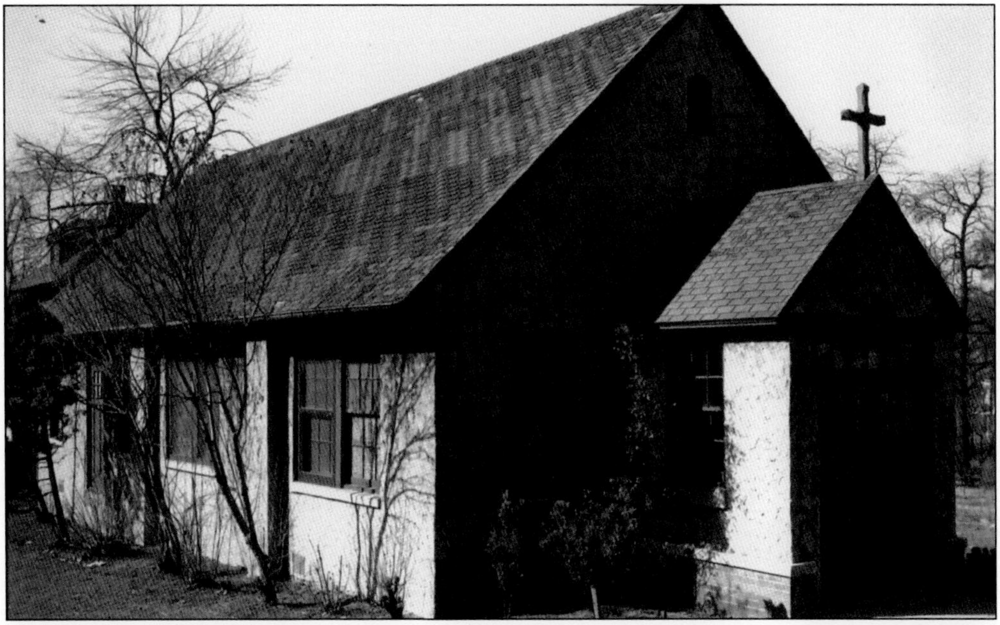

The Church of the Redeemer, pictured here in 1949, was formed after a meeting on March 16, 1925, when 17 members of the Episcopal church met to discuss forming a permanent church. This church was built in August 1927, and the first service was held on September 18, 1927. In 1959, the congregation relocated back to Ridgefield, and the Knights of Columbus bought the property. (Courtesy of *Golden Jubilee of 1949*.)

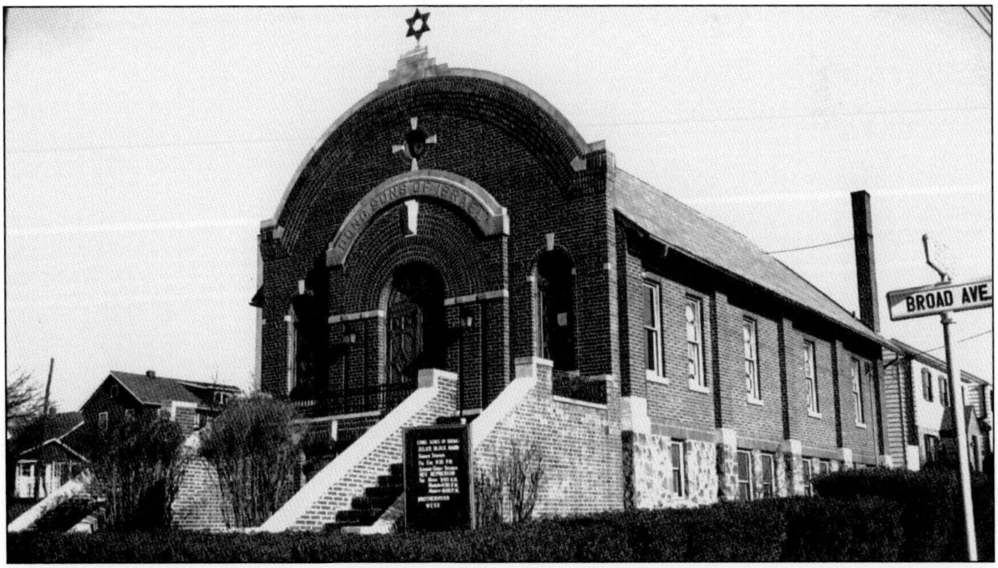

This property, pictured in 1949 and belonging to the Congregation Sons of Israel, was purchased in 1925. Prior to the opening in 1925, members held High Holiday services in a store on Broad Avenue near Homestead Avenue. Shortly after, the Legion Club House in Leonia became the makeshift meeting- and schoolhouse. The synagogue remained here until 1965, when the congregation moved to a new building on Grand Avenue in Leonia. The church is now the home of the Korean Presbyterian Church of New Jersey. (Courtesy of *Golden Jubilee of 1949*.)

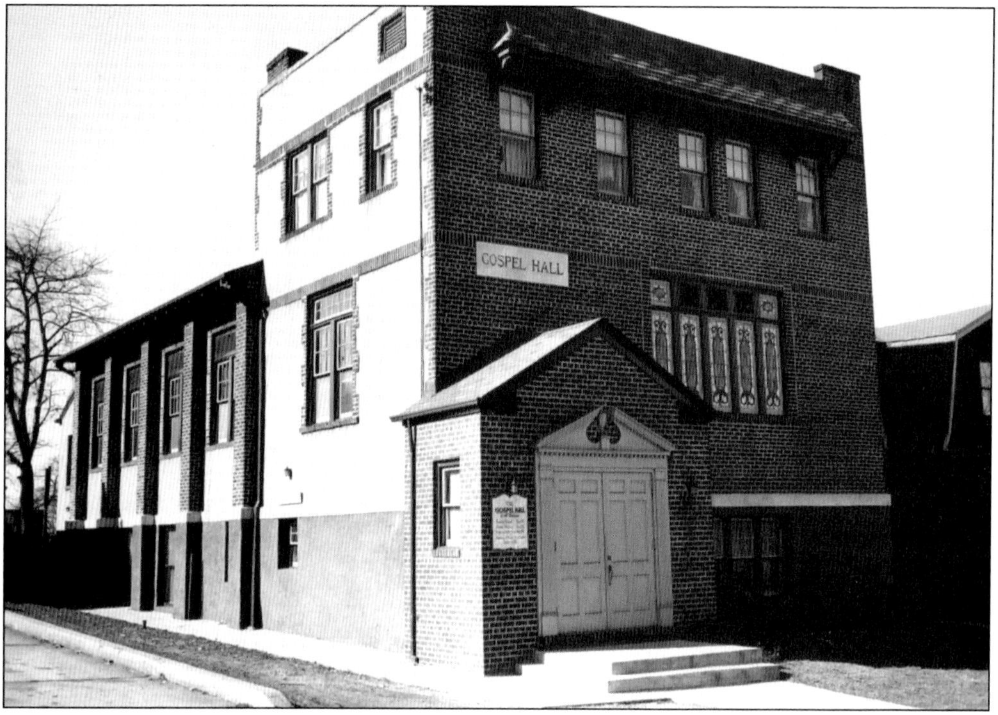

In 1908, 10 members of the Union Church at 219 Grand Avenue left the church and sought their own congregation. They chose to use a hall located in a building on the corner of Grand Avenue and West Central Boulevard and named it Gospel Hall. In 1920, the building was sold, and they erected this building at 14 West Central Boulevard. (Courtesy of *Golden Jubilee of 1949*.)

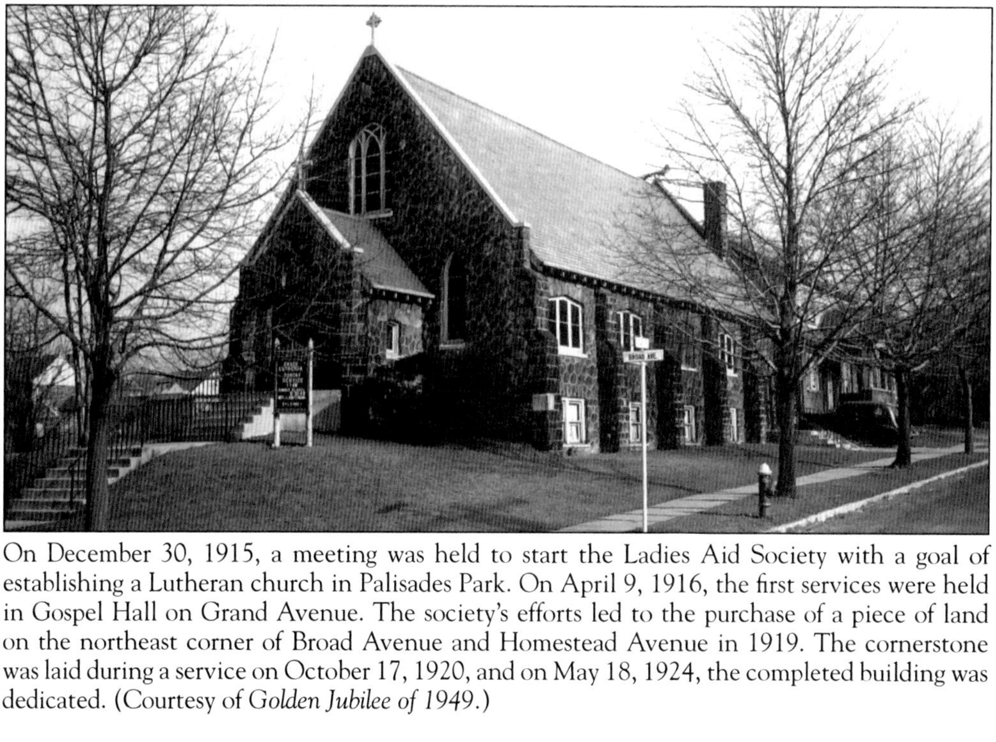

On December 30, 1915, a meeting was held to start the Ladies Aid Society with a goal of establishing a Lutheran church in Palisades Park. On April 9, 1916, the first services were held in Gospel Hall on Grand Avenue. The society's efforts led to the purchase of a piece of land on the northeast corner of Broad Avenue and Homestead Avenue in 1919. The cornerstone was laid during a service on October 17, 1920, and on May 18, 1924, the completed building was dedicated. (Courtesy of *Golden Jubilee of 1949*.)

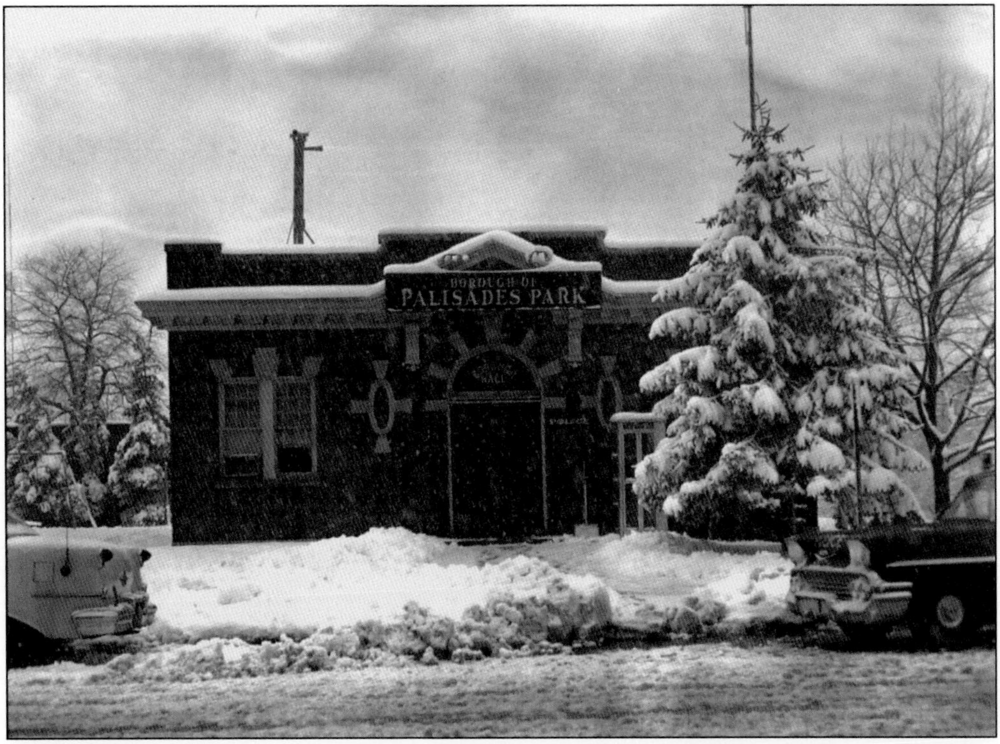

This image from March 21, 1958, shows the borough hall on a snowy day. Four years later, this building was replaced with a new municipal complex. (Courtesy of Leonard R. Cottrell.)

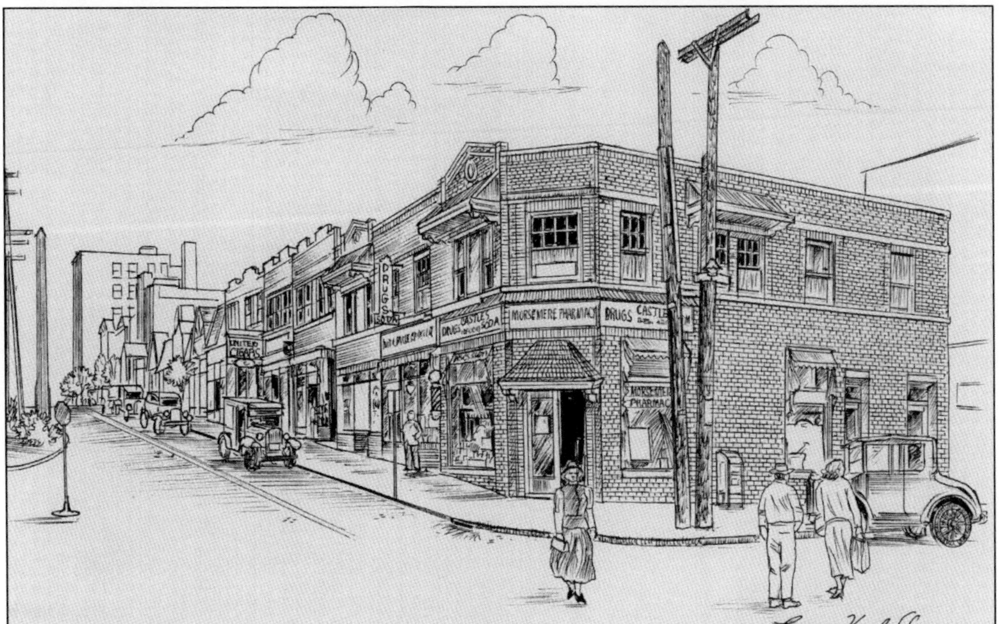

Local artist Eugene Kneloff created this rendition of the Morsemere section of Palisades Park around 1939. The Morsemere section of the town was developed by the Columbia Heights Realty Company. It had its offices on the northeast corner of Columbia and Broad Avenues.

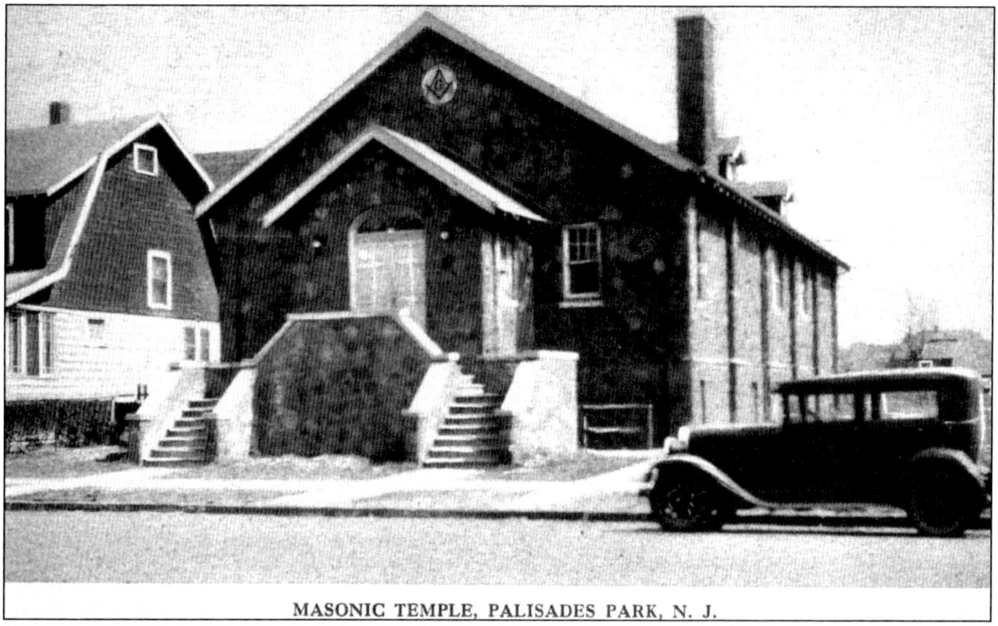

The Masonic temple is pictured here around 1931. In 1919, men gathered in a small back room of John B. Cowan's drugstore to discuss forming a Masonic club. The cornerstone was laid on July 9, 1921, and meetings began on October 13, 1921. Today it is the Armenian-American Support and Education Center.

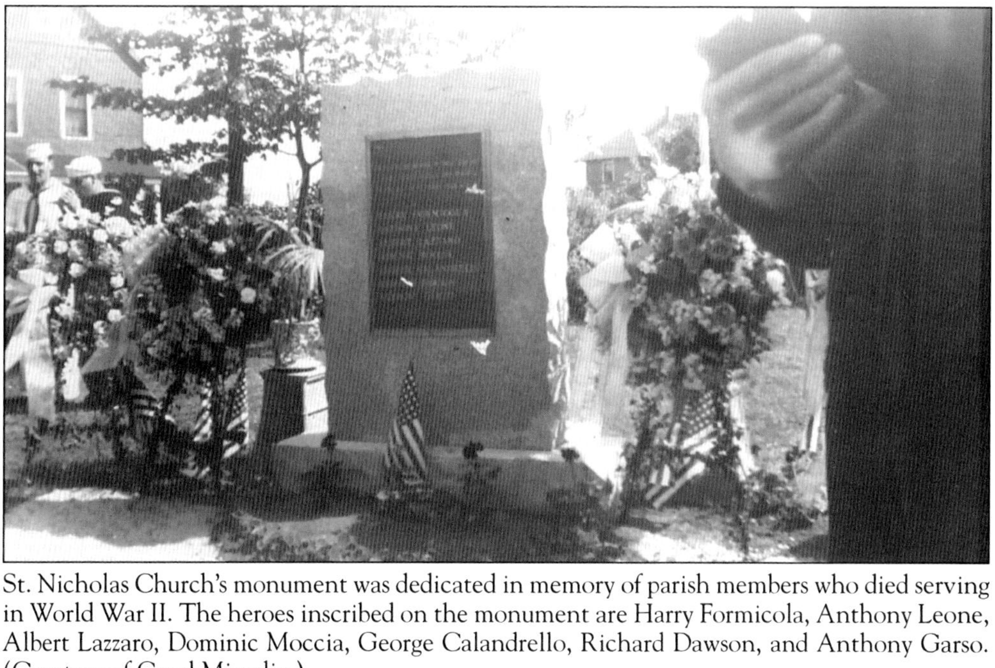

St. Nicholas Church's monument was dedicated in memory of parish members who died serving in World War II. The heroes inscribed on the monument are Harry Formicola, Anthony Leone, Albert Lazzaro, Dominic Moccia, George Calandrello, Richard Dawson, and Anthony Garso. (Courtesy of Carol Miraglia.)

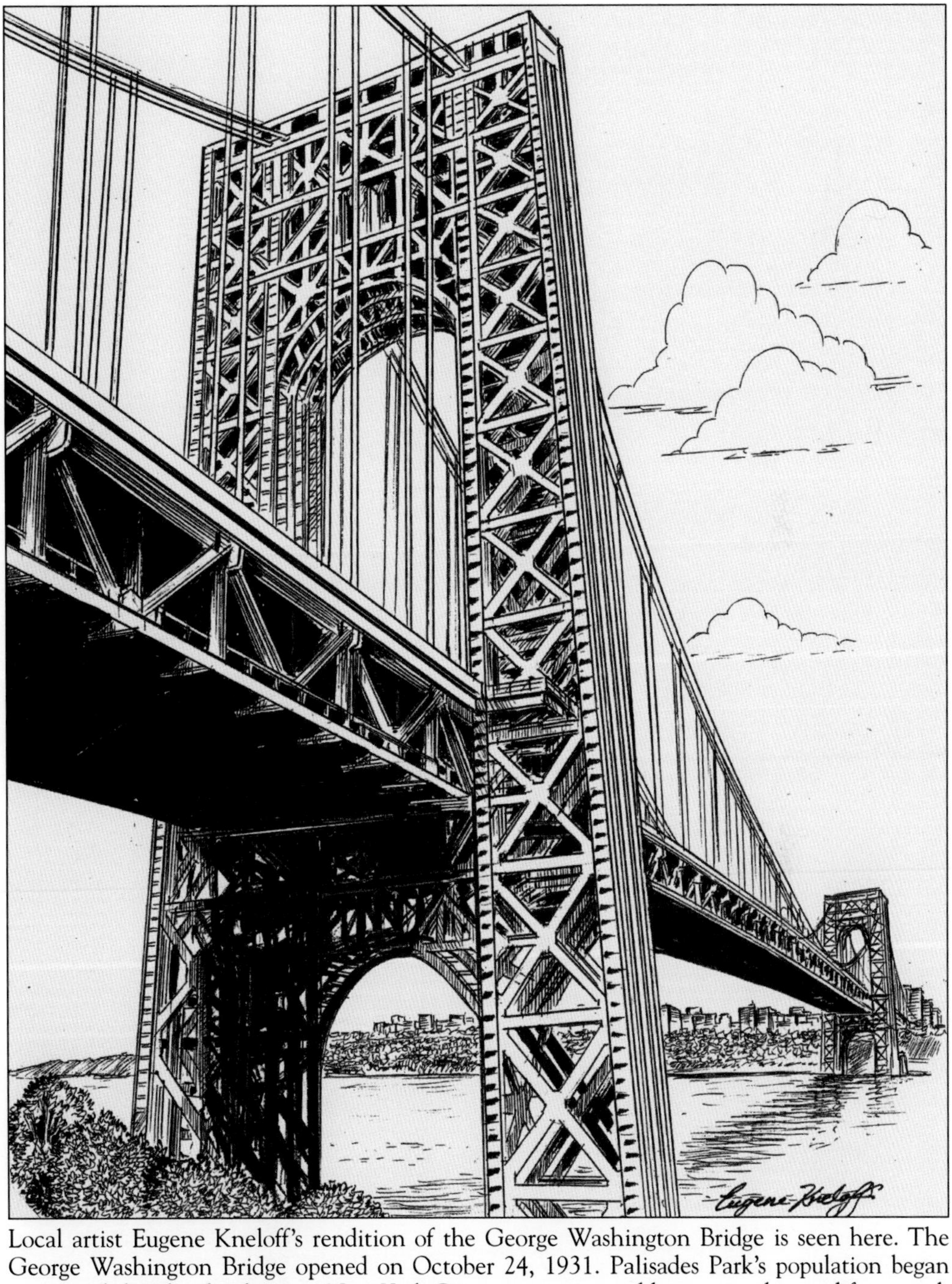

Local artist Eugene Kneloff's rendition of the George Washington Bridge is seen here. The George Washington Bridge opened on October 24, 1931. Palisades Park's population began to expand shortly after because New York City commuters could now travel to and from work faster. Route 46 was built specifically for this bridge. The bridge's lower level was completed on August 29, 1962.

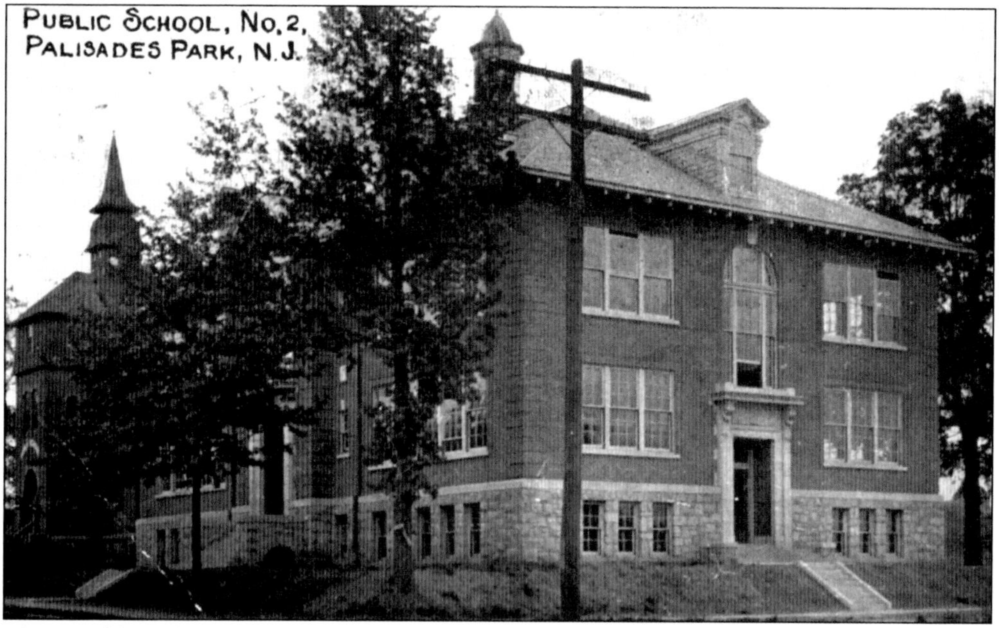

This is Public School No. 2. Palisades Park's school system dates back to 1885. This school was actually called Central Boulevard School, but because it was built after the building on the far left in the photograph, it was deemed Public School No. 2. It is pictured here in 1910.

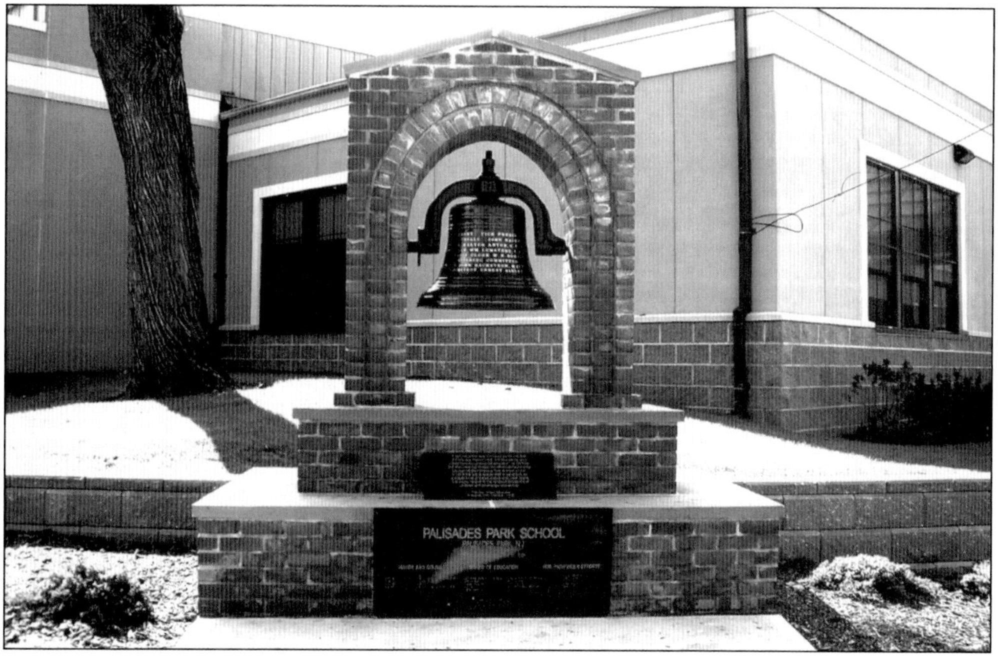

On September 13, 2008, the Palisades Park school bell was dedicated with a plaque affixed to the base. Palisades Park historian Thomas J. Albanese observed, "The bell was first heard by the children of Palisades Park in 1909. . . . In 1981 the bell was restored through the efforts of the Evening Division of the Palisades Park Woman's Club. In 2008 the bell is rededicated in perpetuity as a tribute to all of the educators who over nearly 100 years, helped fill the minds of thousands of children with knowledge and wonder."

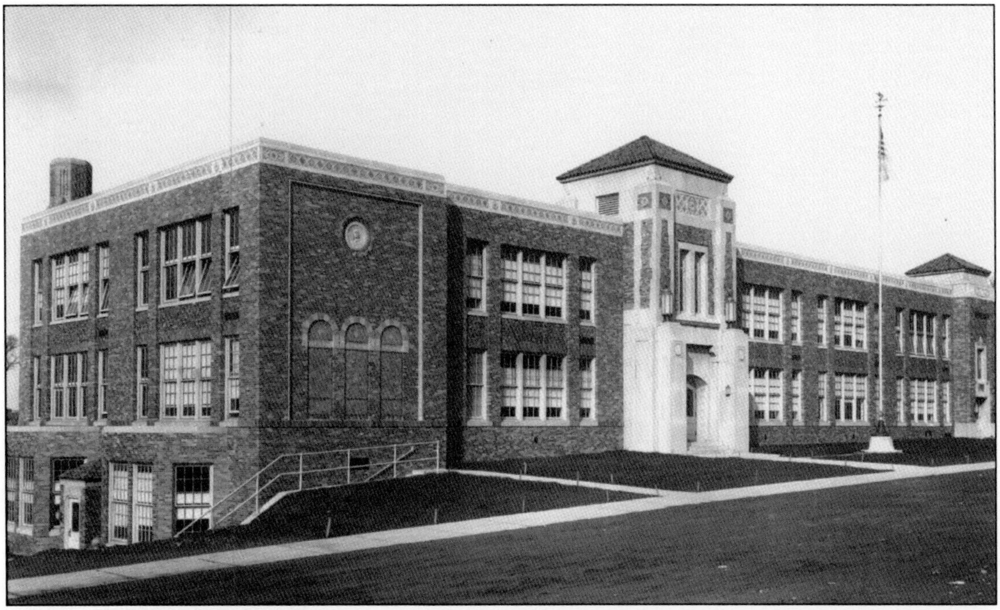

In late September 1928, ground was broken and construction continued through the winter for a new school (above). By August 1929, the building was ready to welcome new students. The board of education permitted the children to decide the name for their new school. The schoolchildren by an overwhelming majority decided to name Lindbergh School in honor of aviator Charles Augustus Lindbergh. The school was officially opened on September 7, 1929. It was equipped with modern classrooms, an auditorium, and a gymnasium. Below is a view of the inside of the original kindergarten. (Courtesy of Tony Bongard.)

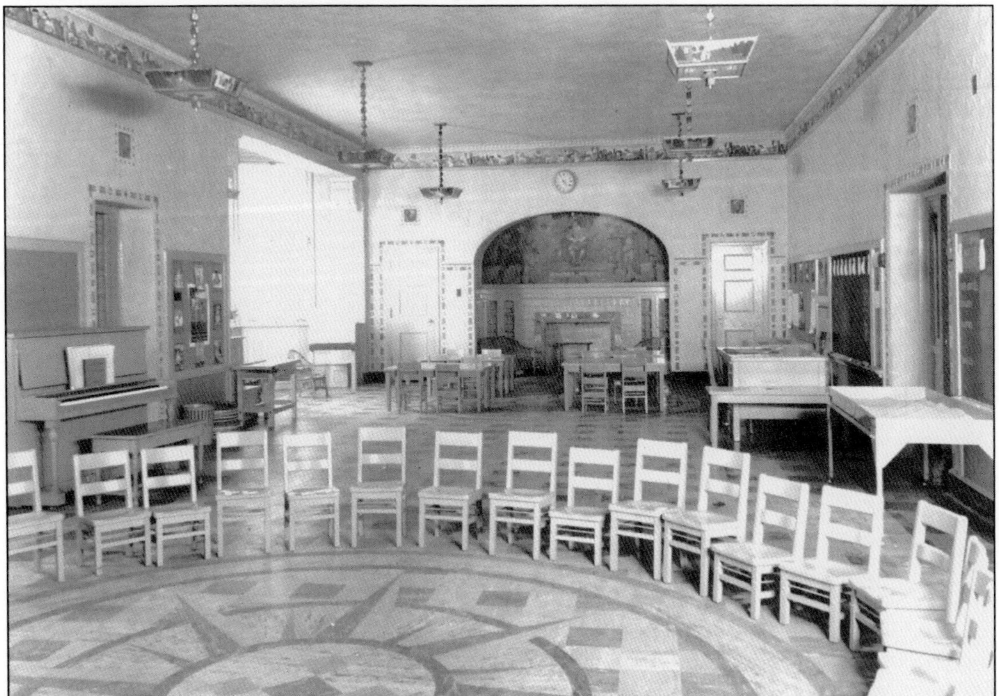

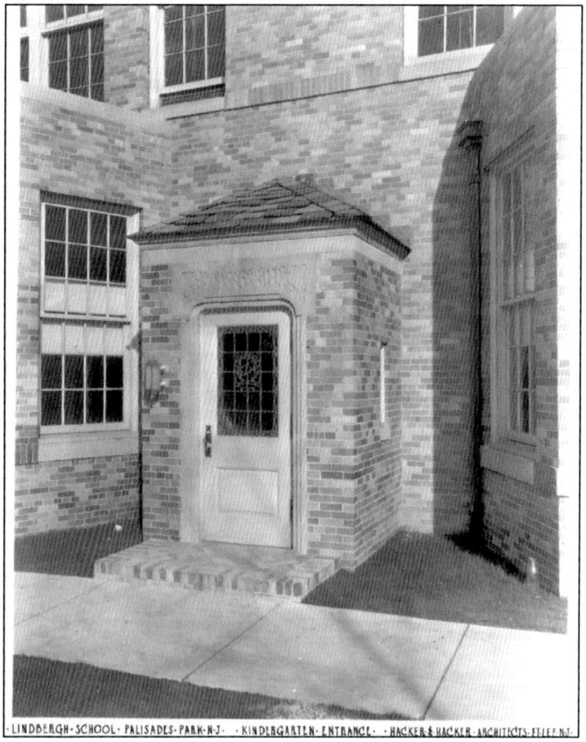

This is a view of the exterior of the Lindbergh School Kindergarten. This school opened on September 7, 1929, with 17 classrooms, an auditorium, and a gymnasium. After the opening, the old Central Boulevard School was also used as a complete elementary school, with classrooms on the first floor and a junior high school, housing grades seven through nine, on the second floor. The basement was used for physical fitness, art classes, and a technical shop. (Courtesy of Tony Bongard.)

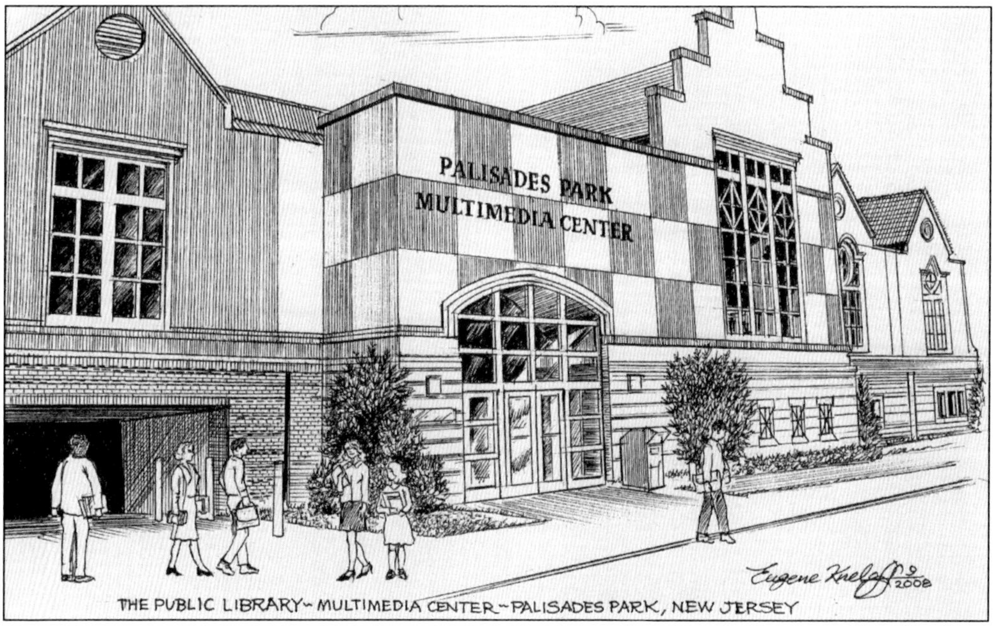

Local artist Eugene Kneloff's rendition of the Palisades Park Multimedia Center is seen here. Lena Harvey's devotion led to a library in the community. On April 15, 1917, a meeting was held in the Central Boulevard School and 104 residents signed cards as borrowers. Harvey was chosen as the first librarian. Residents who wished to be part of the library contributed 50¢ annually for library expenses. However, at the January municipal meeting of 1922, under the leadership of Mayor Robert Todd, a free public library was formed.

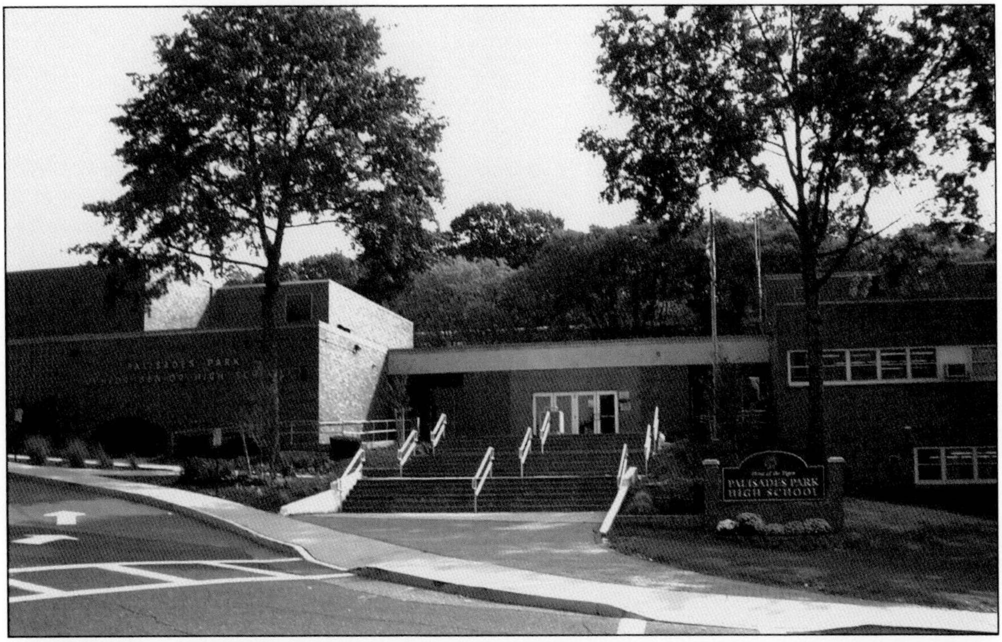

Pictured here is the Palisades Park Junior-Senior High School. Prior to the opening of the Palisades Park Junior-Senior High School in the fall of 1968, students in grades 10 through 12 attended Leonia High School until 1955, when a new contract with Cliffside Park High School was developed.

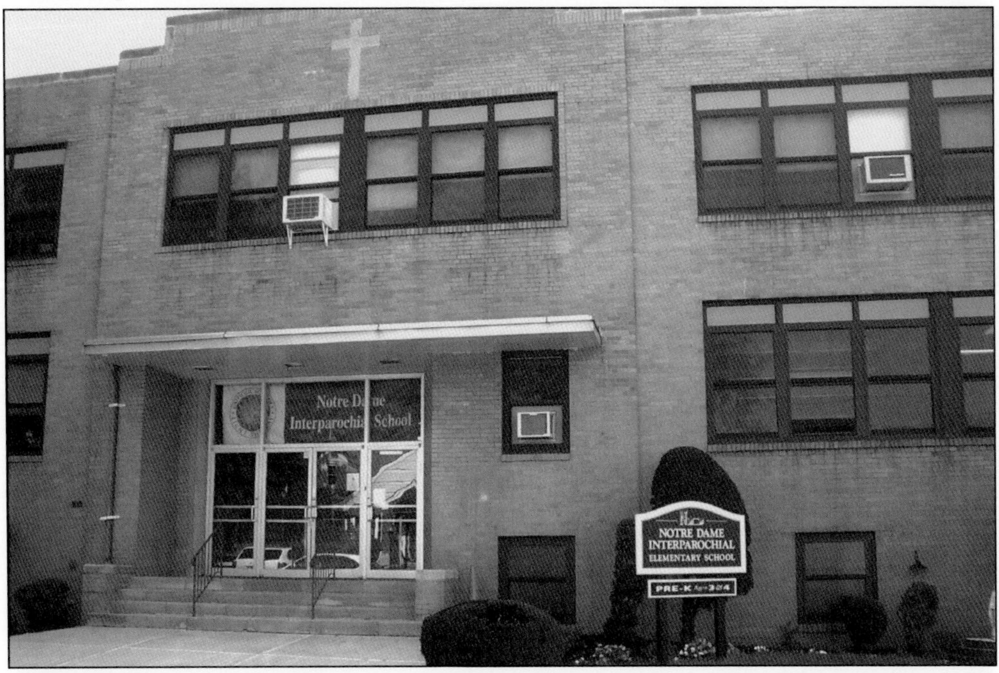

The Notre Dame Interparochial School was founded in September 1991 by merging the schools of St. Michaels, St. Nicholas, and St. Matthews of Ridgefield. Norte Dame Interparochial School was originally St. Michael's school, which was founded on September 8, 1958, and the pictured addition was completed by September 1960.

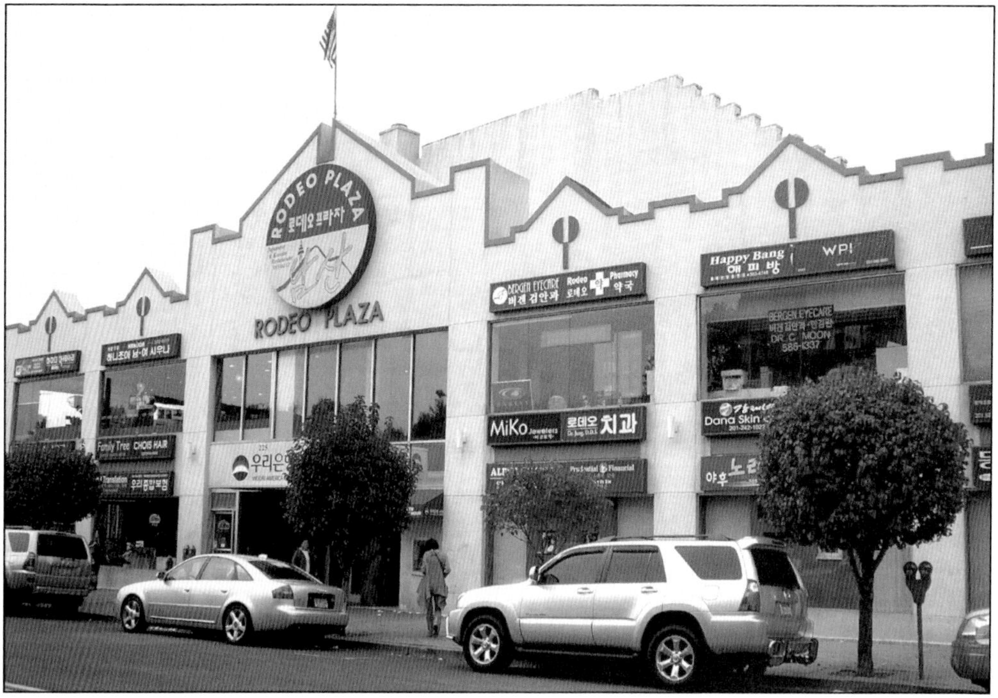

Above is the Rodeo Plaza. This plaza is the former home of the Park Lane Theatre. The Rodeo Plaza is among one of the nicest in the community and includes restaurants, a bank, clothing stores, a pharmacy, and many other fine stores all in one centralized location. Below is a view of the Tamla Plaza, which is located across the street from Rodeo Plaza, between Henry Avenue and East Brinkerhoff Avenue. This plaza has a bakery, restaurant, bank, barbershop, karaoke bar, professional medical and law offices, and other businesses. It has a three-level parking complex in the rear, accessible by East Brinkerhoff Avenue and the Henry Avenue Municipal Lot.

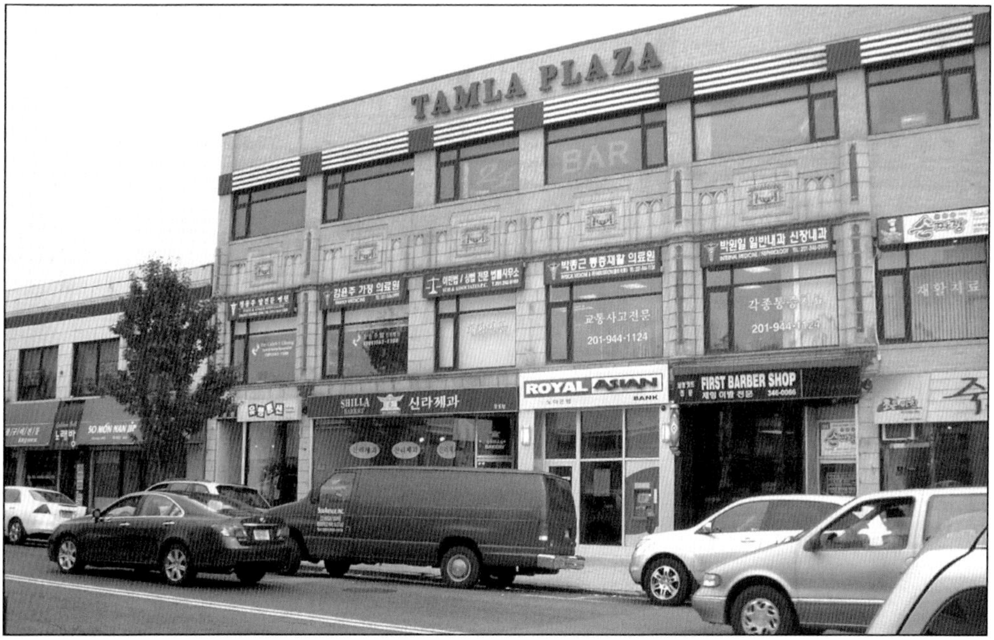

Frank Bellocchio's horse and snowplow are pictured here around 1935. During the 1920s and 1930s, Bellocchio guided his plow along the sidewalks, clearing the heavy snow so residents could move about safely. (Courtesy of Arthur Anderson.)

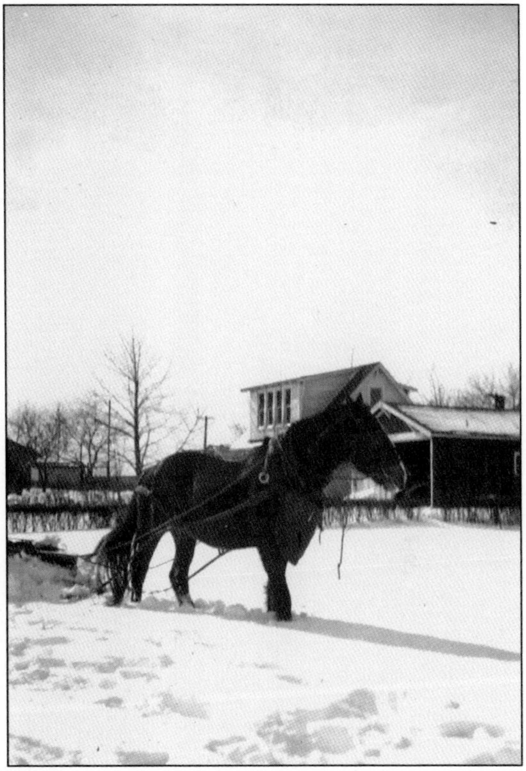

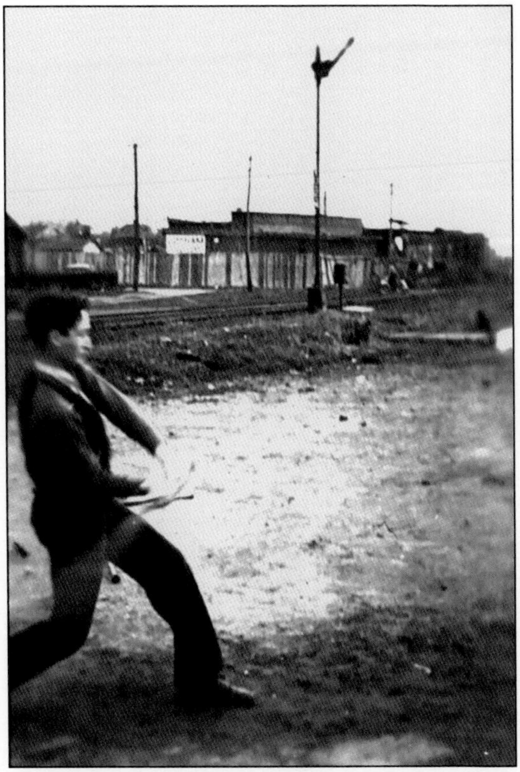

A boy plays baseball along the railroad tracks around 1938. The Palisades Park Lumber Yard is pictured in the background. This area was a popular recreation spot. South of the railroad station was the home field where the Eskimos semiprofessional football team played. (Courtesy of Arthur Anderson.)

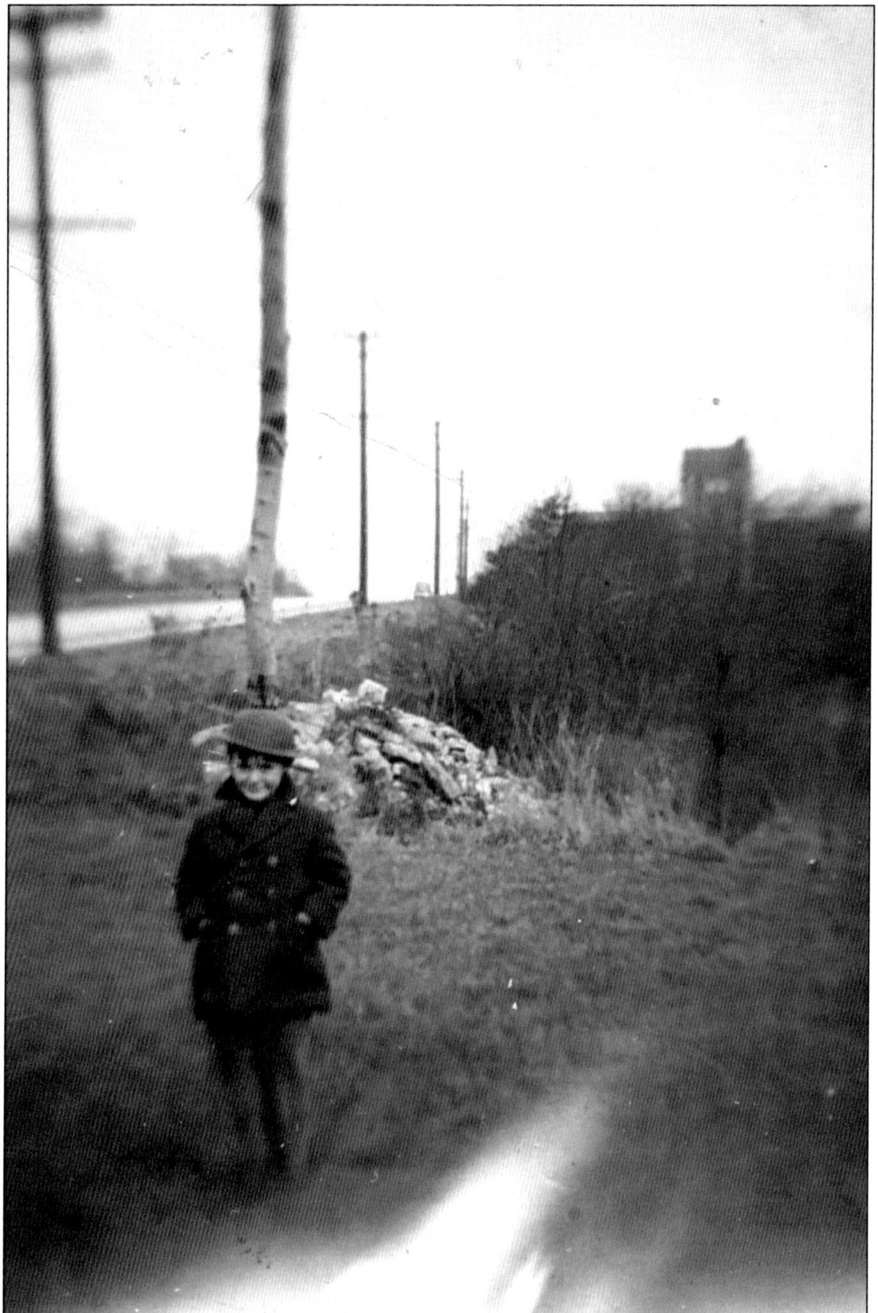

Pictured here in 1945 is Bergen Boulevard, facing north. The old watchtower is pictured in the distance. On May 24 at 8:40 a.m., J. Eves and M. Pollack were stationed in the watchtower and observed planes crash. Their work and rapidity contributed to saving the lives of two valuable pilots and soldiers. They received praise from Air Force major Charles A. Blackwell and regional commander Lt. Col. Davis D. Graves of the First Interceptor Command, New York Region, Ground Observation Section. Vincent Fusco is the boy in the photograph. (Courtesy of Carol Miraglia.)

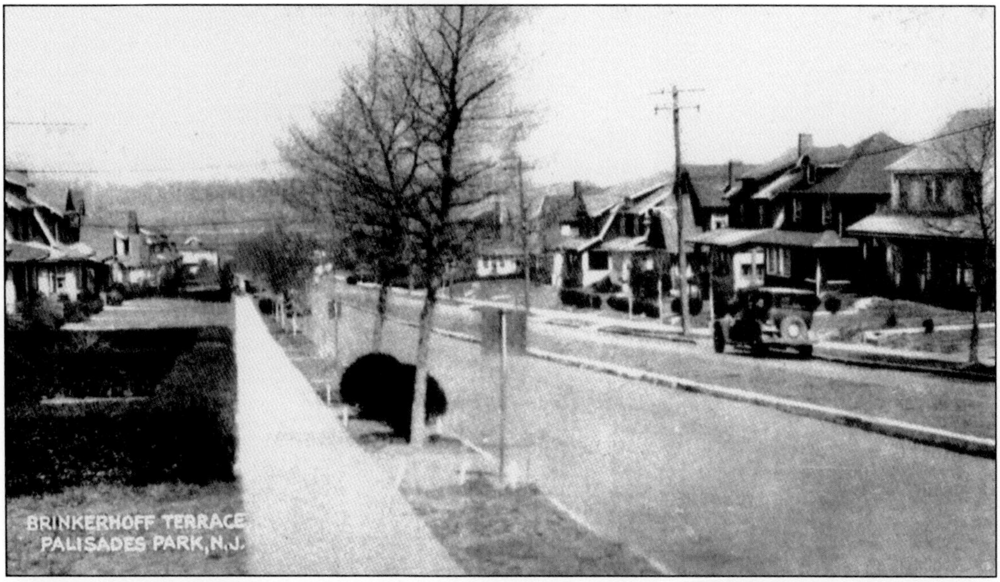

In this *c.* 1932 postcard is Brinkerhoff Terrace looking south from Broad Avenue. This roadway and Henry Avenue were named in honor of Henry Brinkerhoff and the Brinkerhoff family, whose roots are among the deepest in the borough. Before it was developed, the pictured land had a vast amount of apple trees.

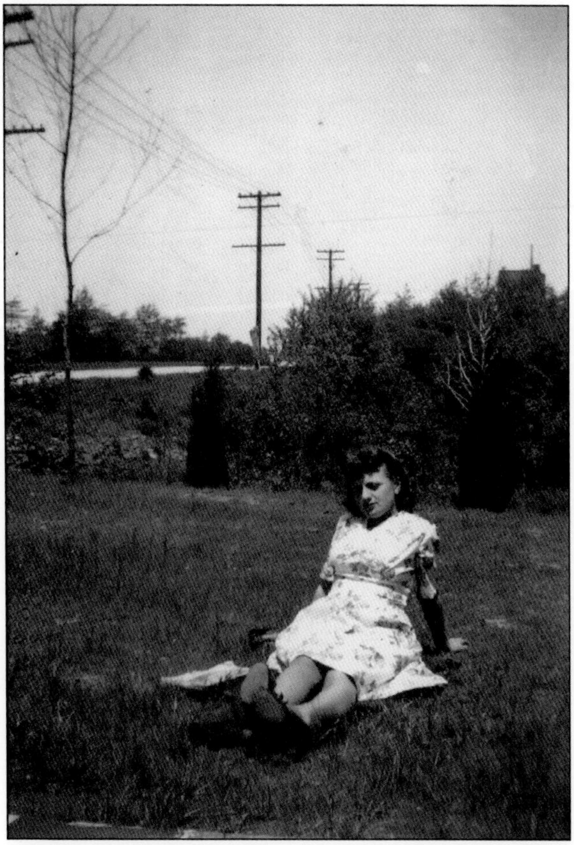

Caroline Miraglia is seen here relaxing in the grass along Bergen Boulevard in 1944. During this time, most of the land was heavily wooded with few dwellings. Bergen Boulevard also had large advertising billboards along the roadway. (Courtesy of Carol Miraglia.)

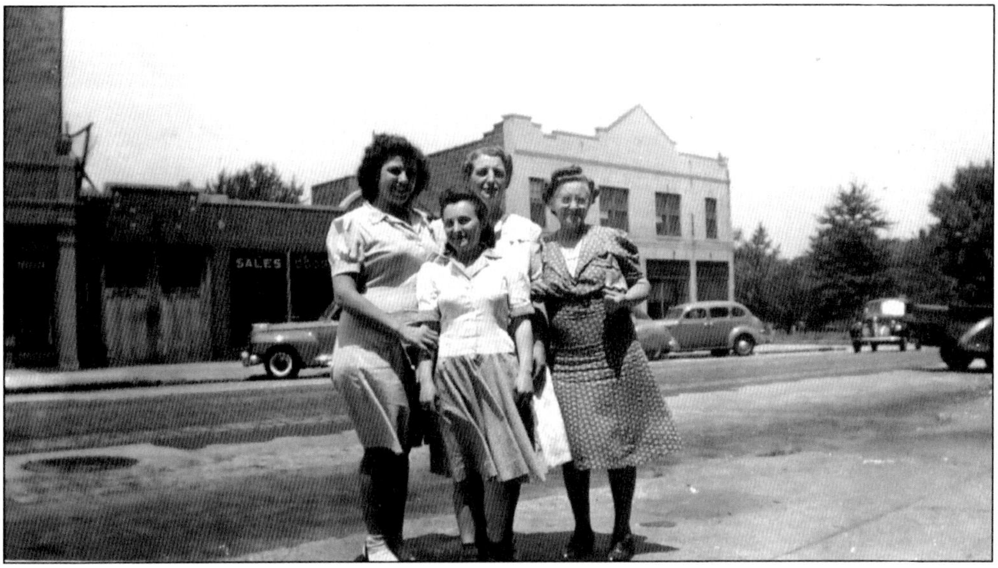

Around 1941, from left to right, Rose Scotti-Perticari, Brenda Fusco, Melissa Trishkin, and Edith Perry stop for a photograph during their lunch break from Solomon's Company, which manufactured ladies' lingerie. This photograph was taken on the east side of Broad Avenue between Palisades Boulevard and Washington Place. Across the street is Bridge Motors, the old Dodge dealership, which was owned by Chester (Chet) Watson. (Courtesy of Carol Miraglia).

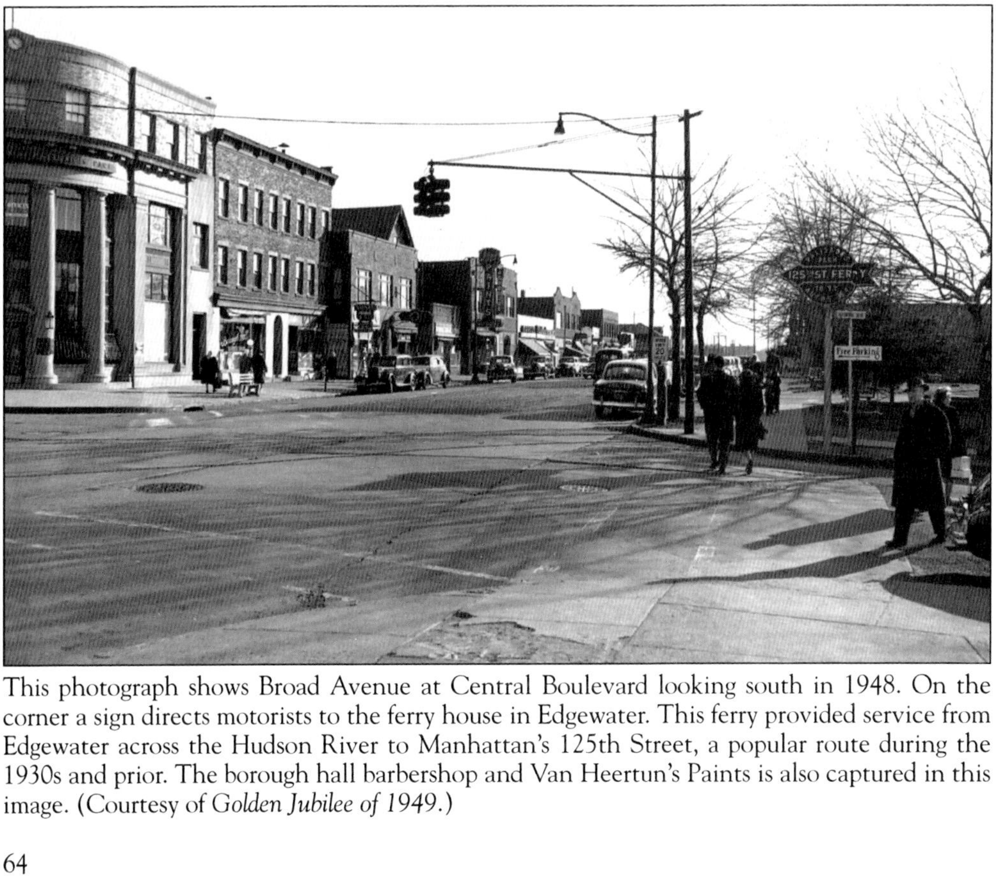

This photograph shows Broad Avenue at Central Boulevard looking south in 1948. On the corner a sign directs motorists to the ferry house in Edgewater. This ferry provided service from Edgewater across the Hudson River to Manhattan's 125th Street, a popular route during the 1930s and prior. The borough hall barbershop and Van Heertun's Paints is also captured in this image. (Courtesy of *Golden Jubilee of 1949*.)

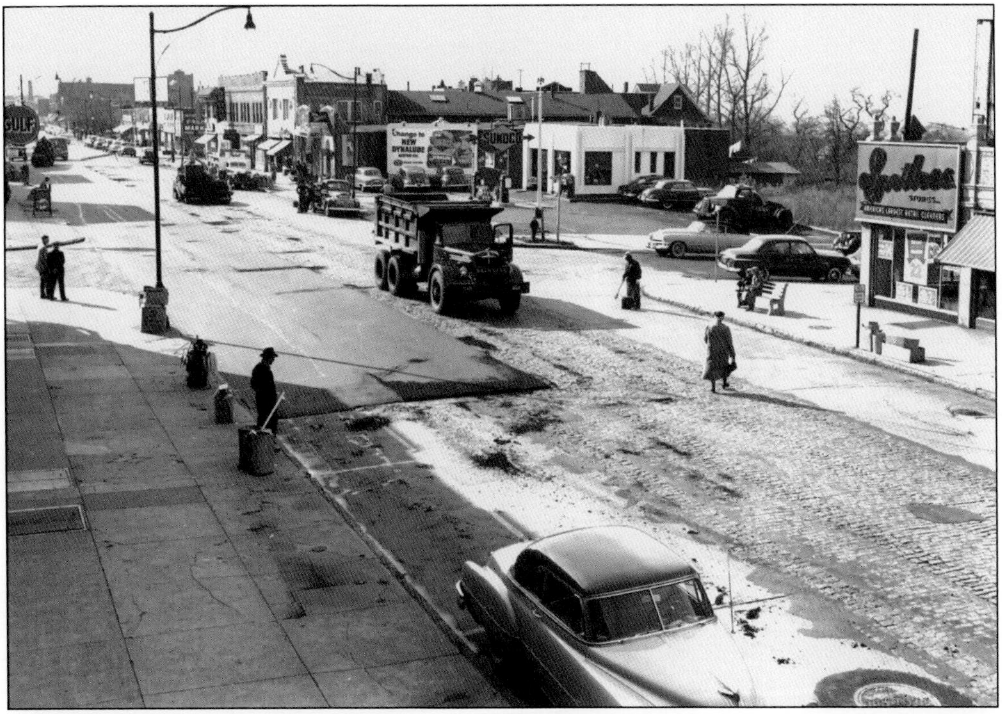

In the above photograph, Broad Avenue is being paved at the intersection of Palisades Boulevard around 1945. During this time, a Gulf gas station was on the east side of the street and Sunoco was directly across. A Pabst Blue Ribbon delivery truck is outside Owen's Hofbrau bar. Fred's Meat Market is pictured on the southwest corner of Belleview Place. In the below *c.* 1950 photograph is a view of Bergen Boulevard looking south at the intersection of East Brinkerhoff Avenue. (Above, courtesy of George J. Farrell; below, courtesy of Charles Martini.)

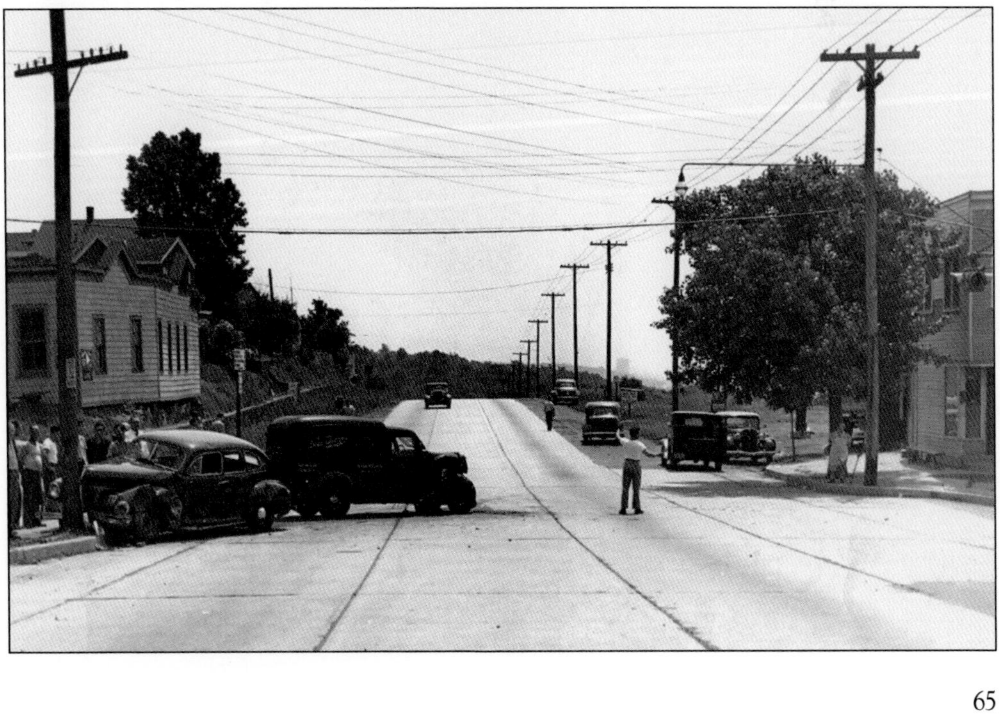

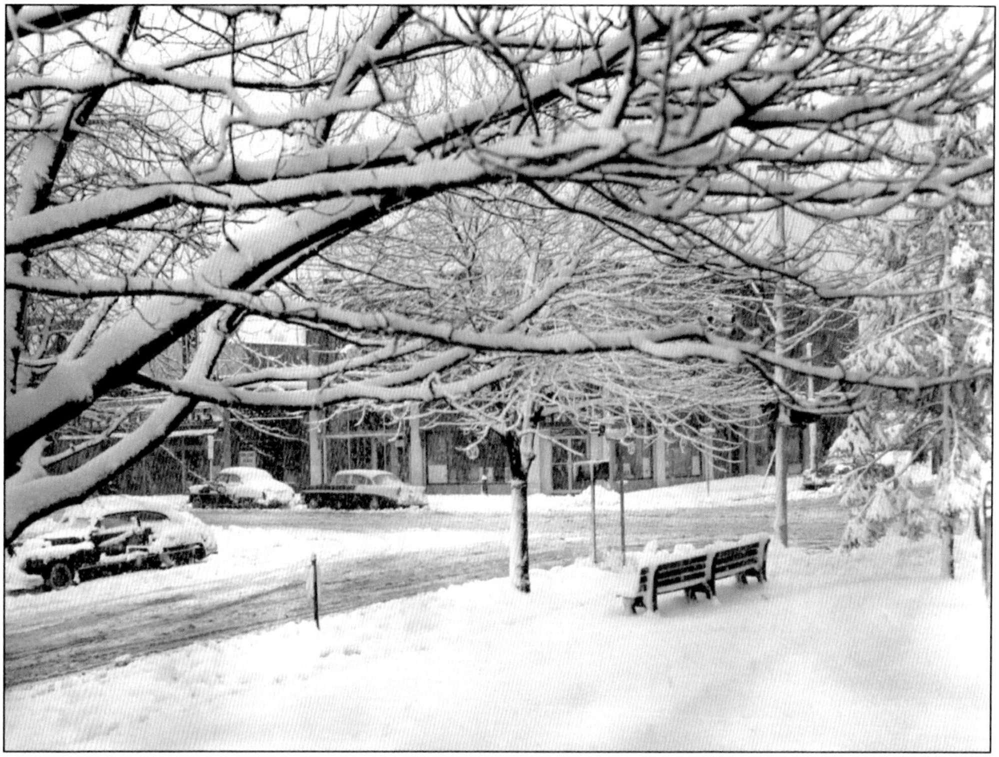

Seen above on March 21, 1958, is a snow scene at the intersection of Central Boulevard at Broad Avenue. In the photograph below, digging out during the blizzard of 1948 are, from left to right, Filomena "Phillie" Longo, Christine Giannantonio, and Filomena "Phillie" Gentile. (Above, courtesy of Leonard R. Cottrell; below, courtesy of Charles Martini.)

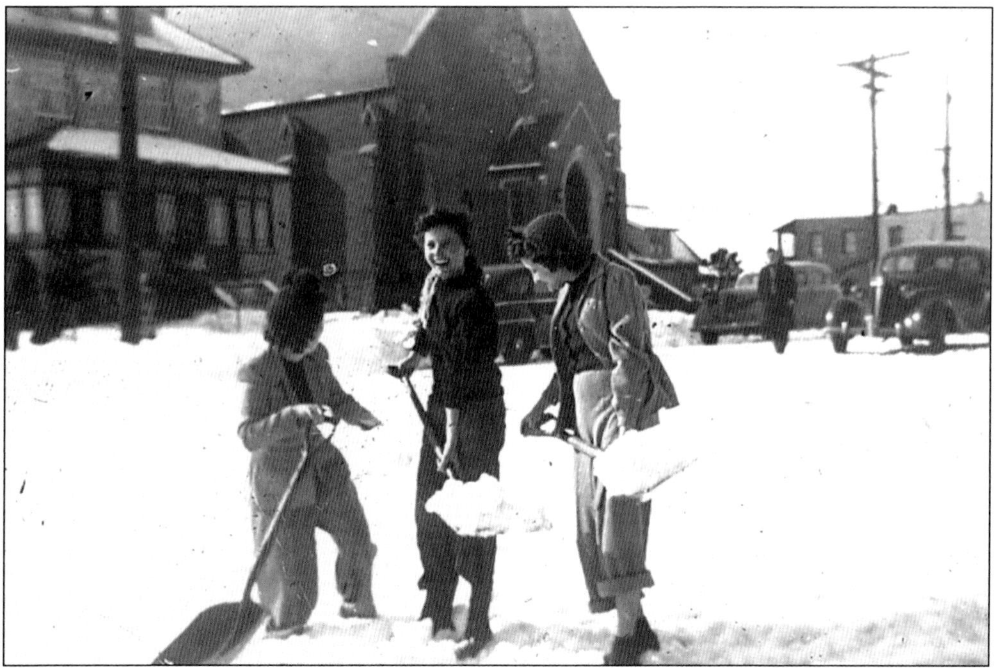

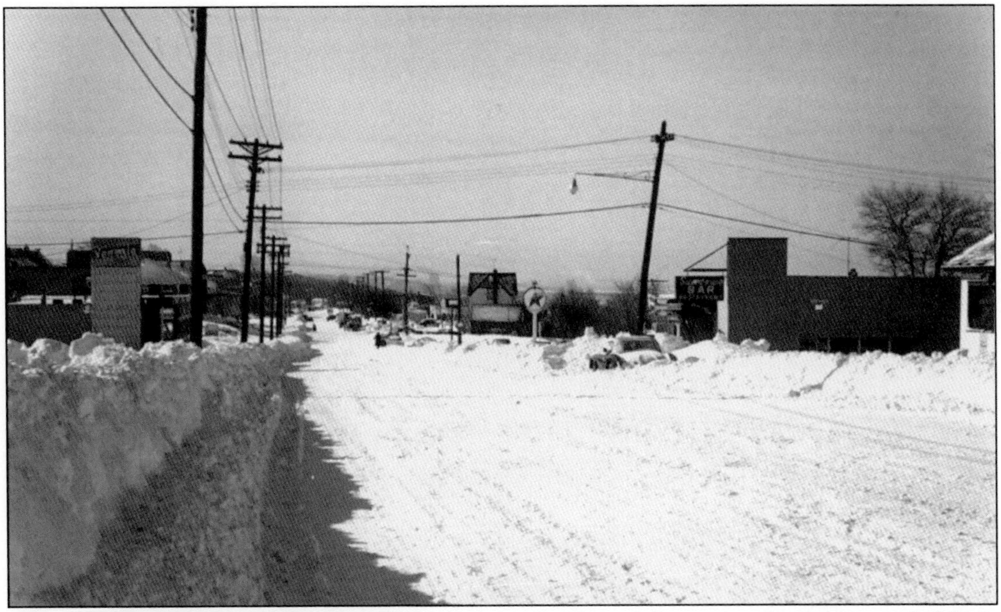

This view from February 5, 1961, shows Bergen Boulevard facing south. Snow is piled high along the roadway. On the west side of the street was Nicholas Sassano's Sundown Lounge and Restaurant. South of the Sundown Lounge was Peter J. Sassano's Broadview Corp/Texaco gas station and repair shop. Across the street on the eastern side was Venezia Restaurant. (Courtesy of Carol Miraglia.)

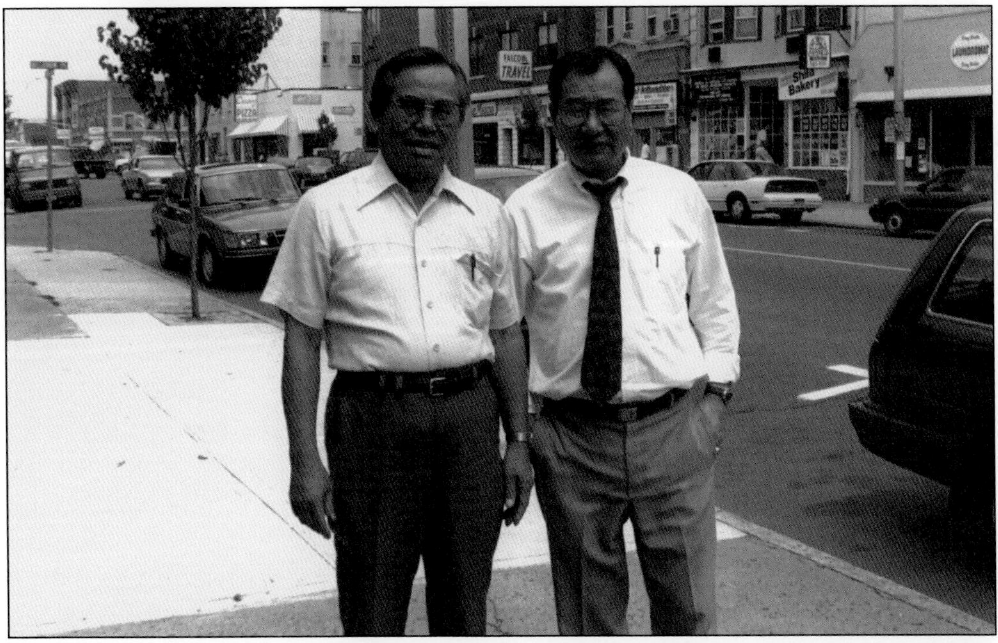

First Korean-American Senior Citizen Association president Suck Hun Sur (left) stands with Andy Nam, president of the chamber of commerce, on Broad Avenue in 1989. Nam has been an active member of the community. His fund-raising efforts in 1992 led to assisting the Palisades Park Beautification Program, which lined the streets of Broad Avenue with beautiful trees. (Courtesy of Andy Nam.)

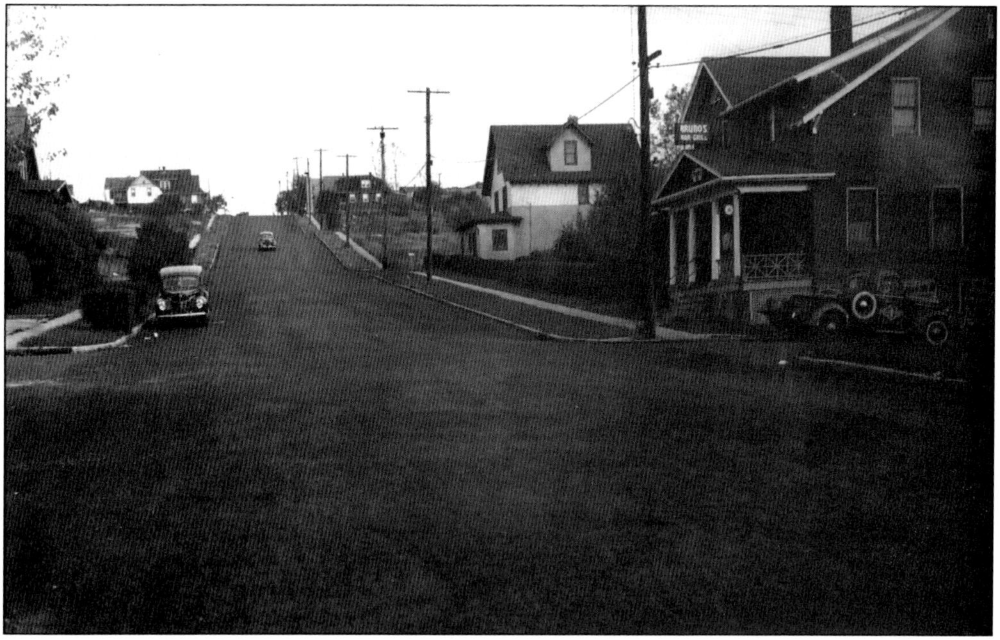

Bruno's Bar and Grill, located on the corner of East Brinkerhoff Avenue and Eighth Street, is pictured here around 1946. This bar later became Pat's Tavern before it was bought by Anthony Sambogna in 1962. Sambogna named it the Shanty Inn. (Courtesy of Robert Payton.)

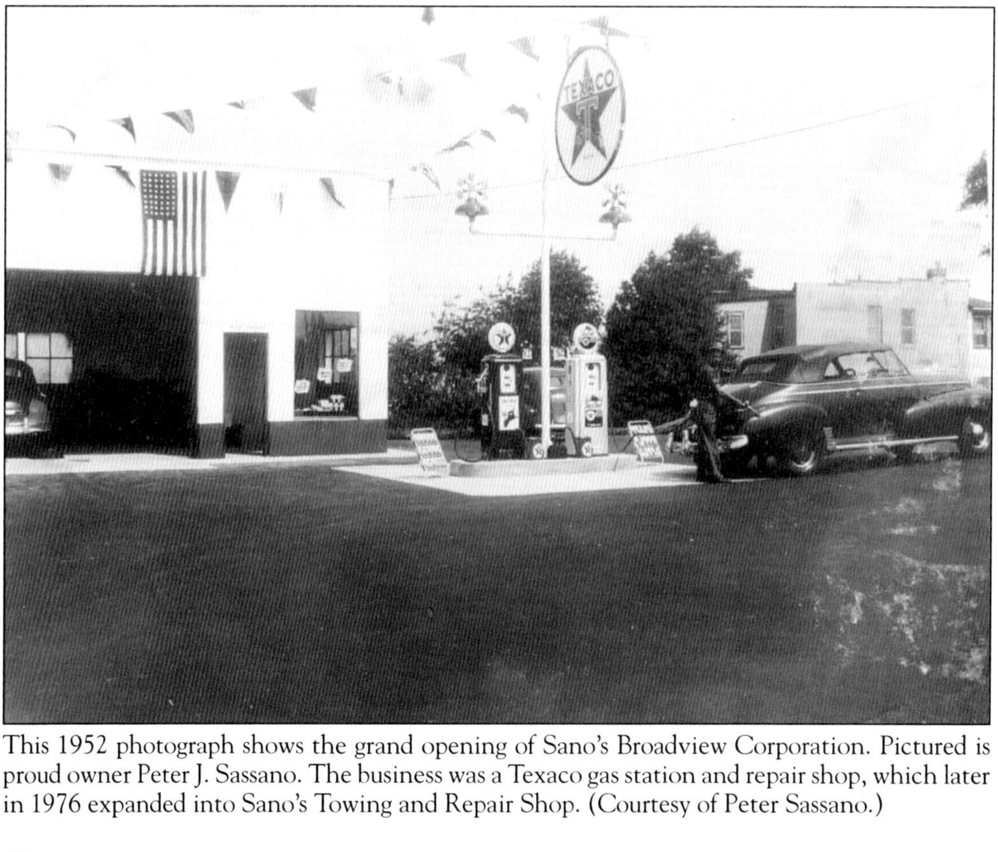

This 1952 photograph shows the grand opening of Sano's Broadview Corporation. Pictured is proud owner Peter J. Sassano. The business was a Texaco gas station and repair shop, which later in 1976 expanded into Sano's Towing and Repair Shop. (Courtesy of Peter Sassano.)

Five

The Life and Spirit of Palisades Park

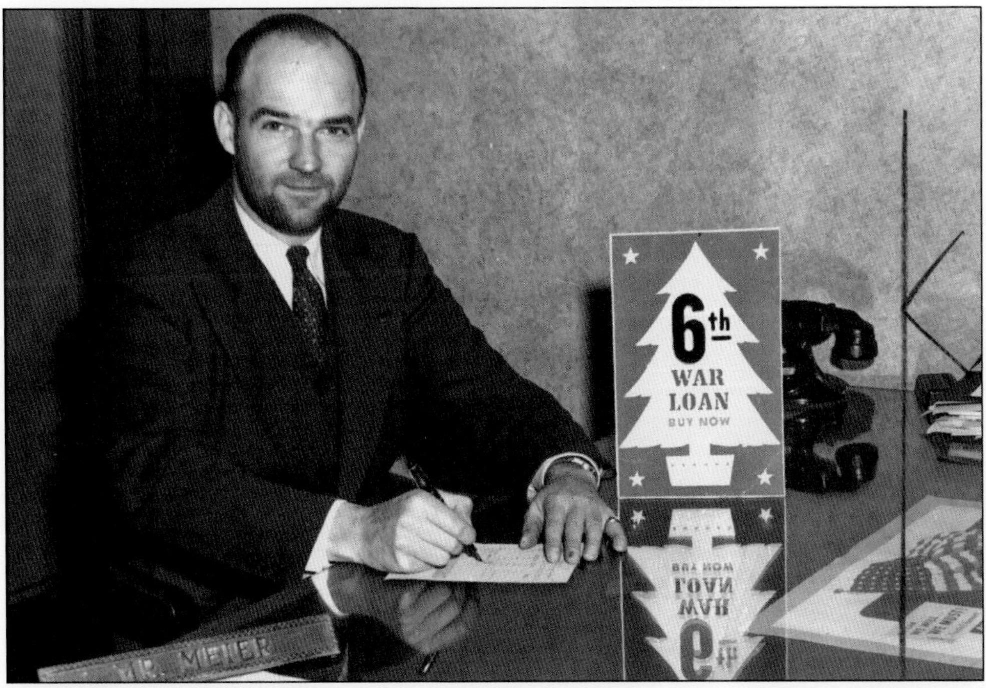

Pictured here in 1946 is proud resident Edward H. Meier, a cashier and director of National Bank of Palisades Park and later bank president, who refused to shave his beard until the war bond drive's goal was achieved. Meier's steadfast commitments raised over $180,000, an accomplishment that brought much praise and recognition from the United States Treasury Department's War Finance Committee. The government was so impressed with the drive that a medium bomber was named in honor of Palisades Park. (Courtesy of Evelyn P. Meier.)

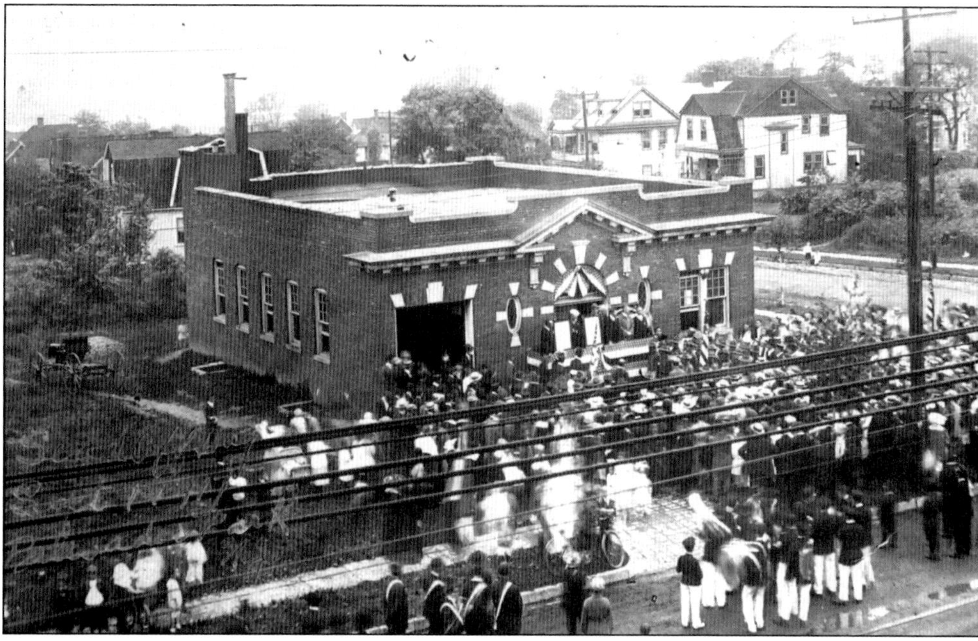

Pictured here is World War I send off day in September 1917. Residents gathered in front of the borough hall to celebrate the brave soldiers heading off to war. (Courtesy of Leonard R. Cottrell.)

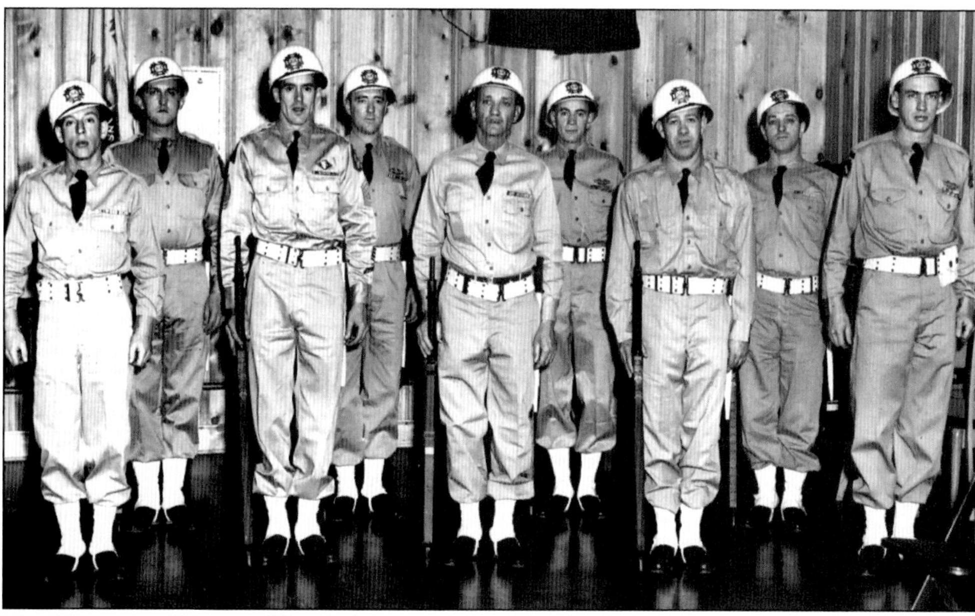

The Veterans of Foreign War Color Guard is pictured here. From left to right are (first row) Jean Senft, Charles Metcalfe, John Peyton, Raymond Meegan, and James Kearney; (second row) John Daneu, Harold Mulligan, William Woltz, and Francis Capicotto. The first VFW was formed in 1899, and since the granting of the Edsall-Lunstedt-Davidson Post No. 4365 in 1945, the post has had the honor of the department of New Jersey recognizing four of its commanders: DeWitt Waack, James McGinley, Bert Tremble, and David Vaughan as all state commanders. (Courtesy of Thomas J. Albanese.)

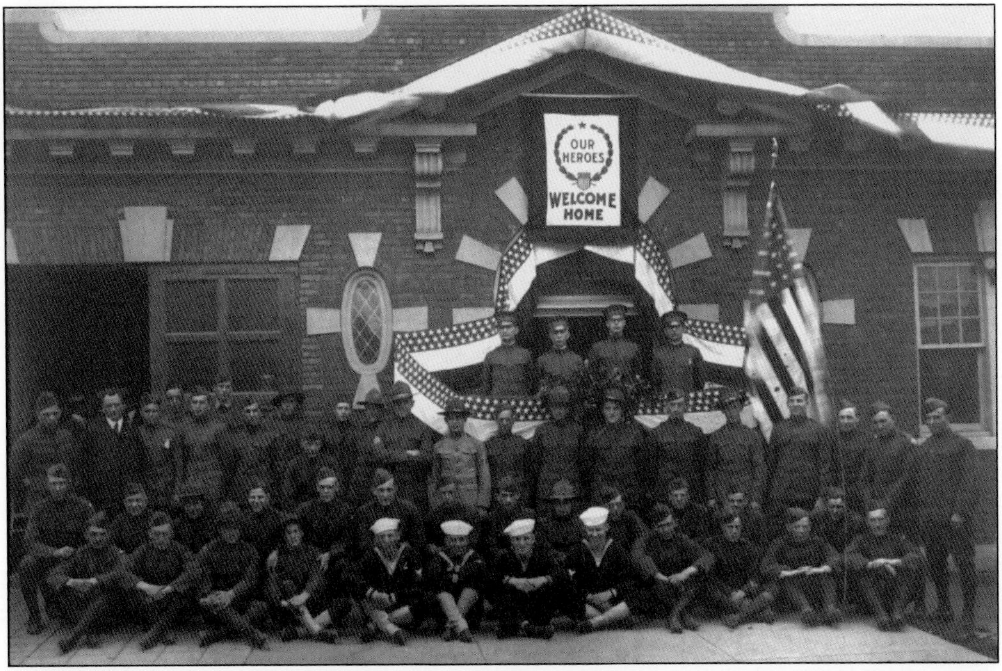

World War I veterans are proudly photographed in front of the borough hall after their homecoming in 1919. Palisades Park lost two soldiers: William Lunstedt Jr. and Edward Parkyn, who died heroically, serving their country. (Courtesy of Palisades Park Public Library.)

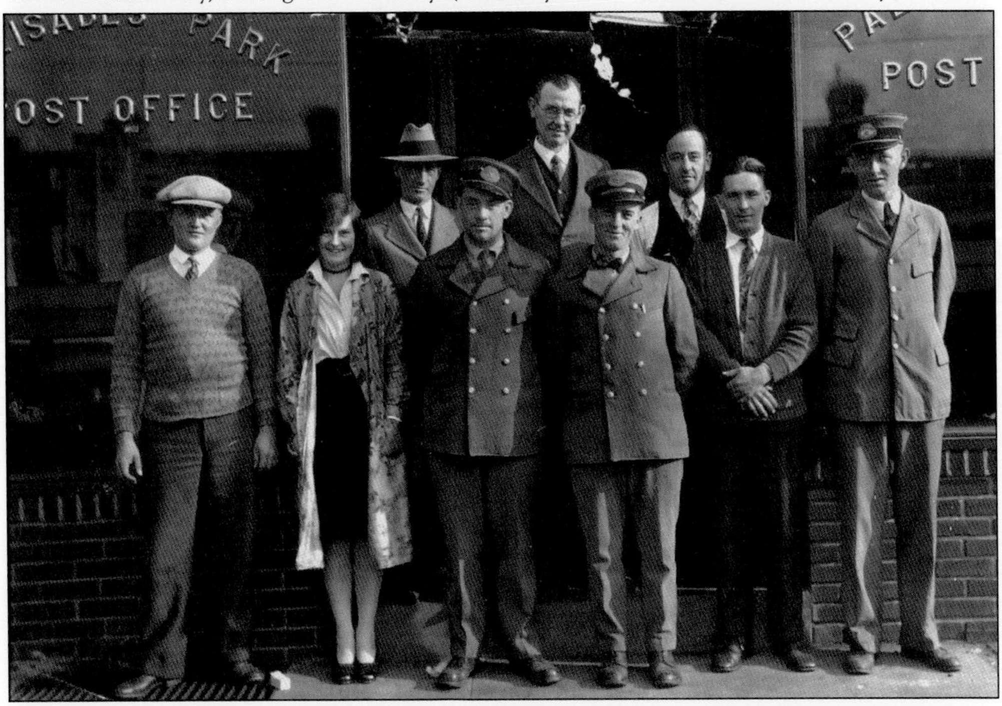

This photograph of the Palisades Park Post Office was taken in front of 312 Broad Avenue on November 1, 1928. Joseph R. Forrest, fifth postmaster, moved the post office to this location upon assuming office on June 23, 1922. (Courtesy of Leonard R. Cottrell.)

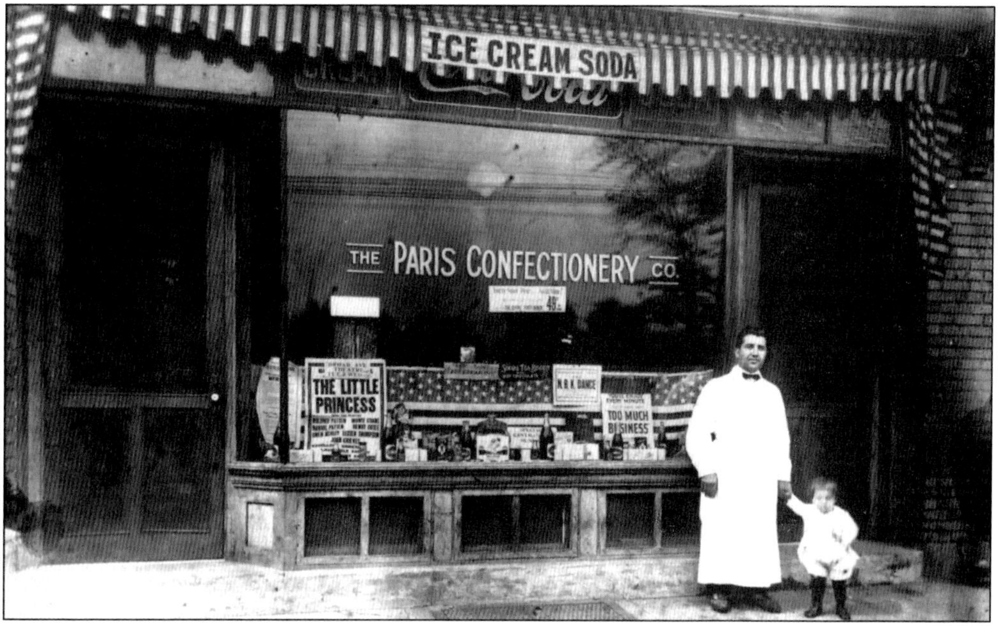

Proprietor Livathares, who co-owned the Paris Confectionery Company with Christos Parigoris, is standing in front of the store with his child in 1916. This ice-cream parlor was opened in 1914 at 313 Broad Avenue. By 1941, the name was changed to Chris' Lunchonette. The sign in the front window is a poster advertising *The Little Princess*, which was featured at the Broad Avenue Theater. (Courtesy of Evelyn P. Meier.)

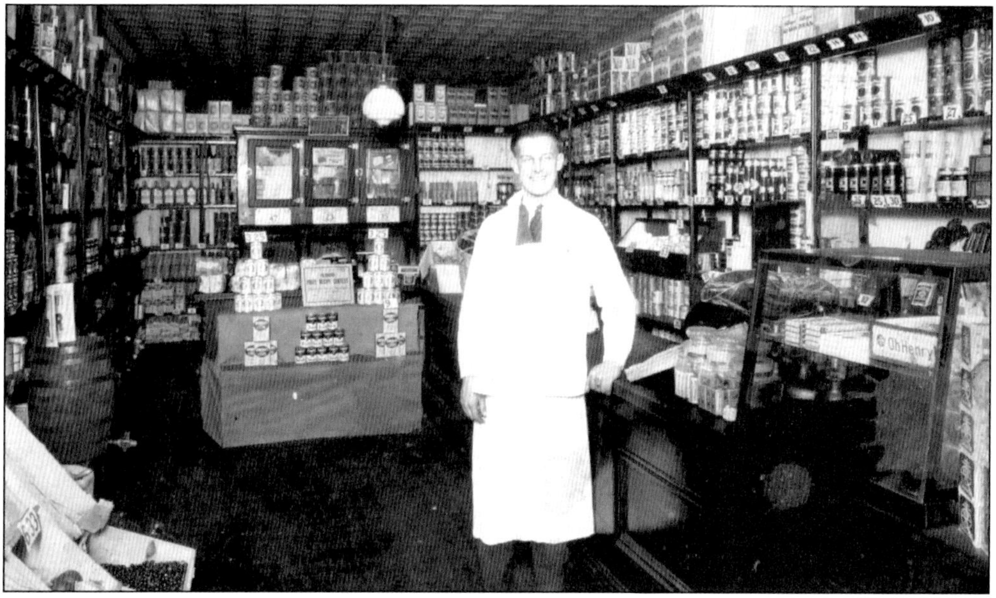

Seventeen-year-old Leonard "Gink" Cottrell is pictured here in 1919, working as the manager of the Daniel Reeves Store. Leonard was a standout on the semiprofessional community baseball team, a volunteer firefighter, and in 1953 became chief of the police department. After an impressive police career, which included many successful endeavors to modernize police services, he retired in 1967. Leonard's father was Abram Cottrell, who was a pioneer of Palisades Park. (Courtesy of Leonard R. Cottrell.)

ALWAYS TWO BIG FEATURES!

PARK LANE

BROAD AVENUE • PALISADES PARK, N. J.

WEEK BEGINNING FRIDAY, JULY 12th, 1935

ARLISS SUPERB AS "CARDINAL RICHELIEU"

A thousand enemies for every friend! Hated! Cursed! Threatened! Yet he walked boldly on! A cat and a wisp of a girl his only friends! His Country and his God his two consuming loves!

GEORGE ARLISS

— in —

"CARDINAL RICHELIEU"

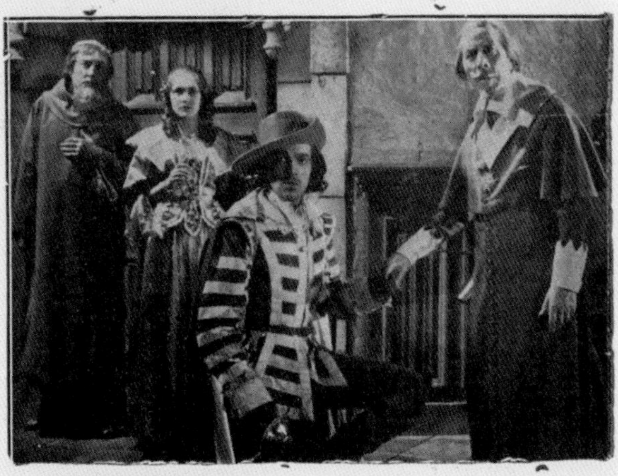

— also —

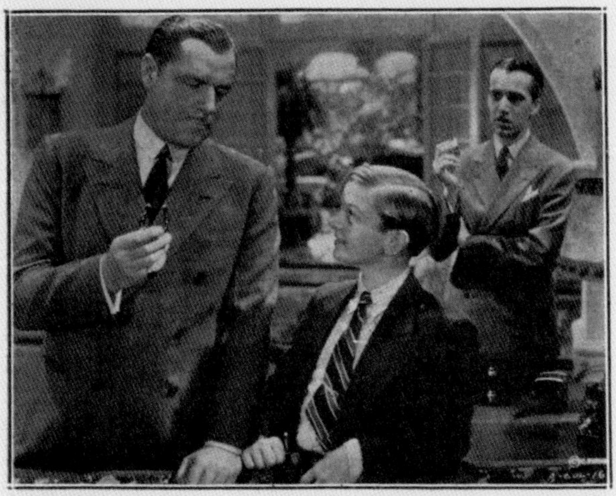

Three on a wish! Wishing against hope—hoping against fear—fearing the love that held them together! The gripping, powerful story of "The Unwelcome Stranger" tells of a man jilted by Lady Luck — until a stranger, whom he feared, spun victory for him on the wheel of fate!

JACK HOLT

— in —

"UNWELCOME STRANGER"

— with —

MONA BARRIE
RALPH MORGAN
JACKIE SEARL

PLAYING HERE FRIDAY and SATURDAY, JULY 12 and 13

On July 12, 1935, the Park Lane Theatre featured George Arliss in Cardinal Richelieu and Jack Holy in *Unwelcome Stranger*. The Park Lane Theatre was built in 1927. Throughout the years, many generations of residents enjoyed the theater and the events held there, which included the graduation exercises of Palisades Park's elementary schools and Leonia's high school. (Courtesy of Palisades Park Public Library.)

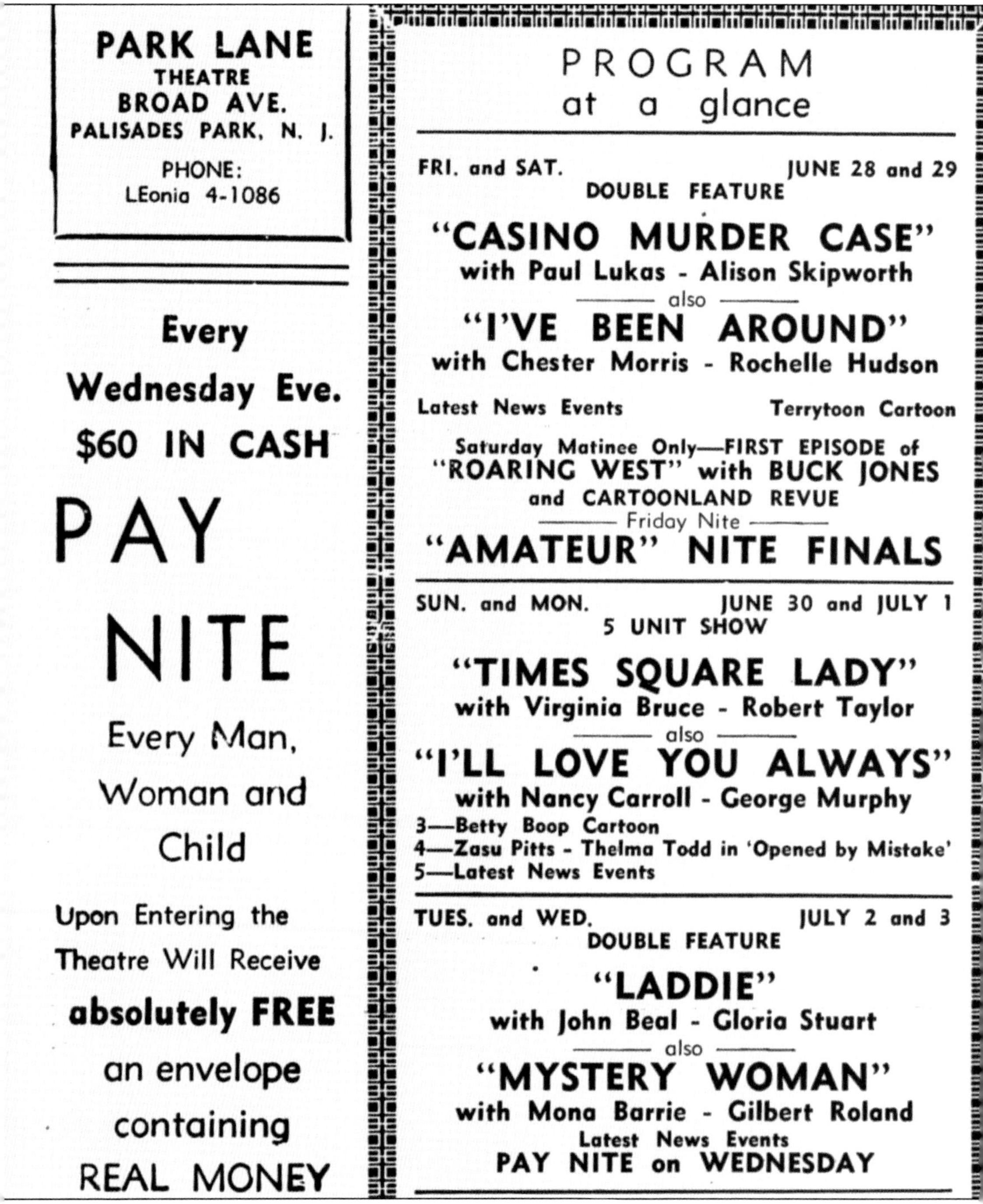

PARK LANE
THEATRE
BROAD AVE.
PALISADES PARK, N. J.
PHONE:
LEonia 4-1086

Every
Wednesday Eve.
$60 IN CASH
PAY
NITE
Every Man,
Woman and
Child
Upon Entering the
Theatre Will Receive
absolutely FREE
an envelope
containing
REAL MONEY

PROGRAM
at a glance

FRI. and SAT. JUNE 28 and 29
DOUBLE FEATURE
"CASINO MURDER CASE"
with Paul Lukas - Alison Skipworth
also
"I'VE BEEN AROUND"
with Chester Morris - Rochelle Hudson
Latest News Events Terrytoon Cartoon
Saturday Matinee Only—FIRST EPISODE of
"ROARING WEST" with BUCK JONES
and CARTOONLAND REVUE
Friday Nite
"AMATEUR" NITE FINALS

SUN. and MON. JUNE 30 and JULY 1
5 UNIT SHOW
"TIMES SQUARE LADY"
with Virginia Bruce - Robert Taylor
also
"I'LL LOVE YOU ALWAYS"
with Nancy Carroll - George Murphy
3—Betty Boop Cartoon
4—Zasu Pitts - Thelma Todd in 'Opened by Mistake'
5—Latest News Events

TUES. and WED. JULY 2 and 3
DOUBLE FEATURE
"LADDIE"
with John Beal - Gloria Stuart
also
"MYSTERY WOMAN"
with Mona Barrie - Gilbert Roland
Latest News Events
PAY NITE on WEDNESDAY

The Park Lane Theatre program is shown here in June 1935. That year was big for the theater, as it bounced back from the low admission following the Depression. Attendees now enjoyed a climate-controlled building with the addition of a modern cooling system, allowing the theater to maintain a temperature of 70 degrees at all times. The theater hosted such gimmicks as free dishes, groceries, cutlery, and other incentives to entice patrons, which included a "Pay Night," where everybody was given an envelope with money ranging from 1¢ to $10 in cash. These

Sunday and Monday **June 30 and July 1**

5 STAR UNIT SHOW!

A race track! A notorious night club! A hockey team! Gambling hells. This was the strange inheritance of "King" Brad'ey's Iowa daughter!

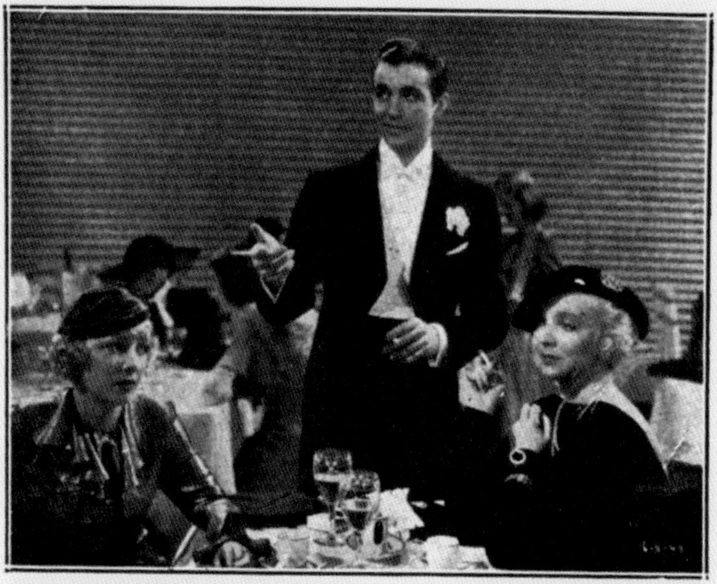

"TIMES SQUARE LADY"

— with —

VIRGINIA BRUCE
ROBERT TAYLOR
HELEN TWELVETREES
ISABEL JEWELL
NAT PENDLETON

——— also ———

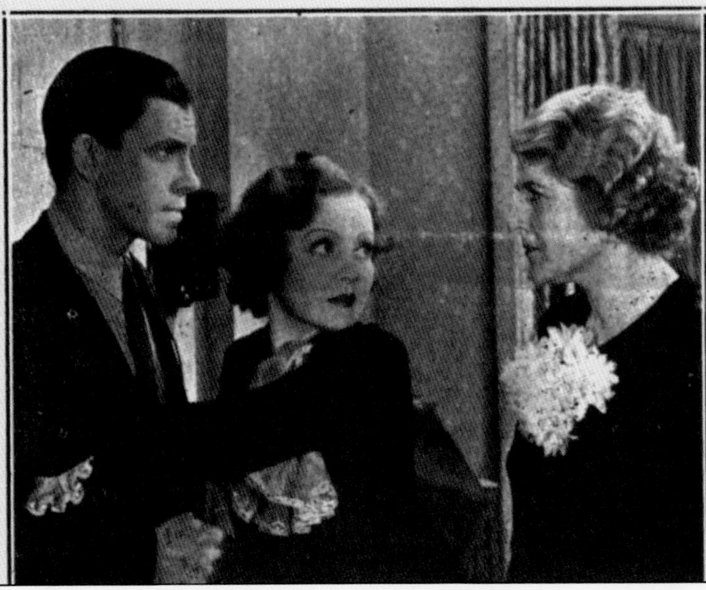

HE WAS BEATEN AND BRUISED . . .

licked by the world . . . but she still cried bravely—

"I'LL LOVE YOU ALWAYS"

— with —

NANCY CARROLL
GEORGE MURPHY

gimmicks proved successful, boosting Saturday night attendance from 400 persons to massive crowds of up to 2,000. The theater also hosted local amateur talent nights. In 1969, manager Chris Stavrou, manager since December 13, 1935, reduced admission to $1, perhaps the greatest gimmick, which resulted in swarms of people from all over the metropolitan area packing the house. (Courtesy of Palisades Park Public Library.)

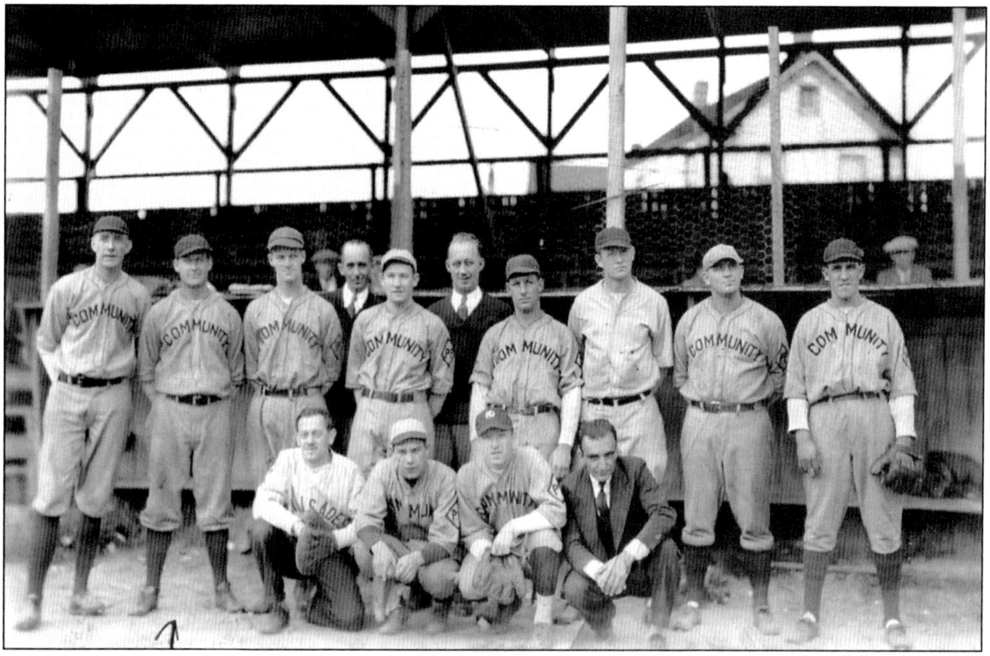

The Palisades Park Community Club, a semiprofessional baseball team, was considered a powerhouse during the late 1920s and early 1930s. This photograph was taken during its first year. From left to right are (first row) Chris Vonderschmidt, Billy Diss, unidentified, and Pete Fusco; (second row) Harrison MacClatchey, Leonard "Gink" Cottrell, Walter "Red" Paulson, unidentified, Buck Brarman, Red Gebhardt, Jake Miller, and unidentified; (third row) ? Urban, who umpired, and Herb Backstrom. (Courtesy of Leonard R. Cottrell.)

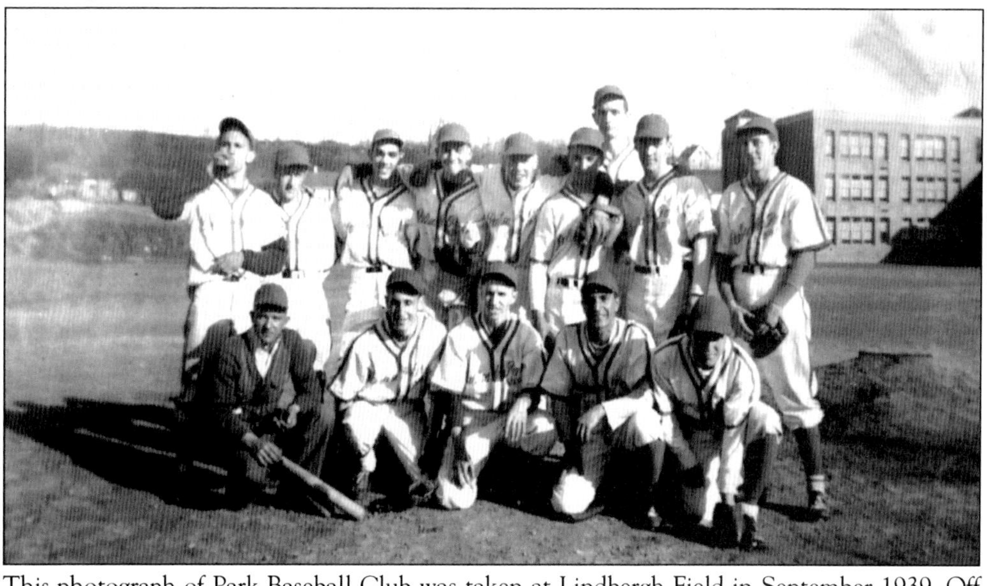

This photograph of Park Baseball Club was taken at Lindbergh Field in September 1939. Off to the right in the distance is the Lindbergh School. It was here on a Sunday afternoon in the 1920s that former Columbia University graduate and later New York Yankee legend, Lou Gehrig, hammered a ball over center field as a member of Everett Millet's All-Collegians against the Palisades Park Arrows. (Courtesy of Thomas J. Albanese.)

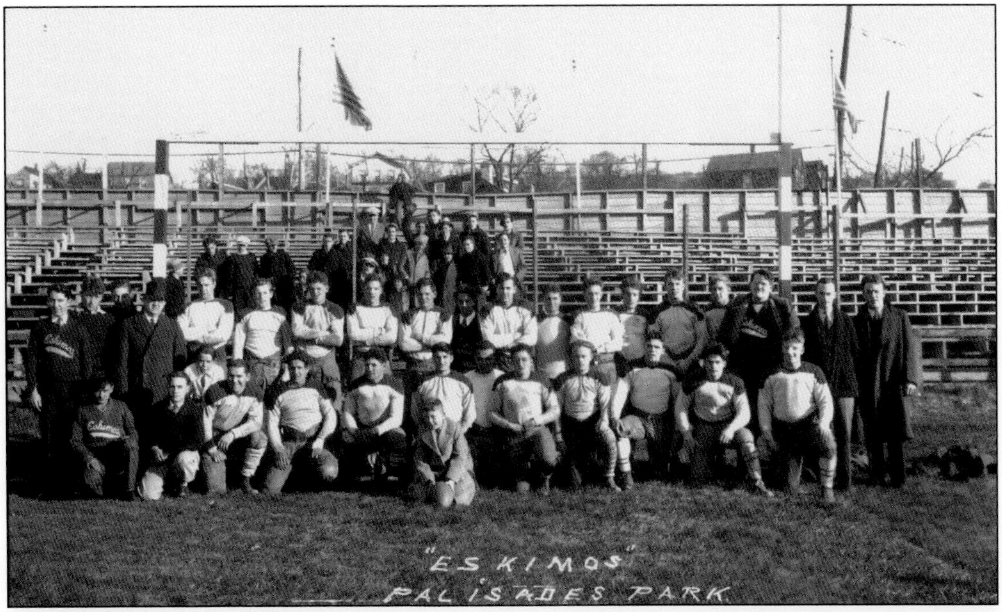

The Eskimos semiprofessional football team is pictured here in 1932. This team was spawned out of Chris Parigoris's ice-cream parlor, the Paris Confectionery Company, in 1926. The team later hired Clayton Loeffel, a former Colgate University player, as its coach. This led to the Eskimos becoming a successful team among the North Jersey semiprofessional football ranks. (Courtesy of Evelyn P. Meier.)

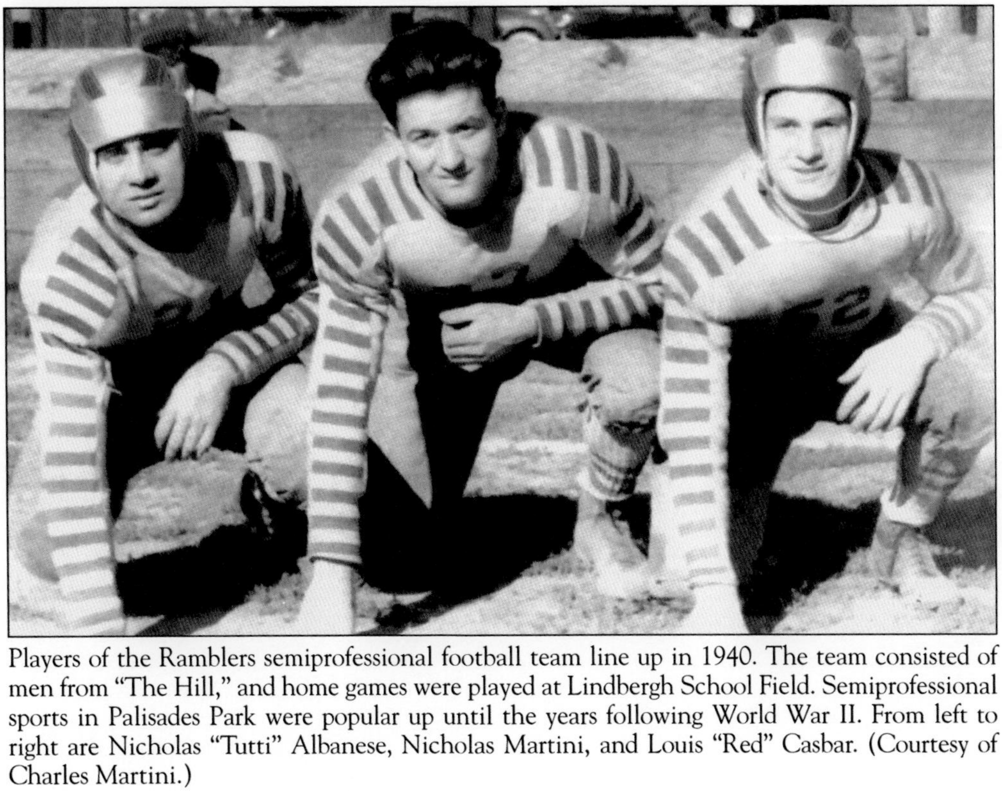

Players of the Ramblers semiprofessional football team line up in 1940. The team consisted of men from "The Hill," and home games were played at Lindbergh School Field. Semiprofessional sports in Palisades Park were popular up until the years following World War II. From left to right are Nicholas "Tutti" Albanese, Nicholas Martini, and Louis "Red" Casbar. (Courtesy of Charles Martini.)

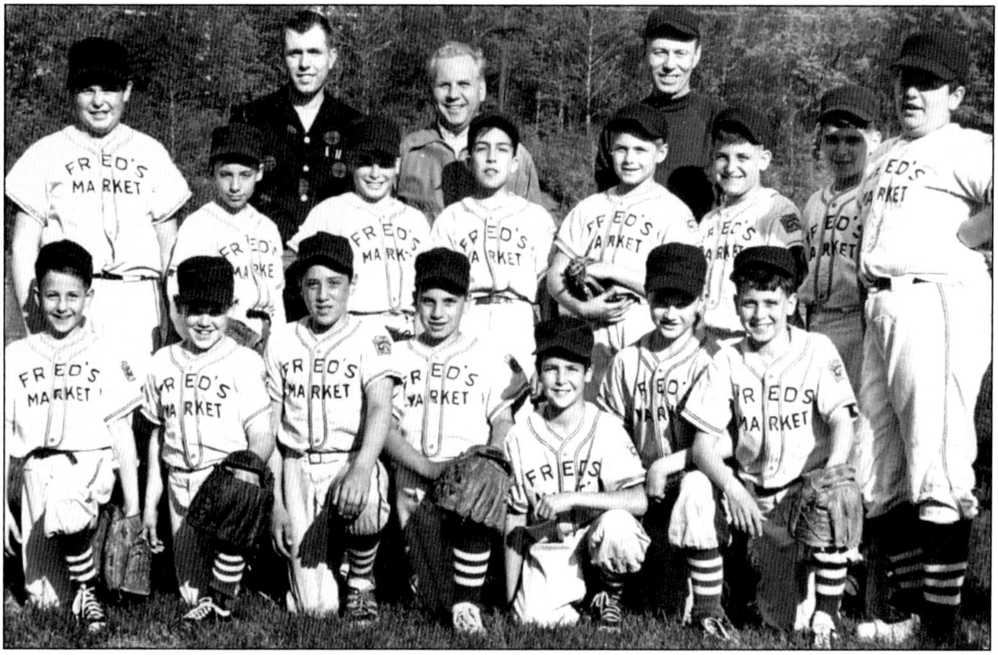

The Fred's Meat Market Little League team poses for a photograph on the present-day high school recess field in 1968. In 1945, the Boys Athletic Association was founded under the direction of police lieutenant Walter Lewandowski. This led to the formation of the Little League during the 1950s and various other organized youth sports in the borough. The Babe Ruth League was organized in 1955 under the leadership of now captain Lewandowski, Frank Hubert, and Thomas Toscano. (Courtesy of Palisades Park Public Library.)

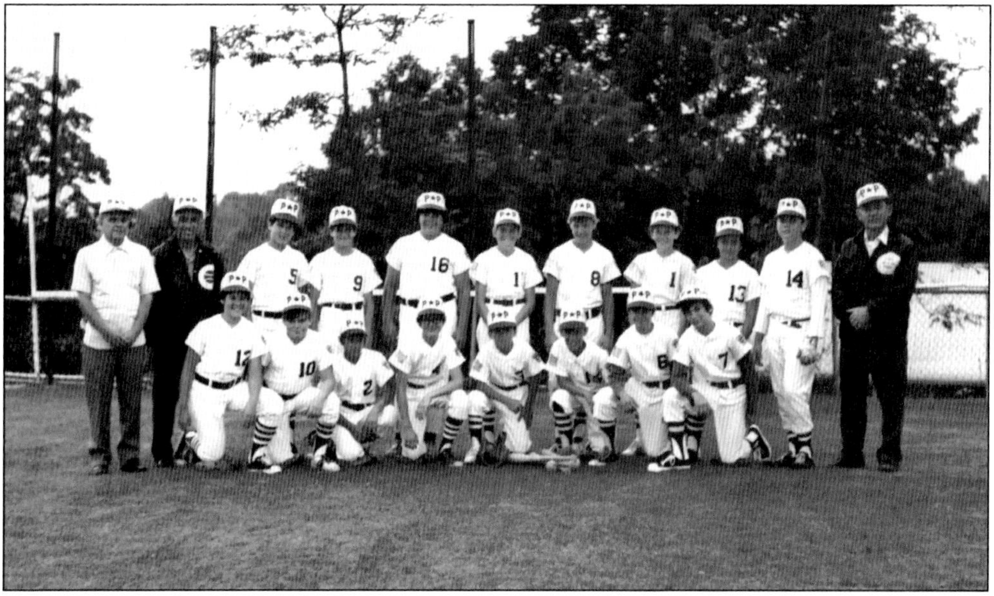

The 1972 Palisades Park Little League All-Stars are, from left to right, (first row) J. Milkman, T. Spain, M. Pucinelli, R. Grow, R. Bell, H. O'Connell, G. Tremble, and M. Bagarazzi; (second row) coach J. Ongione, coach J. D'elia, A. Suttora, J. Benedetto, L. Muccio, S. Beh, D. Kennedy, D. Lynch, T. Grato, J. Noto, and coach J. Noto. (Courtesy of James Benedetto.)

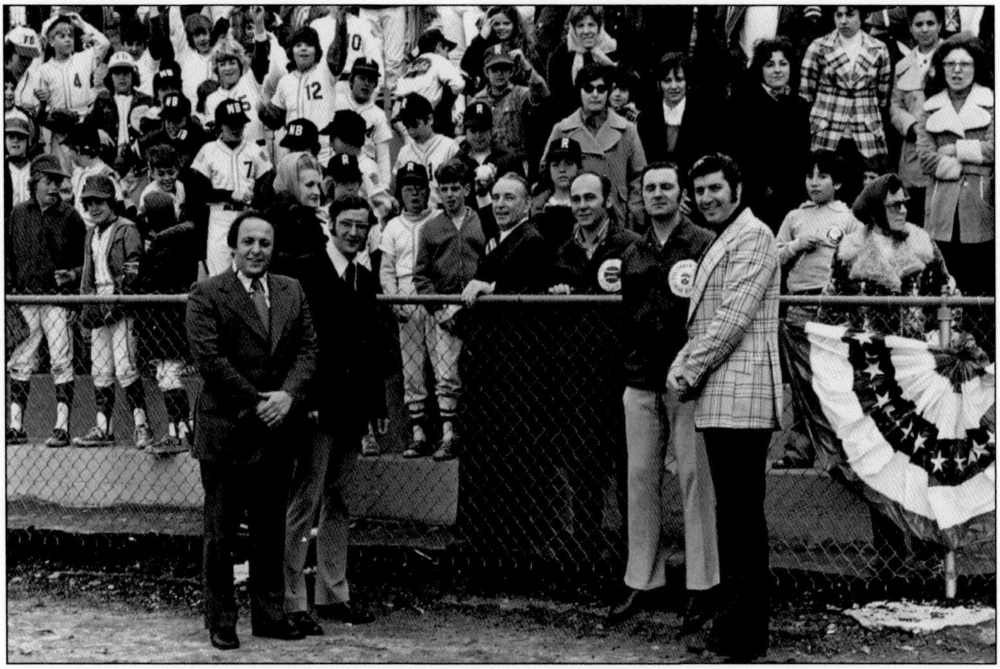

Opening day of the Little League field is shown here in 1970. From left to right are councilmen Peter Sambogna and John Fratinardo, Mayor D. Thomas Toscano, president of Little League Al Giannantonio, Mike Di Paulo, and councilman Robert Pallotta. (Courtesy of Robert Pallotta.)

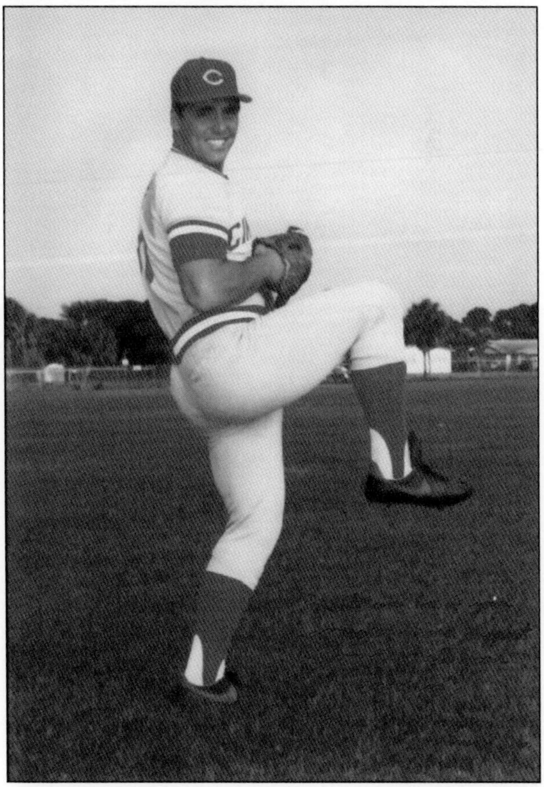

Palisades Park standout and William Paterson graduate Mark Cieslak signed with the Cincinnati Reds in February 1984. The 22-year-old left-handed pitcher sparkled in his first year as a professional, posting a 7-2 record and a 1.49 ERA, with 76 strikeouts. He later played for the Boston Red Sox before returning home and becoming a two-time Coach of the Year in both basketball and baseball. (Courtesy of Mark Cieslak).

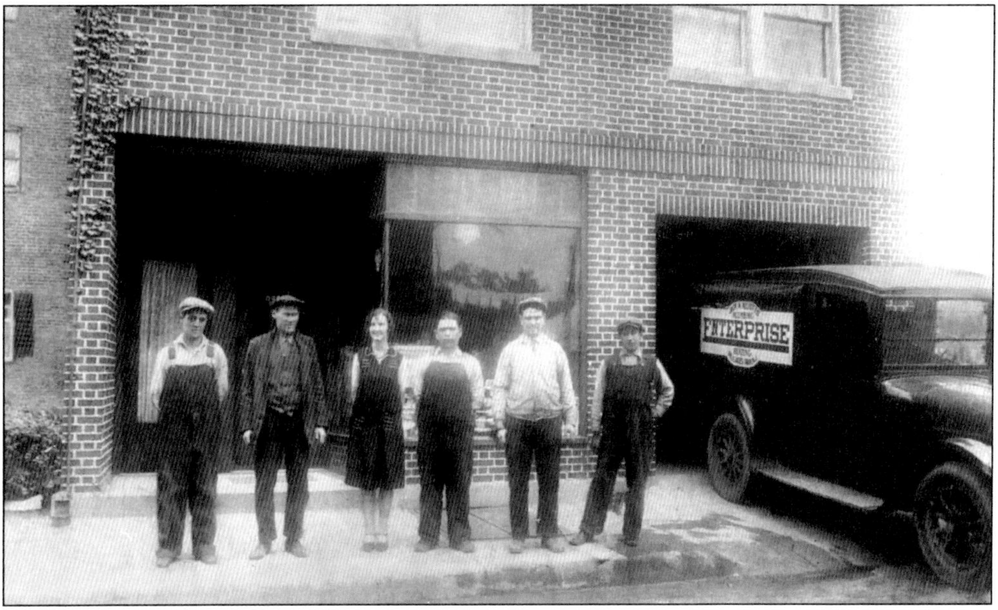

Employees are shown here outside Alliotts Plumbing around 1935. In the 1920s, Charles Alliotts and his brother Jack began as a small plumbing and heating business. In 1985, the business expanded to include a construction and home building company. Pictured from left to right are Anthony Albanese, unidentified, Rachael ?, Charles Alliotts, unidentified, and Charles Pollutt. (Courtesy of Carol Miraglia.)

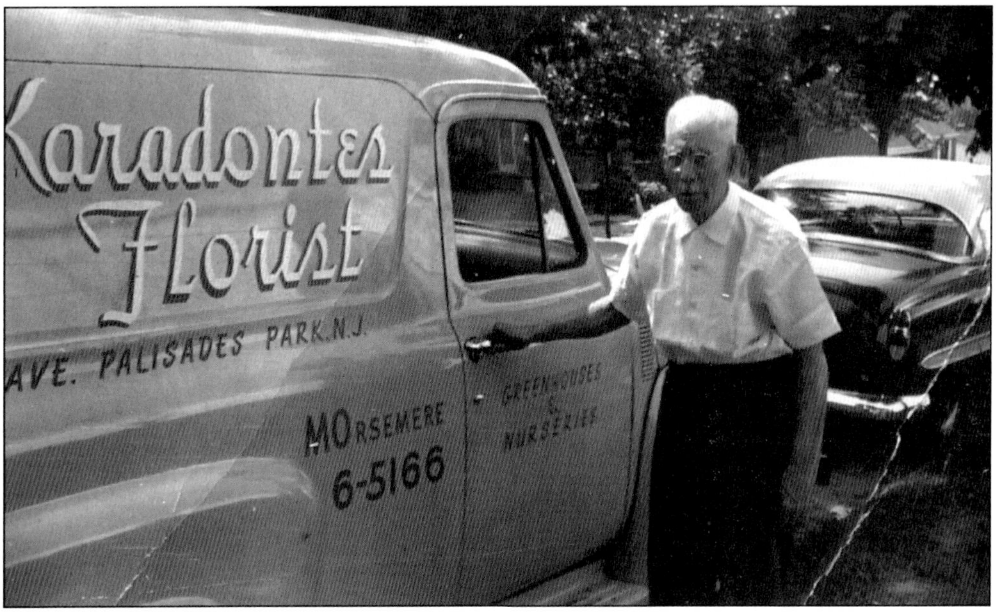

In 1915, the Karadontes brothers—Peter, Chris, Andrew, and James—built their first greenhouse and nursery. They purchased land on West Ruby Avenue from second mayor John G. Edsall. The land was part of Edsall's apple orchard. Here they opened Karadontes Florists and Nursery. The Karadontes family was close friends with the Edsall family. John G. Edsall admired the strong work ethic of the brothers and helped them in any way he could. (Courtesy of Peter Karadontes.)

An employee of Karadontes Nursery cuts fresh flowers for the florists around 1957. The land pictured is John G. Edsall's former apple orchard. After the Karadontes brothers built their first greenhouse in 1915, their business gradually grew and 11 additional greenhouses and a florist shop were established. Over the mid to later part of the last century, most of this land was sold and homes were built. Karadontes Nursery is among one of the oldest businesses currently in the borough. (Courtesy of Peter Karadontes.)

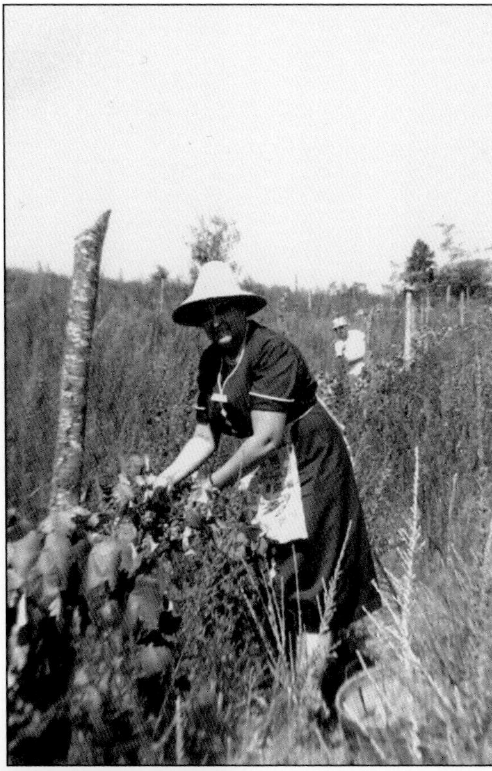

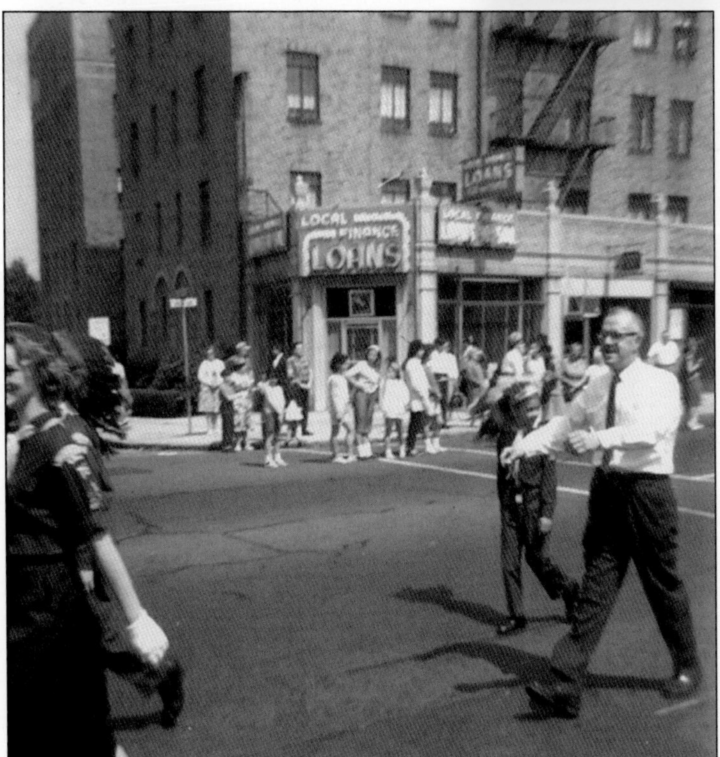

Young Edward C. Meier enthusiastically marches in his Cub Scout uniform in 1963. The Native American headdresses were handmade by each child's parent and were worn for the Memorial Day parades. The photograph was taken at the intersection of Broad Avenue and West Palisades Boulevard. (Courtesy of Evelyn P. Meier.)

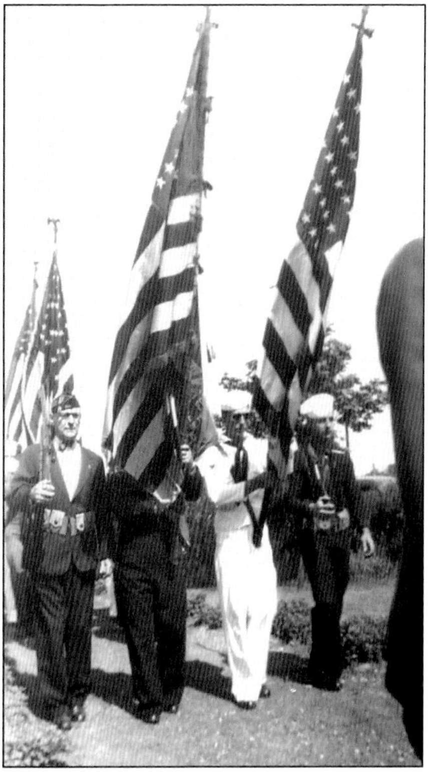

St. Nicholas Church hosted a parade honoring the servicemen that died in World War II on May 30, 1946. Palisades Park lost 27 servicemen during World War II. This parade was dedicated to their heroic service and ultimate sacrifice. Later on in the Vietnam War, Palisades Park lost Jerry Silvia, who died in service. Palisades Park has always had a tradition of its men and women serving proudly and selflessly for their country. (Courtesy of Carol Miraglia.)

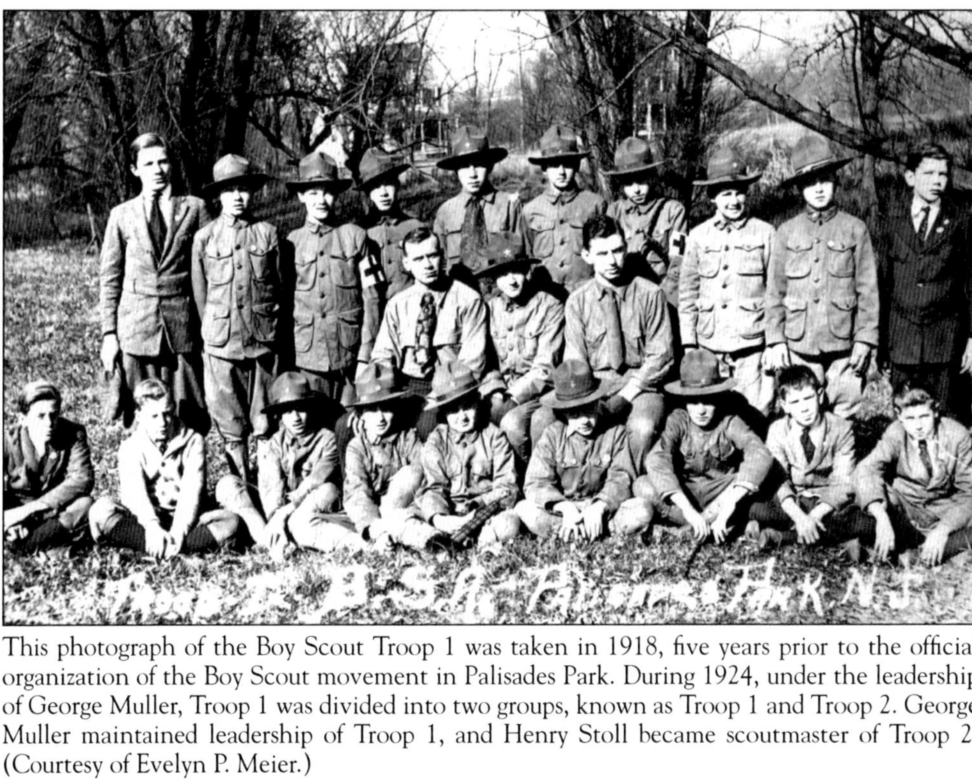

This photograph of the Boy Scout Troop 1 was taken in 1918, five years prior to the official organization of the Boy Scout movement in Palisades Park. During 1924, under the leadership of George Muller, Troop 1 was divided into two groups, known as Troop 1 and Troop 2. George Muller maintained leadership of Troop 1, and Henry Stoll became scoutmaster of Troop 2. (Courtesy of Evelyn P. Meier.)

At right, Boy Scout Troop 161 marches east on Central Boulevard from Broad Avenue. Troop 161 was organized in 1947 with Mr. Slatkin as scoutmaster. Below, Cub Scout Pack 82 on the Lindbergh School stage presents the Cub Scout law. Cub Scout Pack 82 was chartered in November 1942. In November 1960, the Holy Name Society of St. Michael's Church took sponsorship of the pack. (Courtesy of Palisades Park High School.)

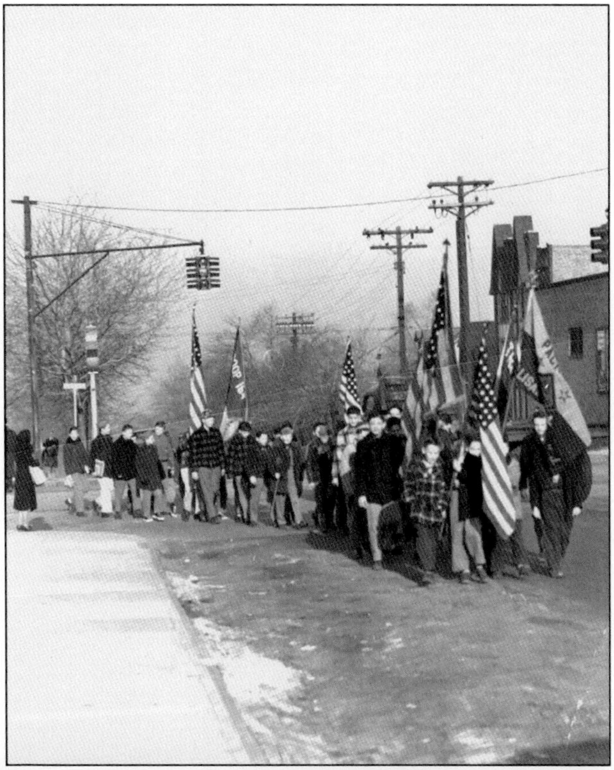

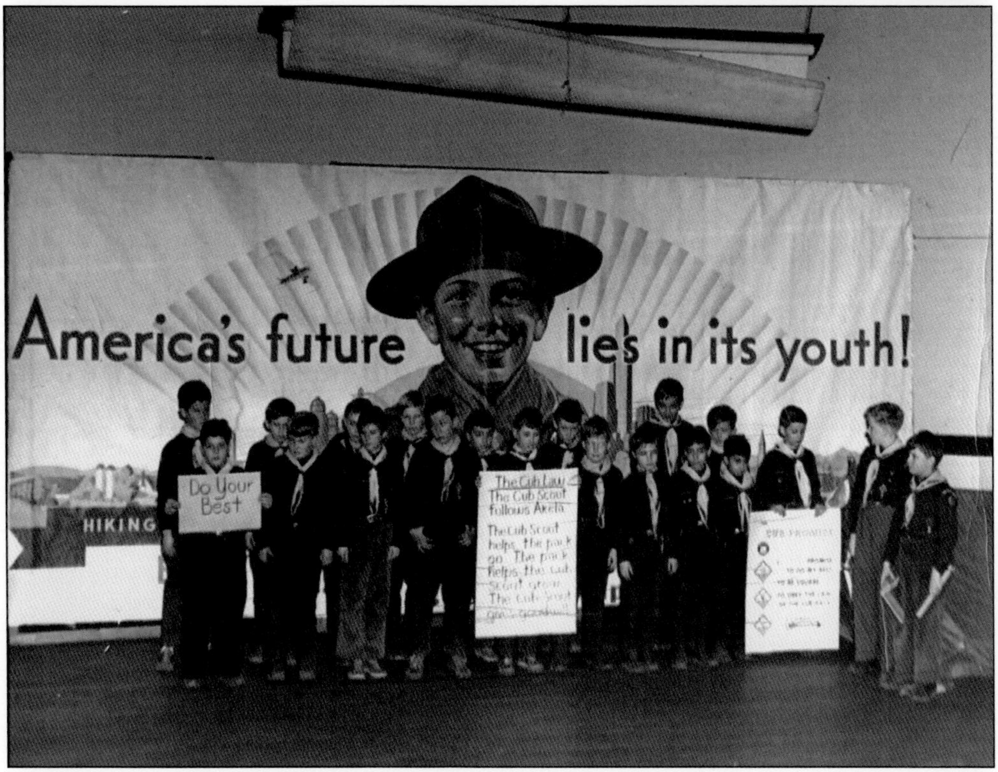

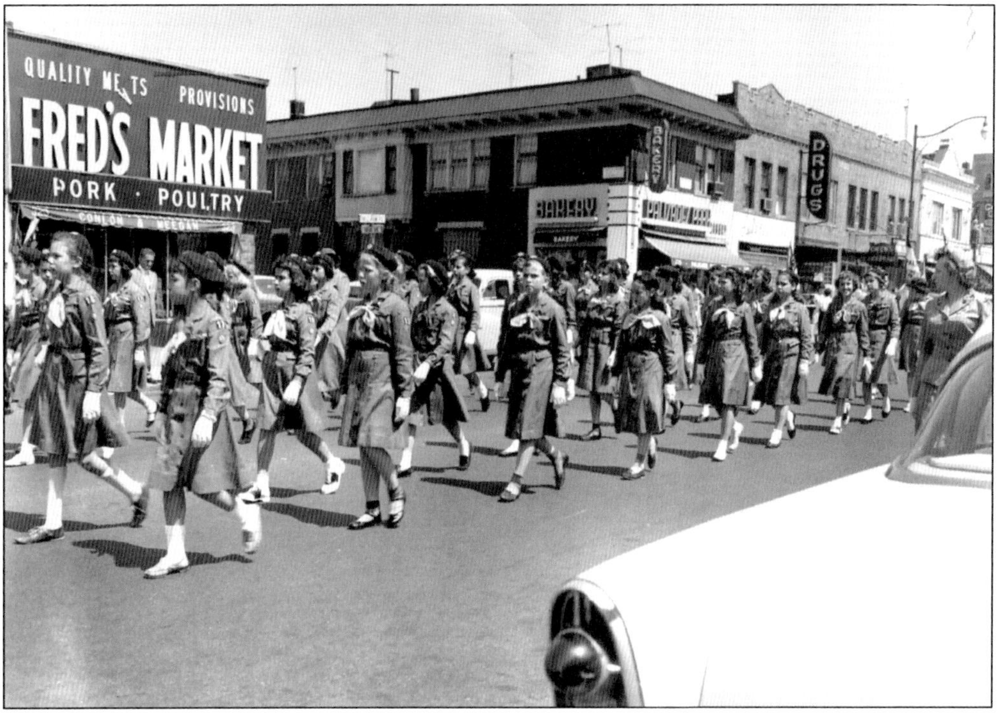

Above, the Girl Scouts are marching past Fred's Meat Market on Broad Avenue. In 1939, Girl Scouting began in Palisades Park. During 1942, the Girl Scout Council was organized. Below, groundbreaking for the Girl Scouts Little House at 440 Fourth Street began on May 25, 1957. Mayor Edward J. Reisch officiated, and the Scouts gathered to celebrate the day. (Above, courtesy of Carol Miraglia; below, courtesy of Evelyn P. Meier.)

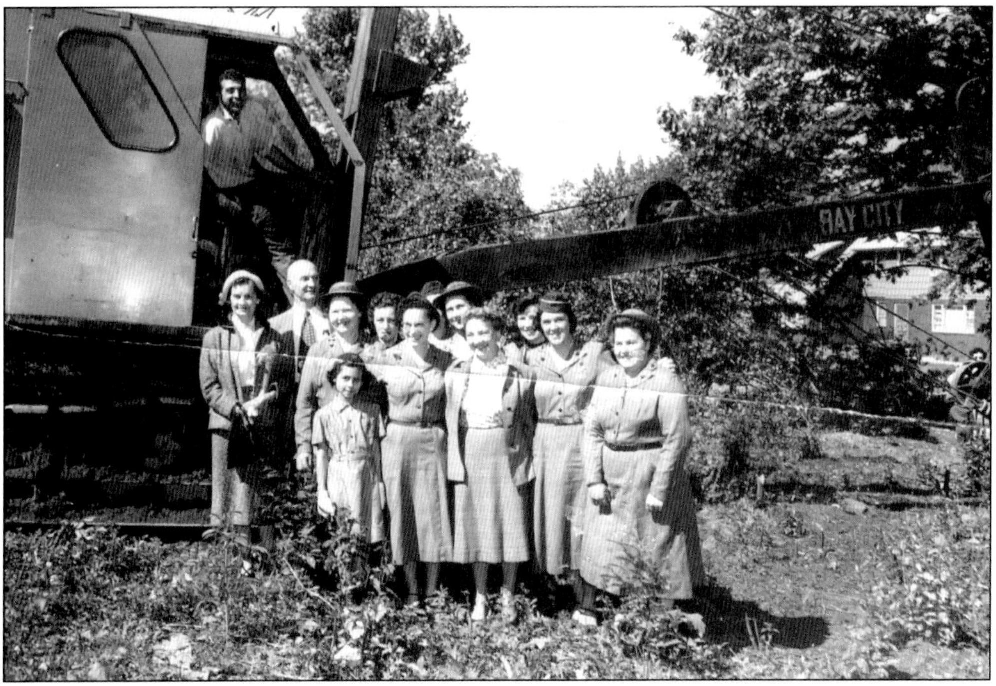

Carol Miraglia stands cheerfully with Eline Meier and the Girl Scouts at the intersection of Broad Avenue and East Brinkerhoff Avenue during the Memorial Day parade on May 29, 1972. Below, drummers are seen marching in the bicentennial parade in 1976. Bertram E. Tremble was chairman of the mayor's bicentennial committee. Palisades Park's bicentennial mayors were Carl Russo (1975–May 1976) and Robert Pallotta (May 1976– 1982). (Courtesy of Carol Miraglia.)

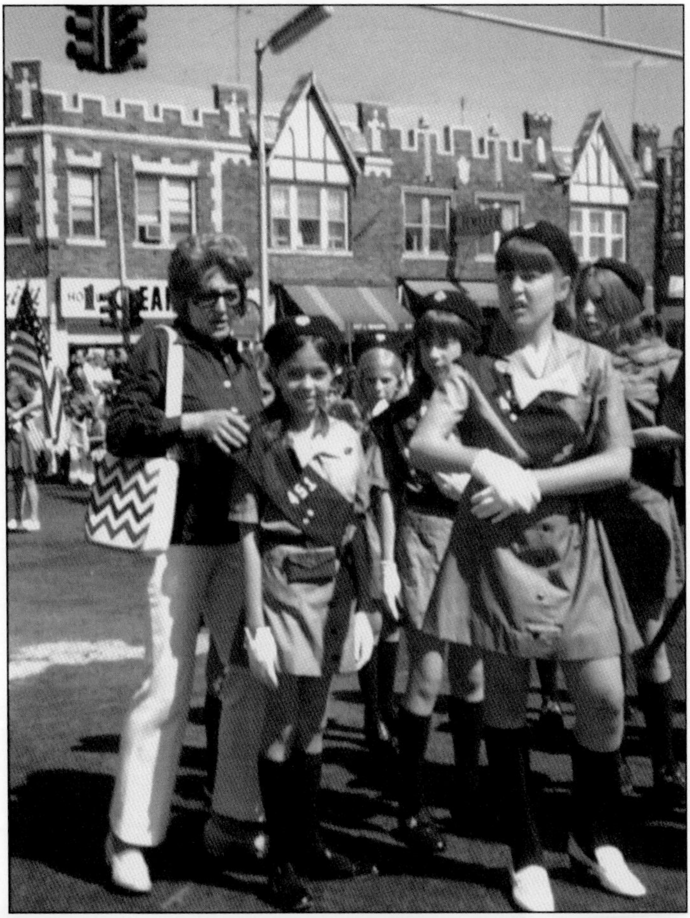

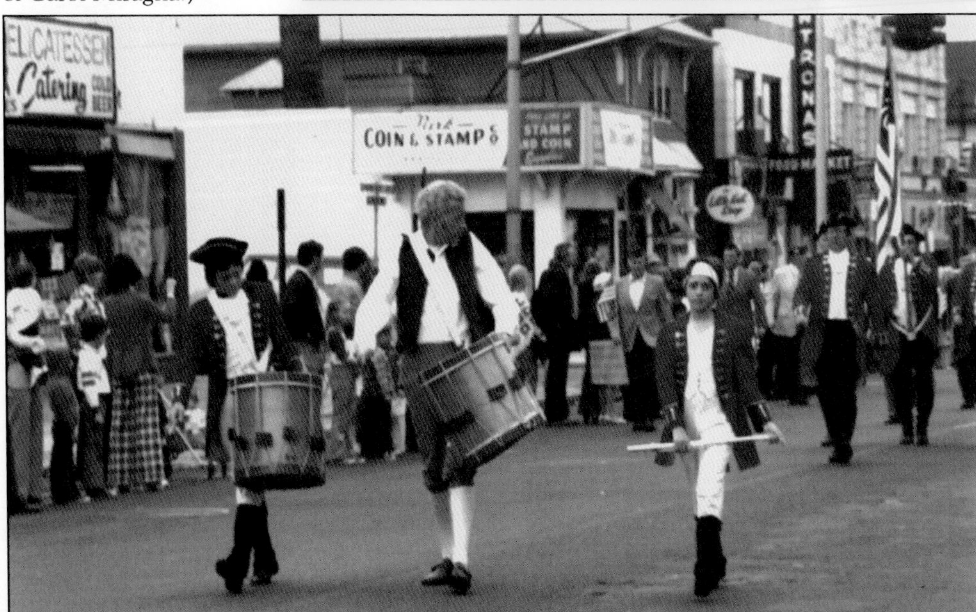

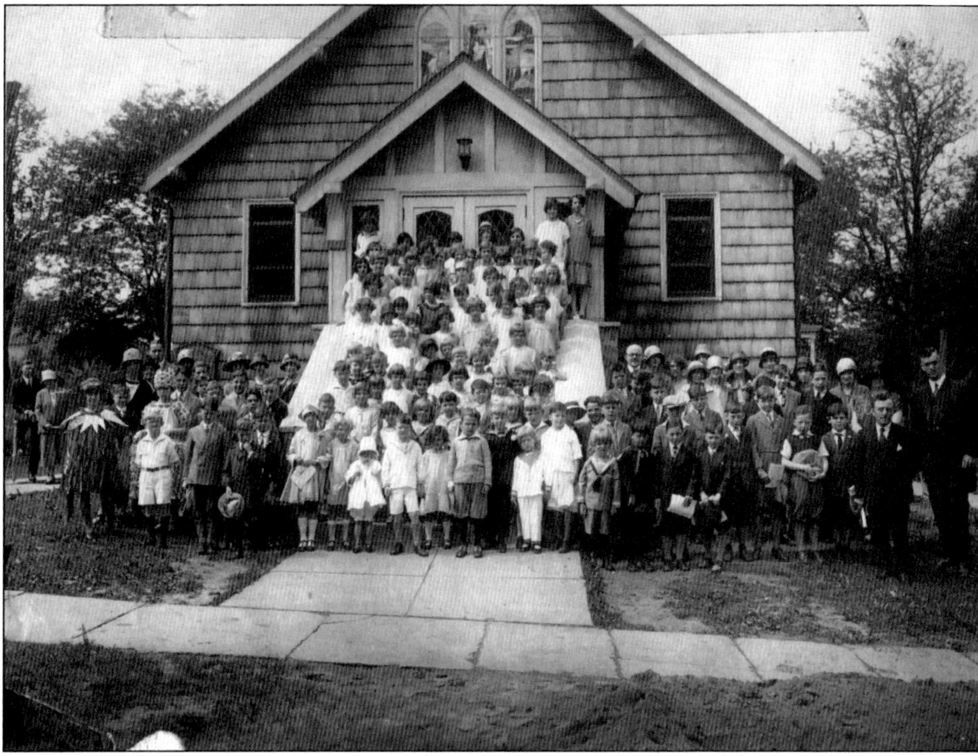

Above, children gather on the front steps of the First Presbyterian Church for Children's Day in 1927. Below is a ticket for a comedy show "Girl Shy," held in the basement of the First Presbyterian Church on March 23, 1933. Admission was 35¢. (Courtesy of Pastor David Peng.)

Christian Endeavor Society
of the First Presbyterian Church
PALISADES PARK, N. J.
PRESENTS
" GIRL SHY "
A THREE ACT COMEDY
Thursday Evening, March 23rd, 1933
IN THE CHURCH BASEMENT
Palisades Blvd. cor. Hillside Ave., Palisades Park, N. J.
Admission 35¢ UNION LABEL 6 at 8:00 P. M.

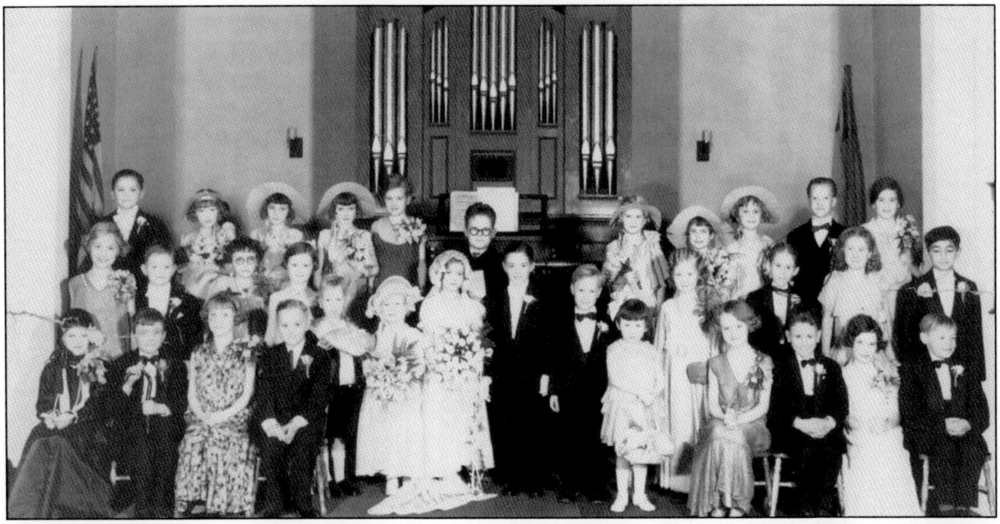

Children gather for a mock Tom Thumb wedding held at the First Presbyterian Church on West Palisades Boulevard and Highland Avenue in the above *c.* 1931 photograph. The photograph below is of the First Presbyterian Church confirmation class of 1936. (Courtesy of Arthur Anderson.)

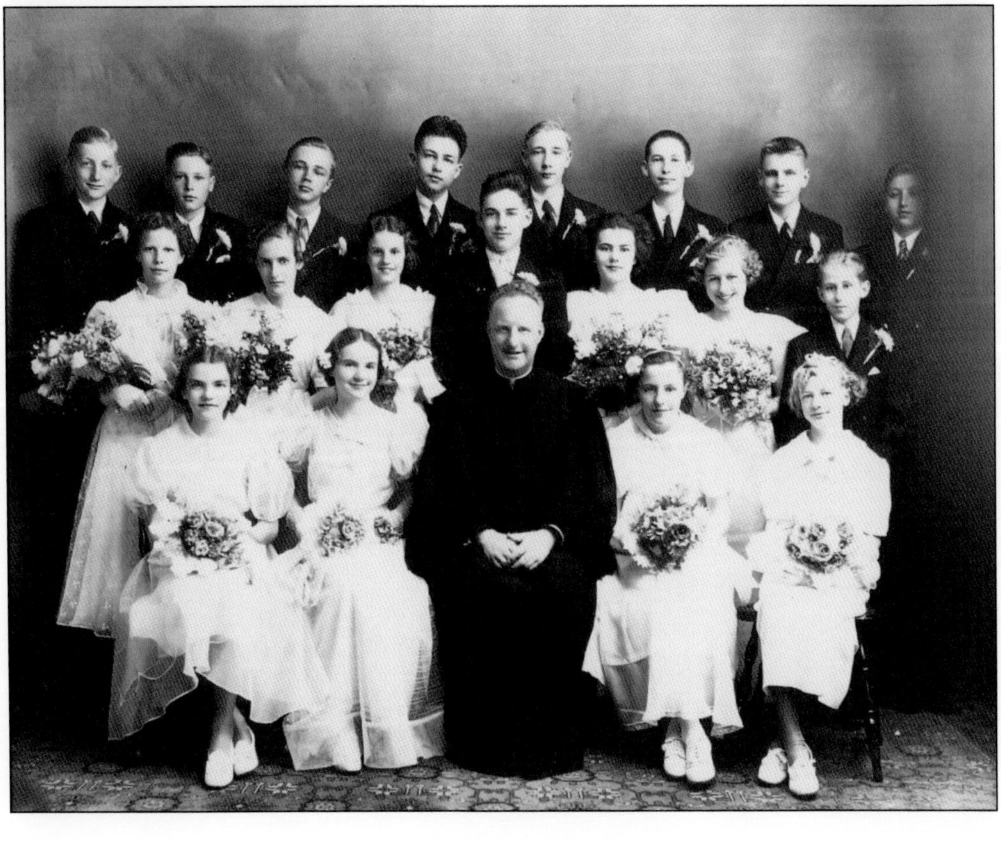

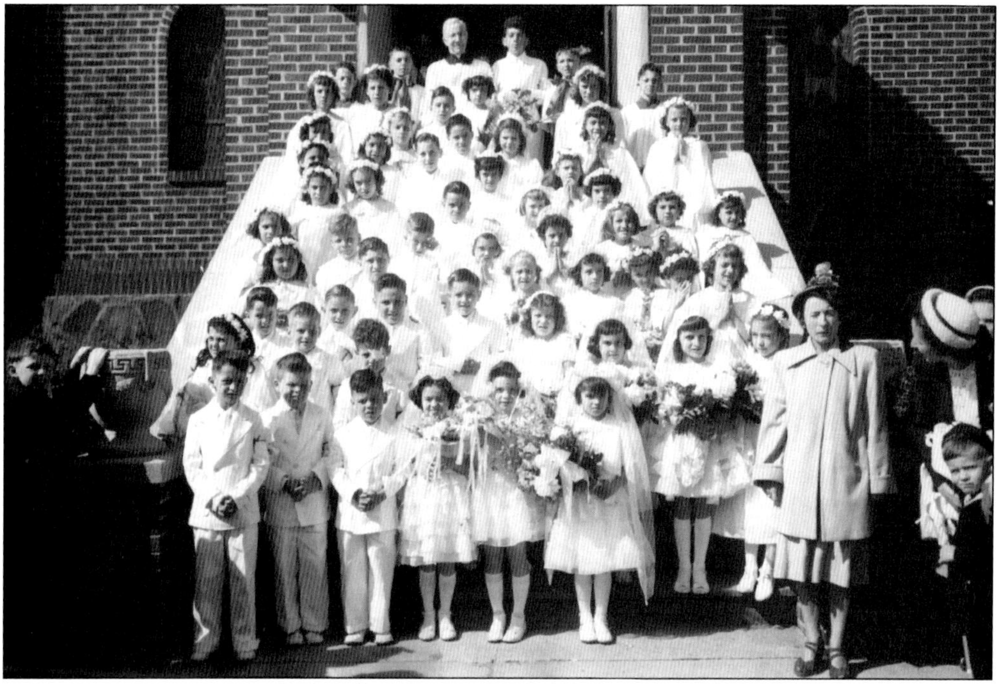

First communion at St. Nicholas Church is pictured above in 1945. The children's instructor was Mildred Pollut. Below, children are seen walking from St. Nicholas Church on the day of their first communion. (Above, courtesy of Robert Pallotta; below, courtesy of Charles Martini.)

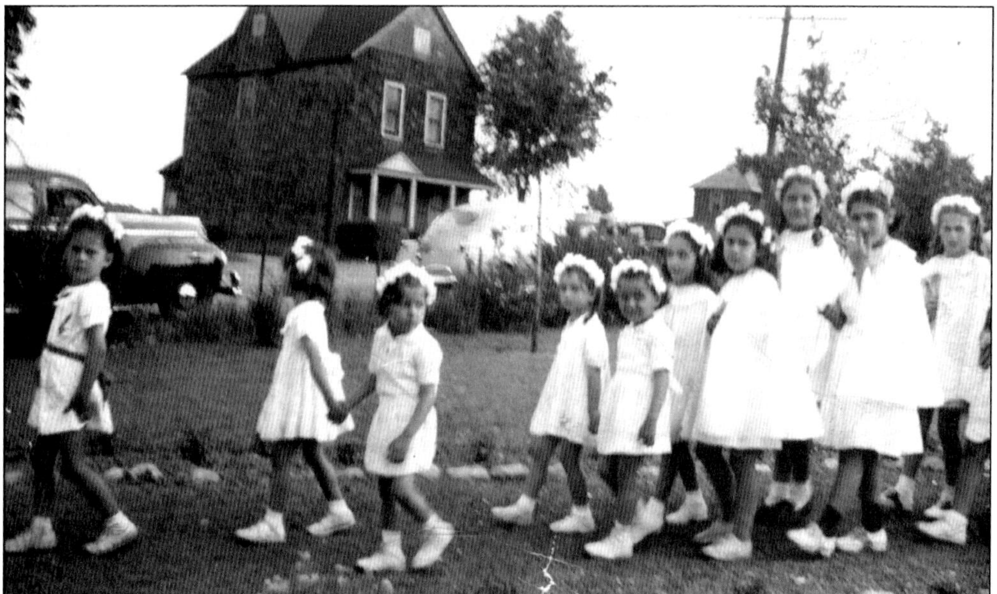

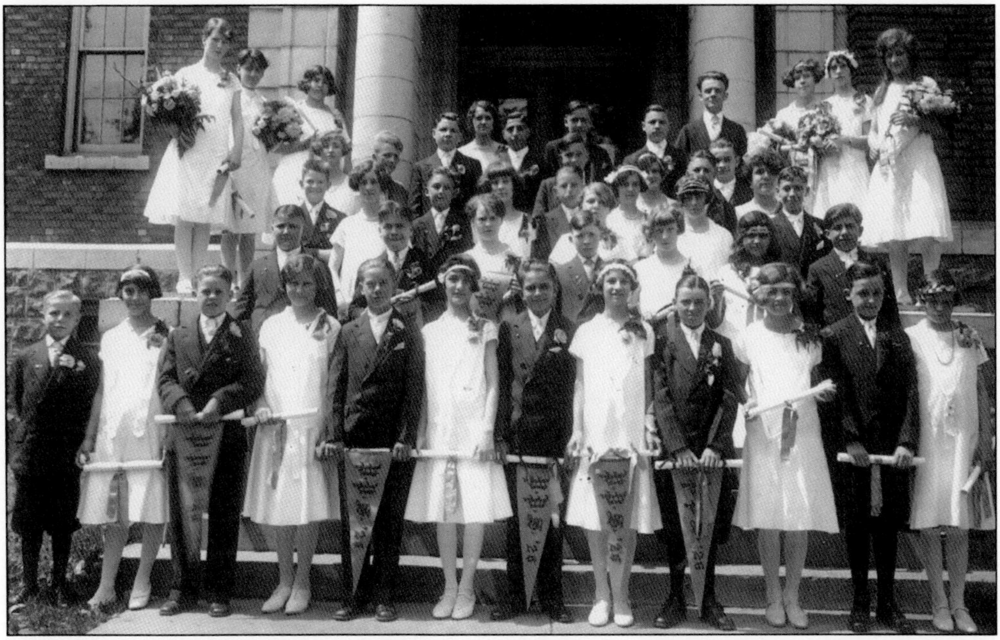

The Central Boulevard School graduating class of 1926 is pictured above. The photograph below is of the graduating class of 1927. In 1894, Central Boulevard School was built. The school grew rapidly from 1896, when it consisted of one graduate, Horace Collins. The following year the graduating class increased to six students, and growth continued with the formation of the borough in 1899 and the subsequent years ahead. (Above, courtesy of Thomas J. Albanese; below, courtesy of Palisades Park High School.)

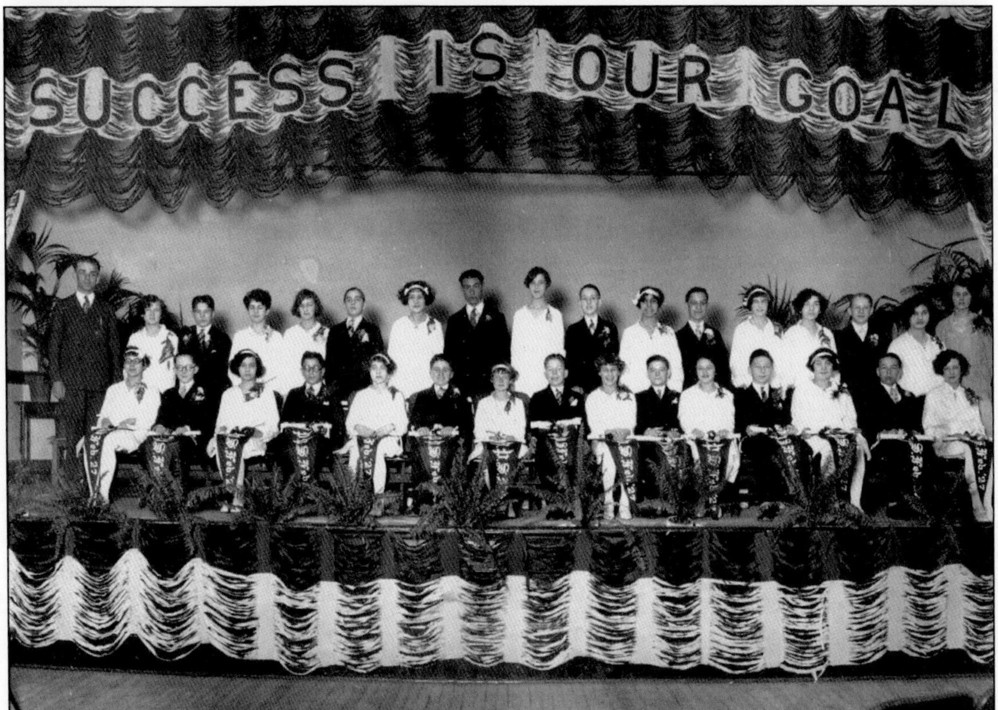

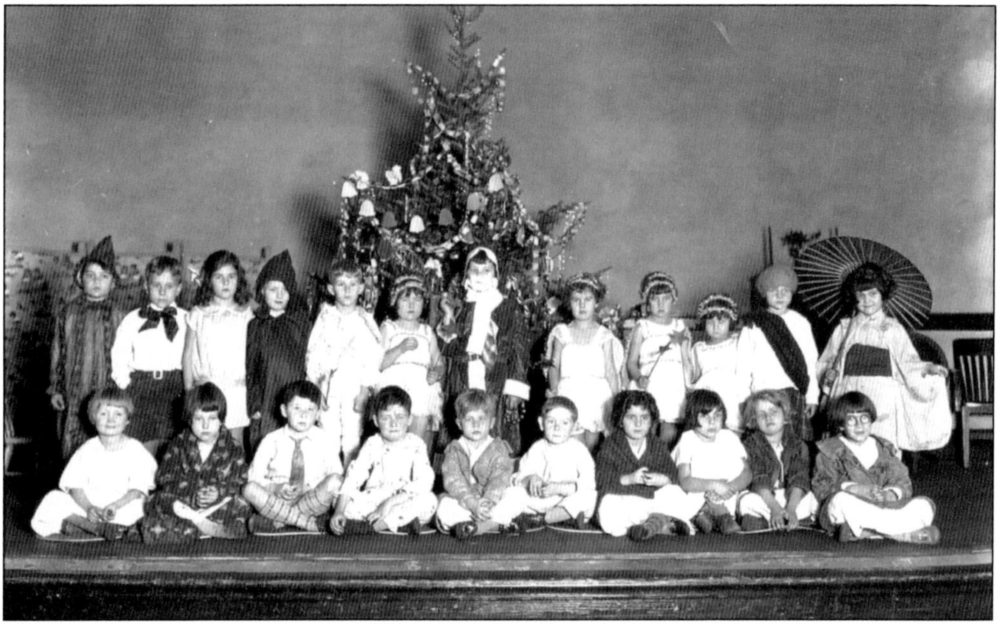

The kindergarten class of 1930 performs a Christmas play in the above photograph. Below, Arthur Anderson was the guest of honor at his Columbus Avenue home in 1938. The party was for his classmates and was a wonderful evening of games and refreshments. The guests were Alice Anderson, Nettie Anderson, Mary Barker, Lena Brooks, Peter Carney, James Dorgan, Robert Downing, George J. Farrell, Marjorie Heitz, Meta Jaegar, Mrs. H. Jaegar, Doris Lesti, Philip Katz, Grace Keefer, Dorothy Madden, Arthur Popkin, Francis Primershank, Dolly Stevens, and Andrew Watson. (Courtesy of Arthur Anderson.)

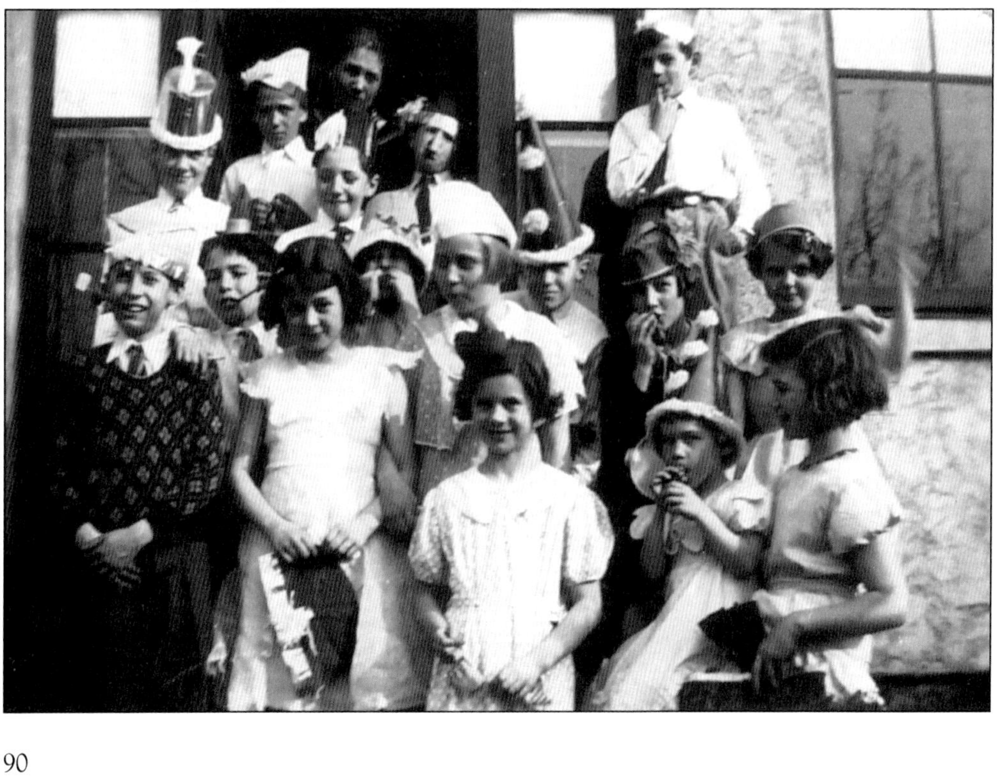

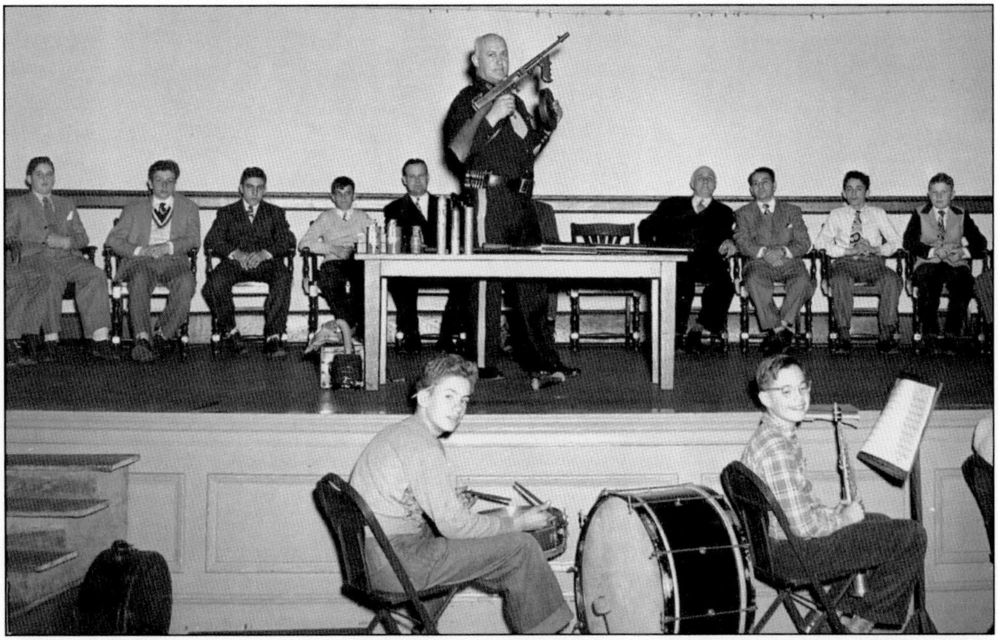

Above, children gather for an assembly at Lindbergh School, where a police officer shows students a Thompson submachine gun. Chief Leonard Cottrell is pictured sitting in the center of the photograph behind the uniformed police officer. Below, Lindbergh School children participate in a mock presidential debate of 1948. The election of 1948 was considered one of the biggest election upsets in American history, where incumbent president Harry S. Truman defied all odds and predictions, defeating Republican Thomas E. Dewey. (Courtesy of Palisades Park High School.)

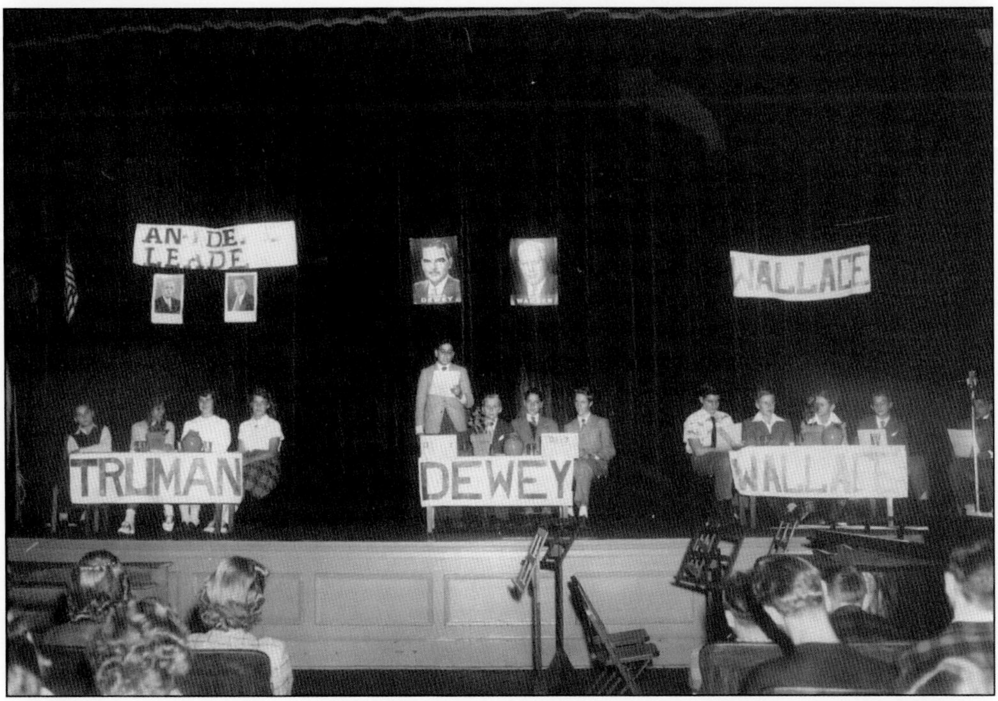

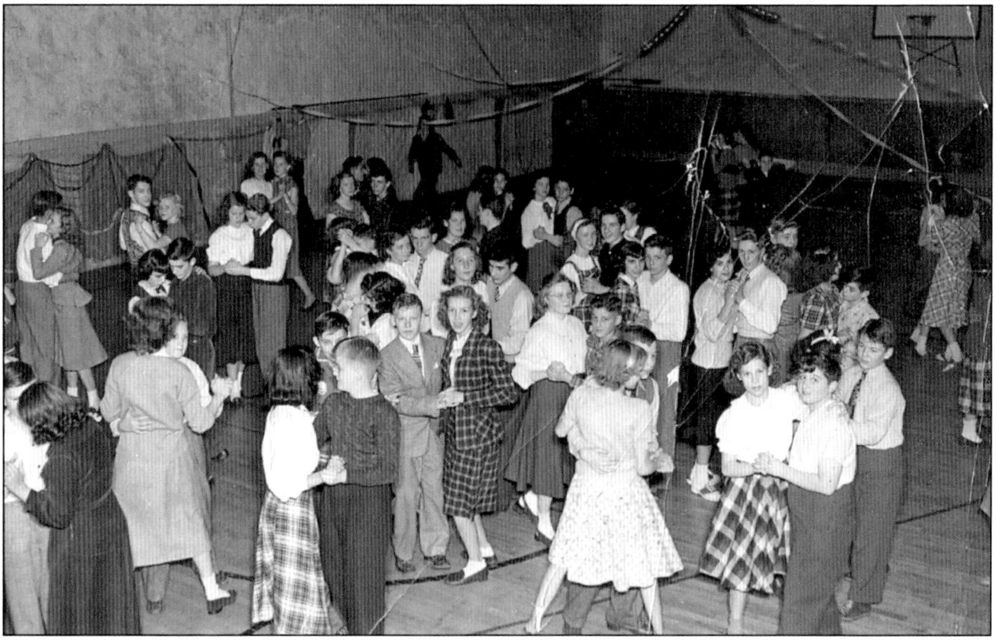

Students are dancing in the gymnasium at Central Boulevard School in this *c.* 1950 photograph. (Courtesy of Palisades Park High School.)

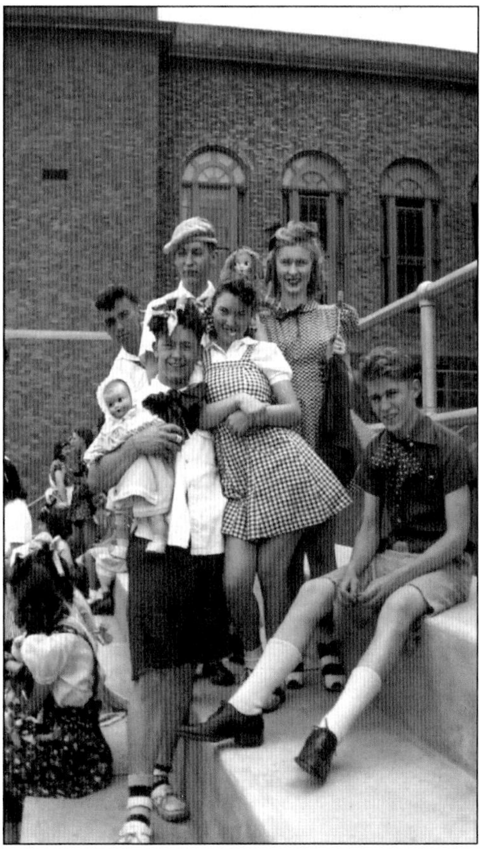

Baby Day at Leonia High School is seen here around 1940. Palisades Park students from 10th to 12th grade attended Leonia High School prior to 1955. When the sending arrangement ended in 1955, a new arrangement was made and the same-aged students attended Cliffside Park High School until the fall of 1969 when the Palisades Park Junior-Senior High School opened. Arthur Anderson is sitting on the bleachers in the photograph. (Courtesy of Arthur Anderson.)

Santa Claus visits the children of Central Boulevard School in this c. 1944 photograph. (Courtesy of Palisades Park High School.)

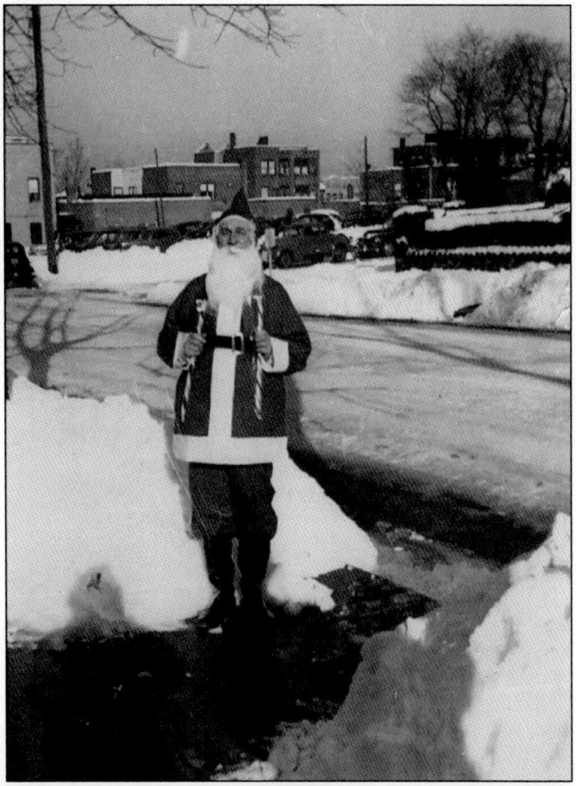

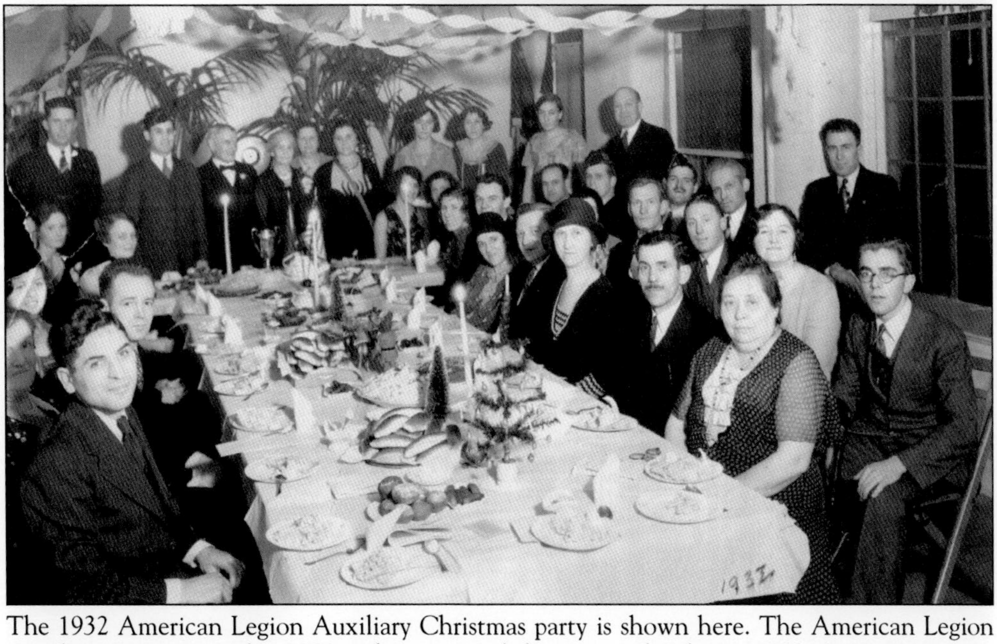

The 1932 American Legion Auxiliary Christmas party is shown here. The American Legion Auxiliary was organized in 1920 and was granted charter membership in 1923. As a requirement of membership, one needed a family connection with a veteran of World War I. The Presbyterian church's social room was used for meetings and social events. Disabled veterans were brought from nearby hospitals to be entertained. (Courtesy of Thomas J. Albanese.)

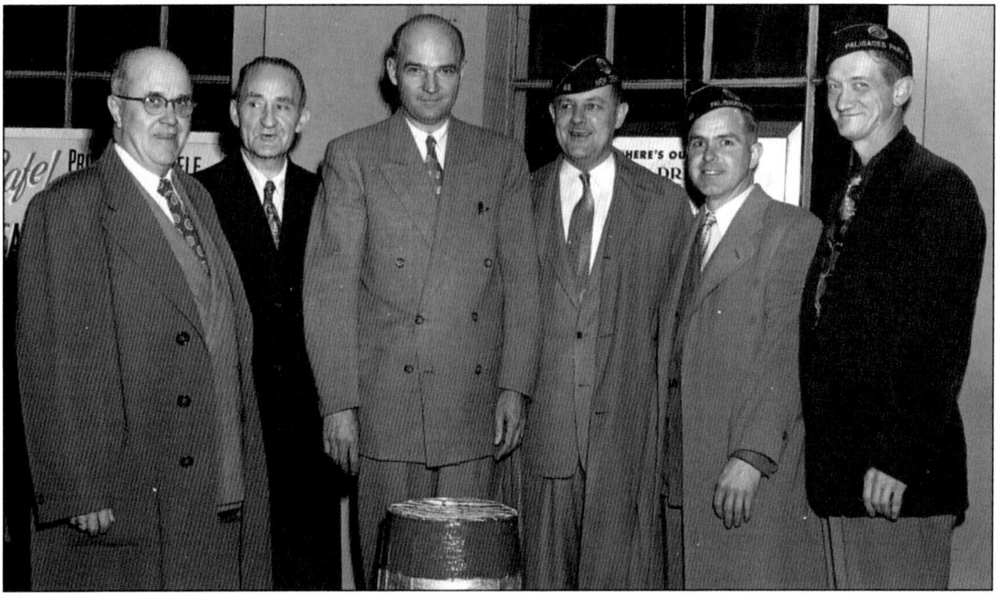

Edward H. Meier, chairman of the American Legion penny drive, stands in the center with his men to celebrate their fund-raising success around 1945. Throughout the years, the American Legion was actively involved in philanthropic endeavors that contributed to the betterment of the community. (Courtesy of Evelyn P. Meier.)

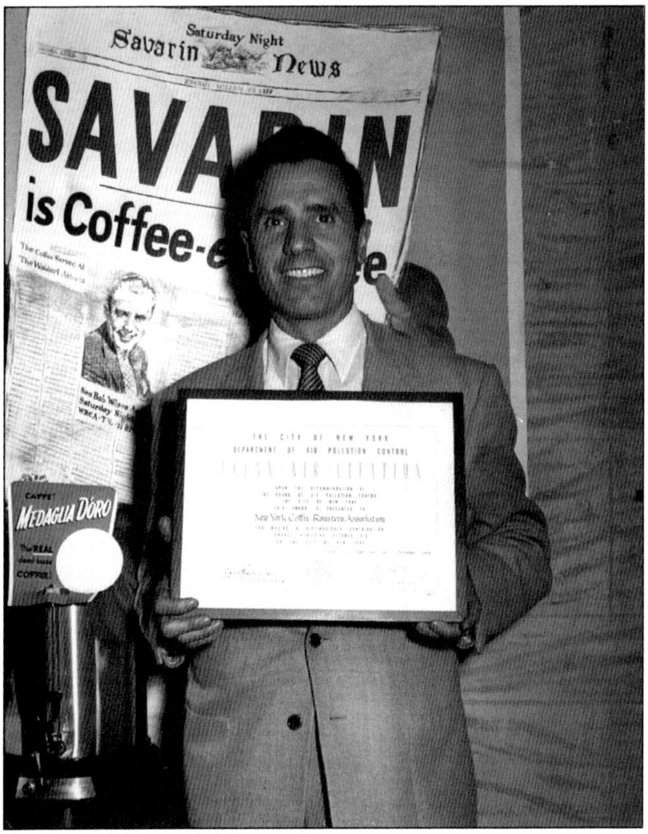

John Mazzei, late husband of Ada Mazzei, cheerfully accepts a Clean Air Citation on behalf of the New York Coffee Roasters Association in October 1955. Mazzei, a longtime resident of Palisades Park, was instrumental in selecting the new location of the S. A. Schonbrunn and Company, which opened on Grand Avenue and West Ruby Avenue in 1958. The coffee plant, known by residents as Savarin, employed hundreds of people and manufactured and marketed both instant and ground coffees. Schronbrunn's popular brands were Savarin, Medaglia D'Oro, El Pico, and Brown Gold. (Courtesy of James Benedetto.)

The color guard of the American Legion Veterans of Foreign Wars is raising the flag during the dedication of the new and current post office, located at 201 Broad Avenue, on June 19, 1960. The post office began as a one-man office in 1889 and throughout the years has grown to serve the expanding postal needs of the community. (Courtesy of Thomas J. Albanese.)

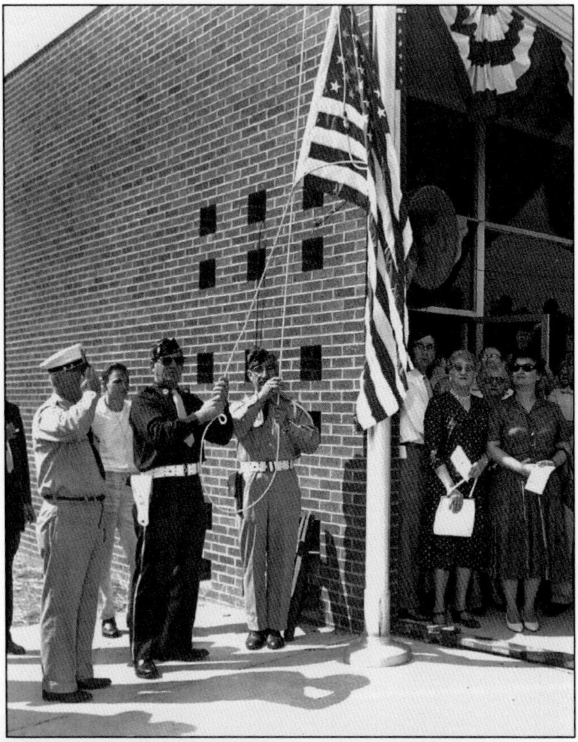

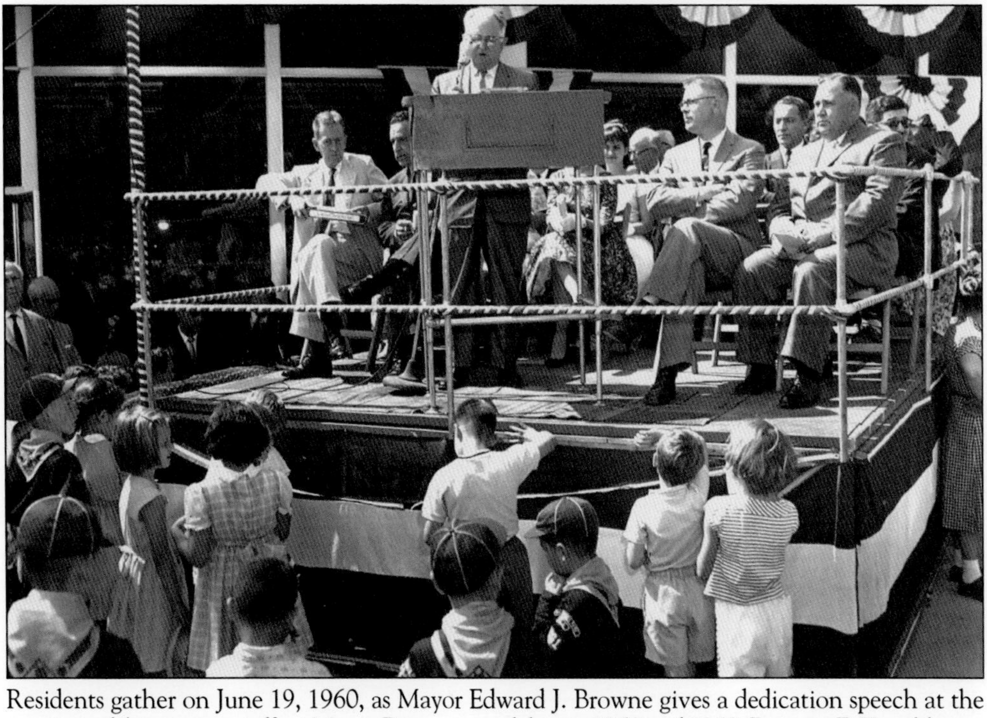

Residents gather on June 19, 1960, as Mayor Edward J. Browne gives a dedication speech at the opening of the new post office. Mayor Brown served during 1959 and 1960. Bertram E. Tremble was the postmaster, and his dedication committee consisted of chairman Victor W. Farris, Mrs. Wallace Doremus, Edward H. Meier, and Joseph A. Testa. (Courtesy of Thomas J. Albanese.)

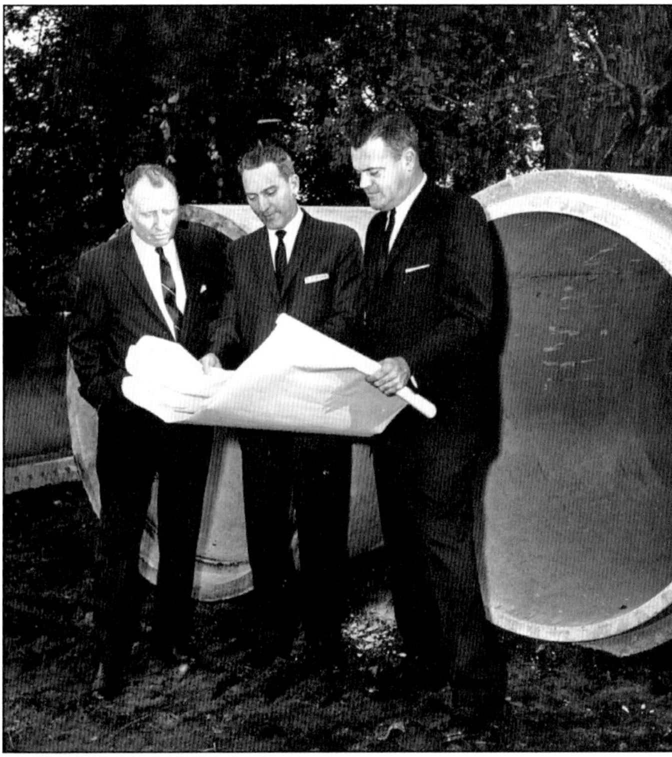

Mayor William J. Dorgan (center) is discussing the plans for a new sewer system in the borough on October 11, 1961. He is pictured with Bergen County freeholder Cassius Daly Jr. (left) and borough engineer Thomas Fox (right). (Courtesy of Thomas J. Albanese.)

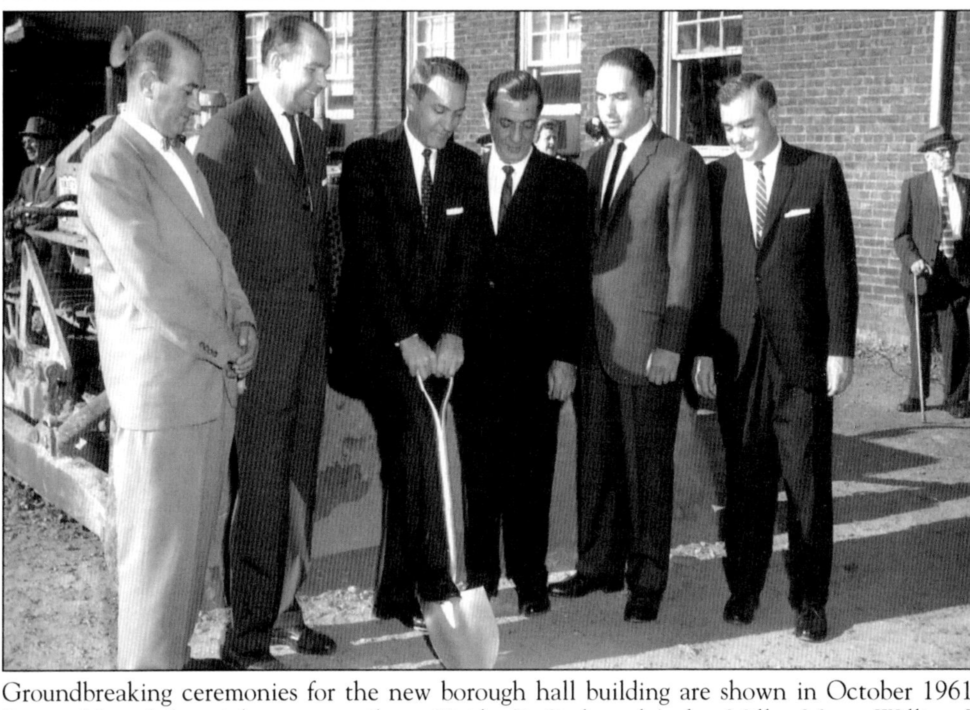

Groundbreaking ceremonies for the new borough hall building are shown in October 1961. Pictured from left to right are councilmen Visidor DeCarlo and Arthur Miller; Mayor William J. Dorgan; Dr. Vincent Lolordo; and councilmen Stanley Goldstein and Joseph Christini. (Courtesy of Thomas J. Albanese.)

Mayor William J. Dorgan is standing on the front steps of the old borough hall building with his son William (center) and builder Martin Luccarelli during the groundbreaking ceremony for the new borough hall. (Courtesy of Thomas J. Albanese.)

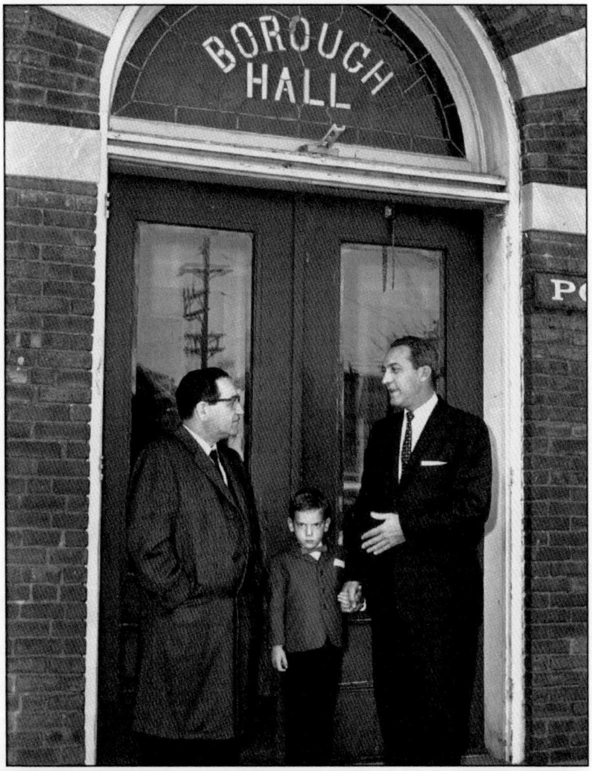

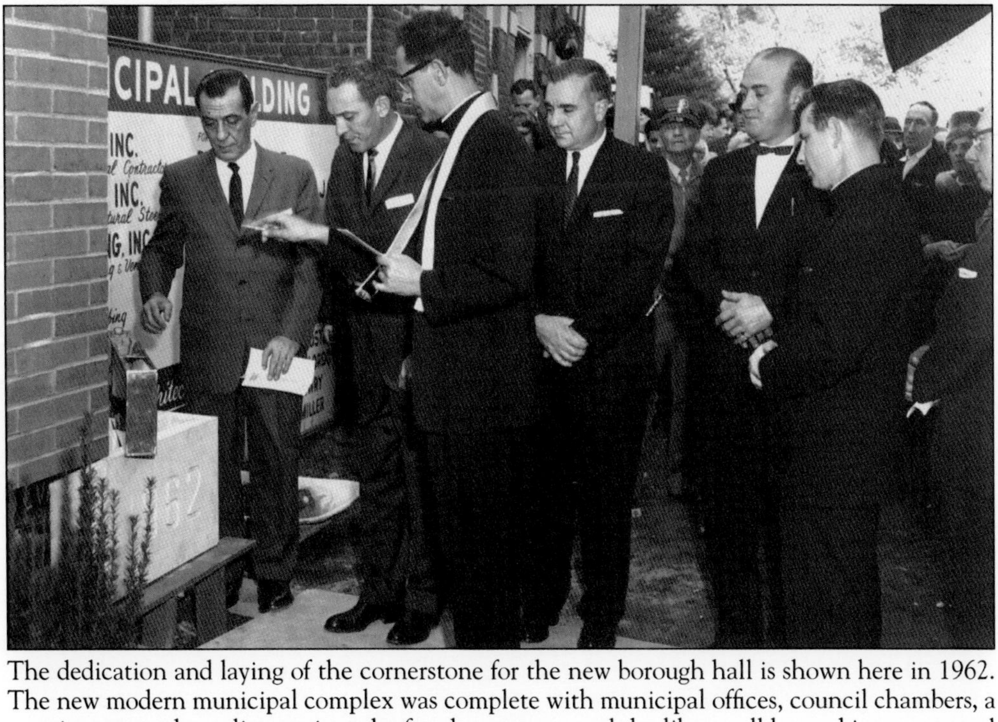

The dedication and laying of the cornerstone for the new borough hall is shown here in 1962. The new modern municipal complex was complete with municipal offices, council chambers, a meeting room, the police station, the fire department, and the library all housed in one central location. (Courtesy of Thomas J. Albanese.)

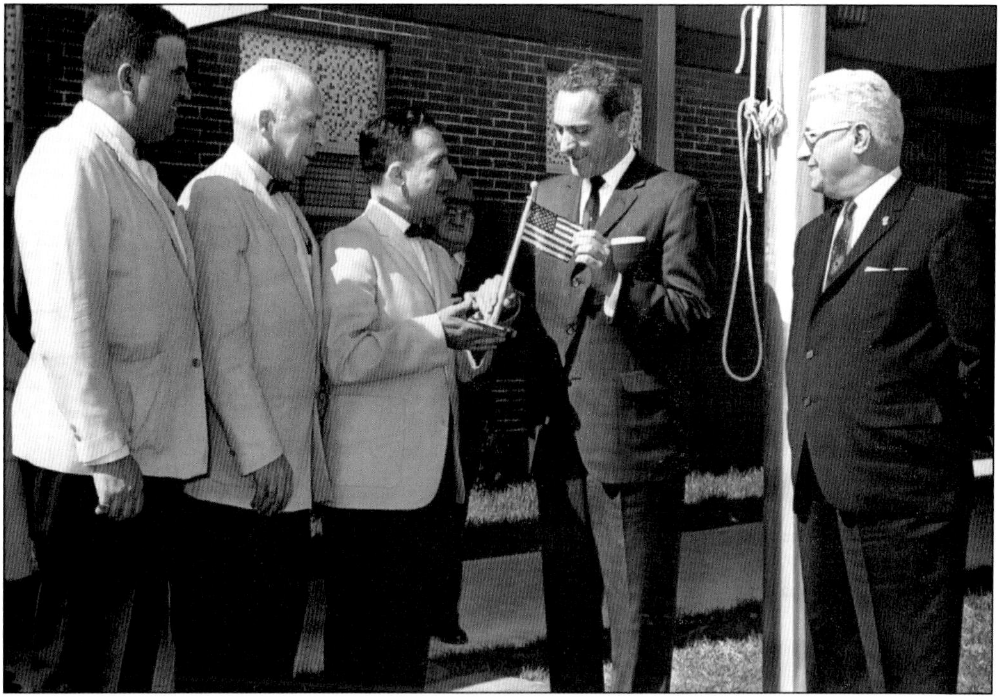

President of the Lions Club Frank Silva and his board dedicated a flagpole to Mayor William J. Dorgan in front of the newly built municipal building on April 1, 1963. From left to right are Lions secretary John Costello, chairman of the flagpole committee Alex Gasser, Lions Club president Frank Silva, Mayor William J. Dorgan, and Lions Club treasurer Mark Lombardini. (Courtesy of Thomas J. Albanese.)

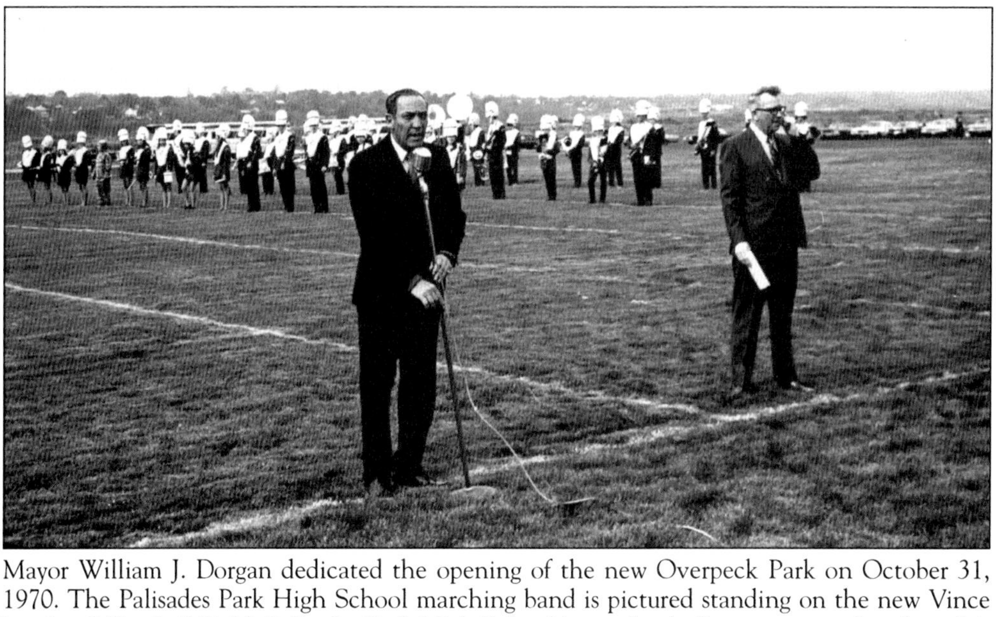

Mayor William J. Dorgan dedicated the opening of the new Overpeck Park on October 31, 1970. The Palisades Park High School marching band is pictured standing on the new Vince Lombardi Football Field. Palisades Park High School home football games were played on this field, which recently was replaced with a modernized turf field and sports complex. (Courtesy of Thomas J. Albanese.)

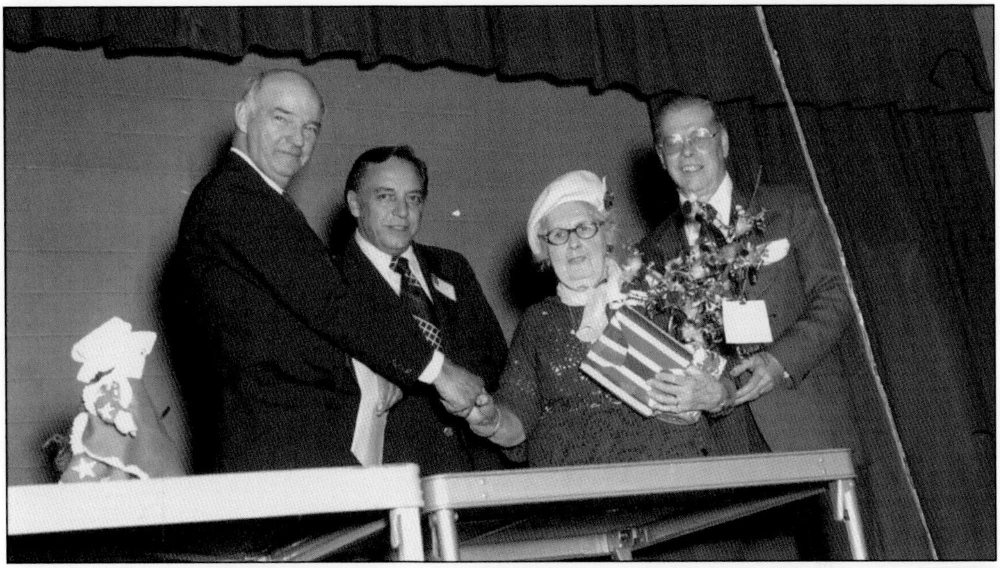

Irene Monaghan is celebrated as the oldest borough-born resident in 1976. Born on July 10, 1893, at 326 First Street, she was married to Mayor Thomas J. Monaghan, who served from 1931 to 1936. After graduating grammar school in 1907, she attended high school in Hackensack, because the borough at that time did not have a high school. A special school bus trolley transported the children to and from Hackensack High School. From left to right are chairman of Old Timers' Day Edward H. Meier, Mayor Carl Russo, Irene Monaghan, and bicentennial chairman Bertram E. Tremble. (Courtesy of Thomas J. Albanese.)

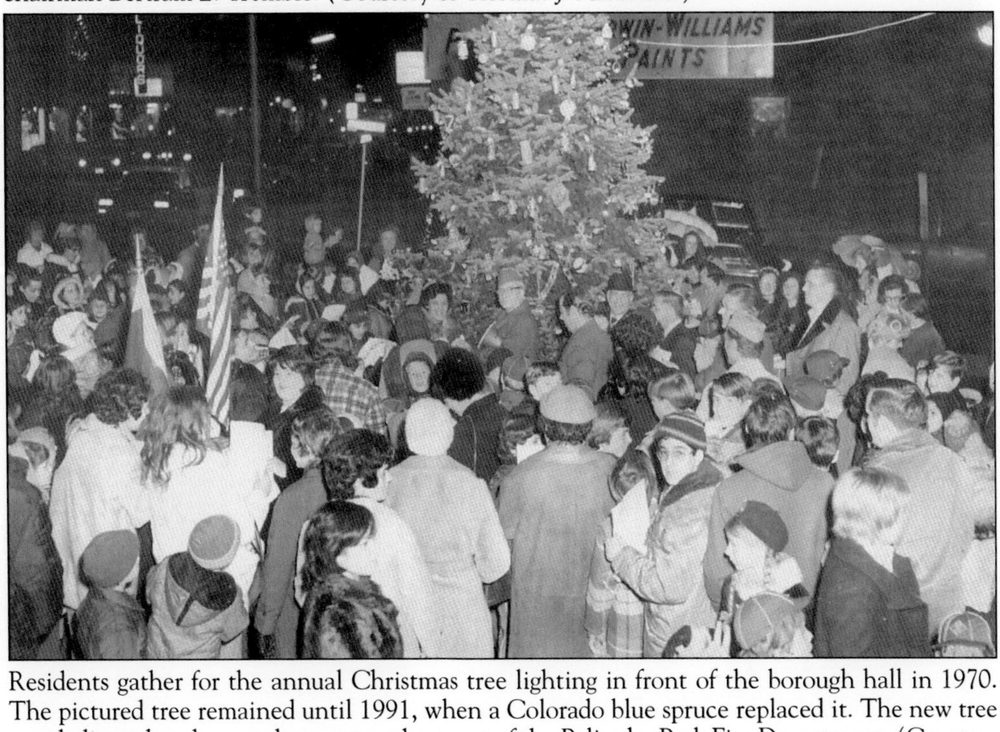

Residents gather for the annual Christmas tree lighting in front of the borough hall in 1970. The pictured tree remained until 1991, when a Colorado blue spruce replaced it. The new tree was dedicated to the members past and present of the Palisades Park Fire Department. (Courtesy of Robert Pallotta.)

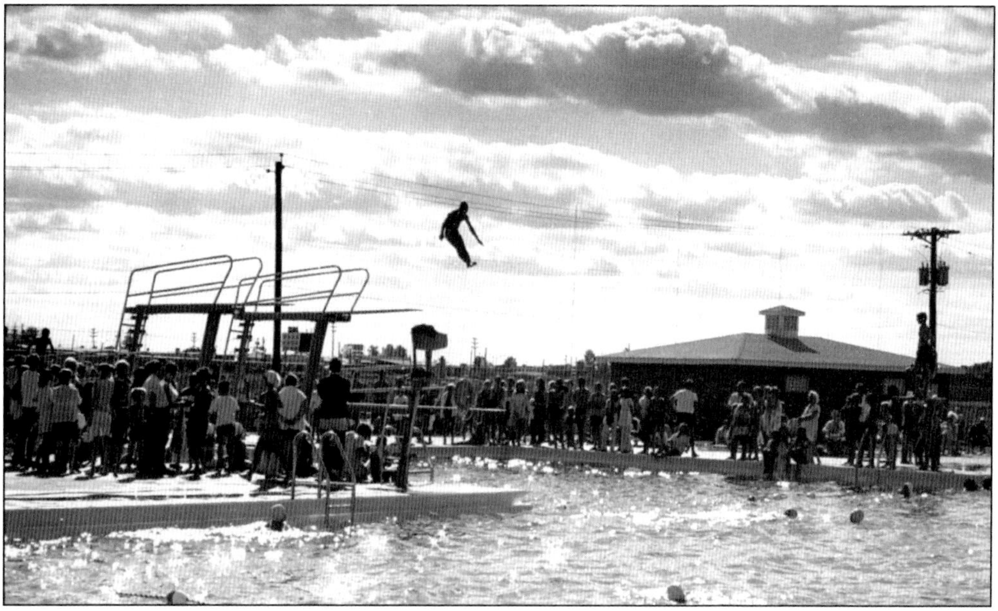

A swimmer jumps from the high dive on the opening day of the Palisades Park Swim Club on August 1, 1970. During February 1970, Ihnen and Son Pool Builders began constructing the pools. The swim club has three pools: 50 meters, 25 meters, and a kiddie pool. There are also basketball, handball, and volleyball courts. Other activates include shuffleboard, horseshoes, picnic areas, and acres of grass for sunbathing. The complex is equipped with a large eating pavilion with a snack bar and a parking facility. Throughout the years, residents have enjoyed the beautiful pools and aesthetically maintained grounds. It is considered among the best swim clubs in New Jersey. (Courtesy of Robert Pallotta.)

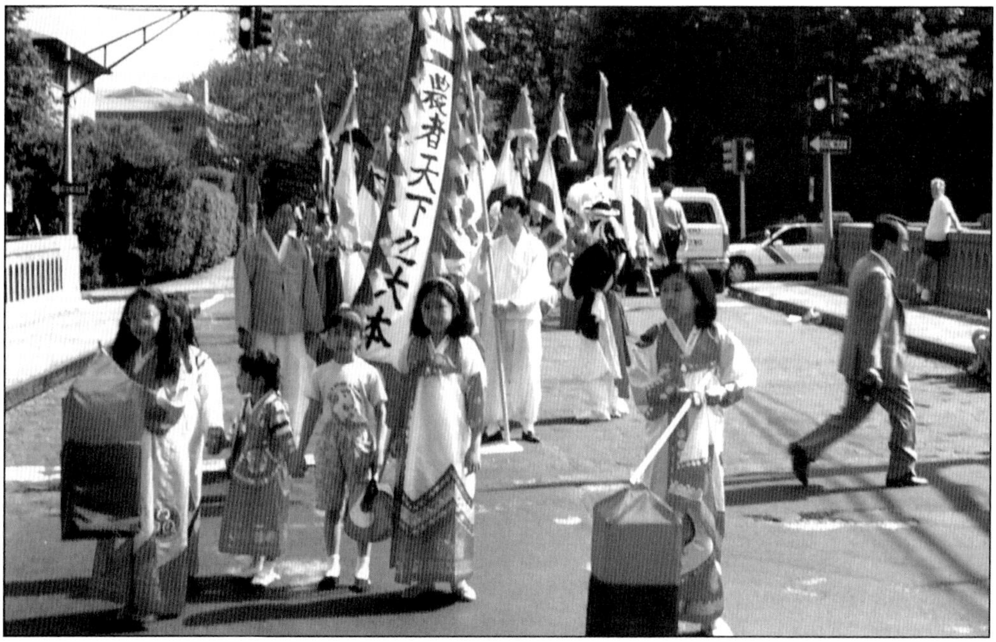

Korean American children celebrate Memorial Day in Korean traditional dress around 1990. This traditional attire is worn on holidays and special occasions. (Courtesy of Charles Park.)

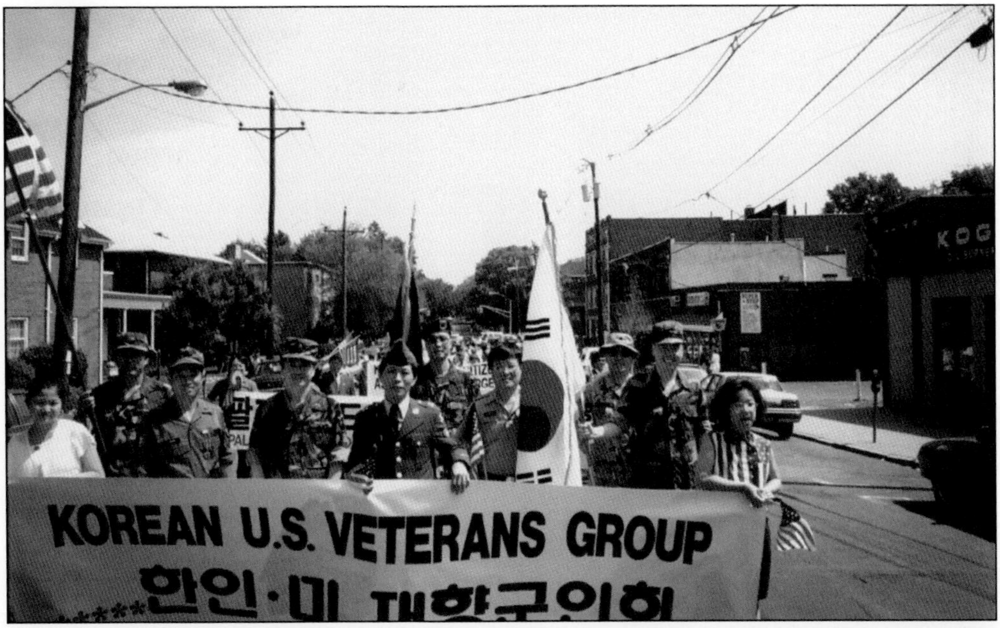

Korean United States Veterans Group is marching with honor and enthusiasm during the Memorial Day parade on May 30, 1993. This group is made of Korean Americans who bravely served in the U.S. military. (Courtesy of Charles Park.)

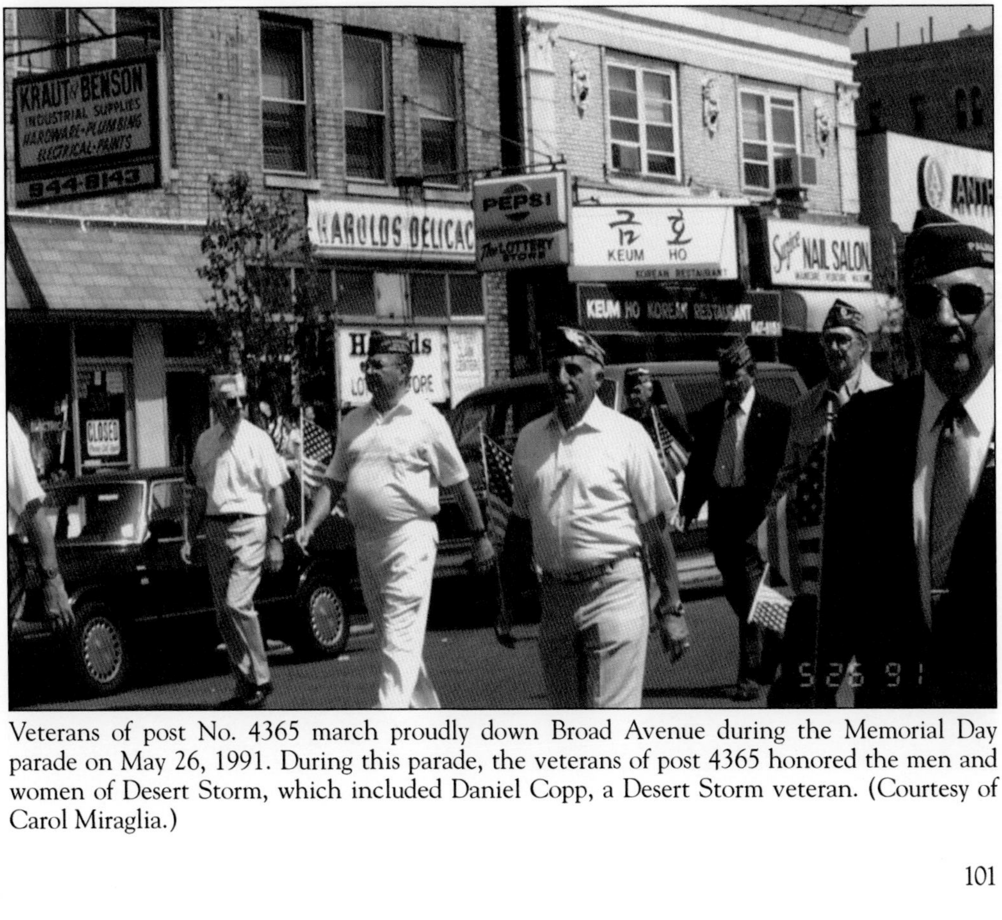

Veterans of post No. 4365 march proudly down Broad Avenue during the Memorial Day parade on May 26, 1991. During this parade, the veterans of post 4365 honored the men and women of Desert Storm, which included Daniel Copp, a Desert Storm veteran. (Courtesy of Carol Miraglia.)

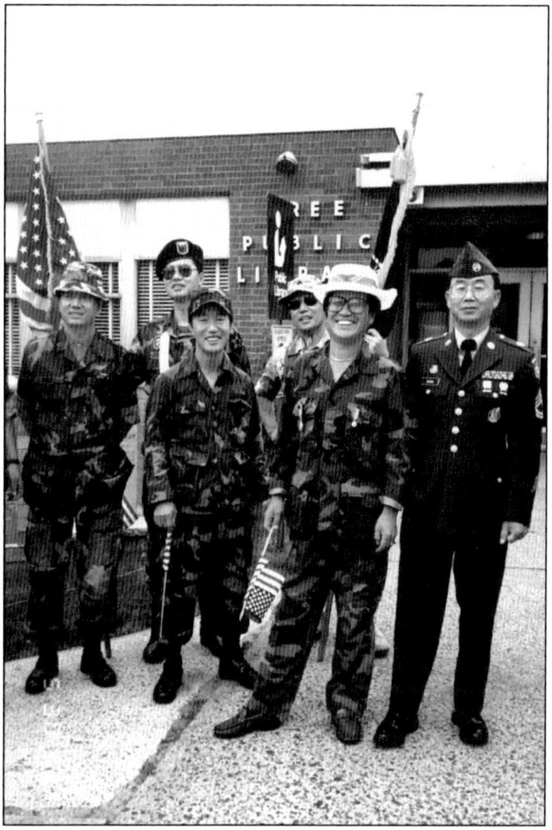

Members of the Korean United States Veterans Group stand proudly in front of the borough hall on May 30, 1993. From left to right are Spec. 4 Jung, Staff Sergeant Lim, Sergeant Lee, Sgt. Charles Park, and Staff Sergeant Moon. Sgt. Charles Park served in the U.S. Army 101st Airborne Division from 1975 to 1978. He settled in Palisades Park in 1989, when he opened his store New Seoul Carpets on Broad Avenue. He also served as president of the Korean United States Veterans Group, chamber of commerce/Korean American Business Association. (Courtesy of Charles Park.)

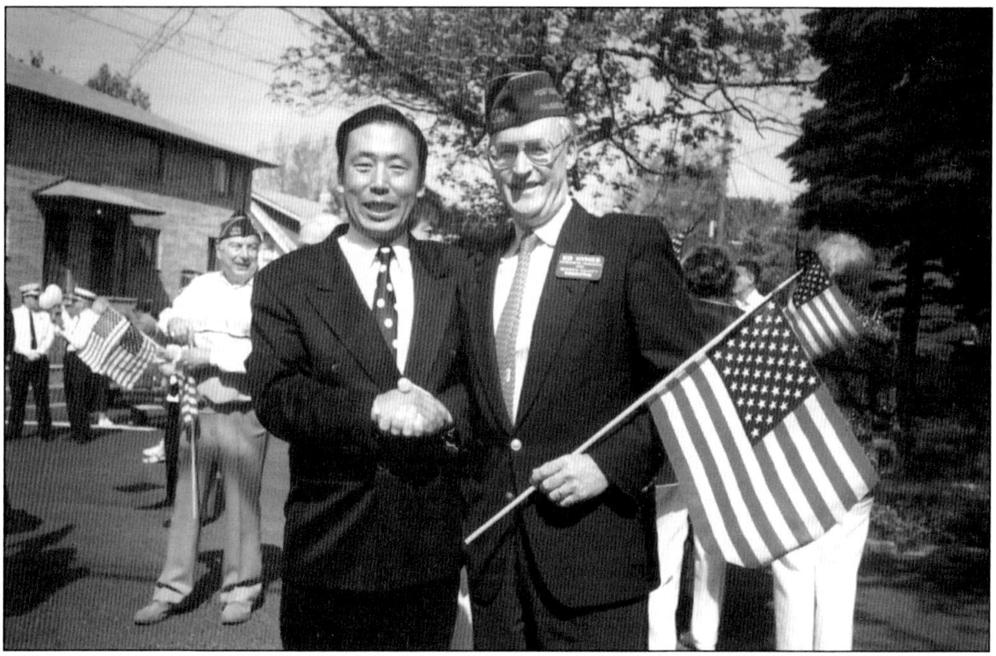

Palisades Park Chamber of Commerce member Byung Jo Jung celebrates Memorial Day with veteran Ed Hynes around 1992. (Courtesy of Charles Park.)

Six

PALISADES PARK'S FINEST

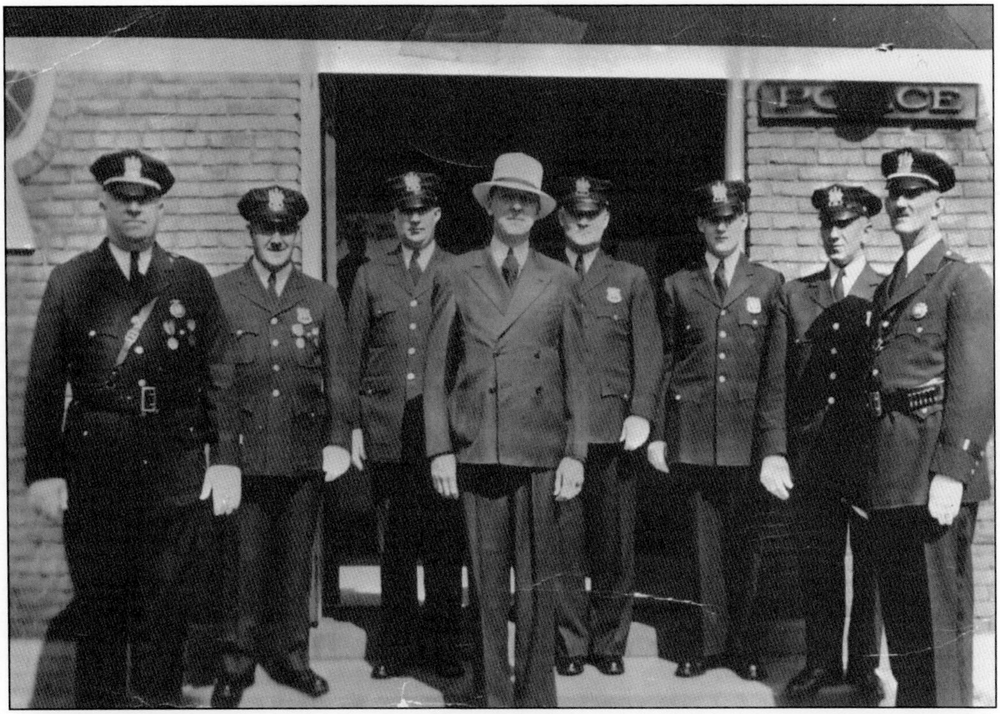

Chief David J. W. Bell stands on the front steps of the borough hall with his men in 1936. From left to right are Capt. Joseph J. Shokoff, patrolman George Farrell, patrolman George Shokoff, Chief David J. W. Bell, patrolman Charles E. Simmons, patrolman Wallace B. Dorremus, patrolman Anthony Ribello, and Lt. Robert E. MacDonald. (Courtesy of Robert Payton.)

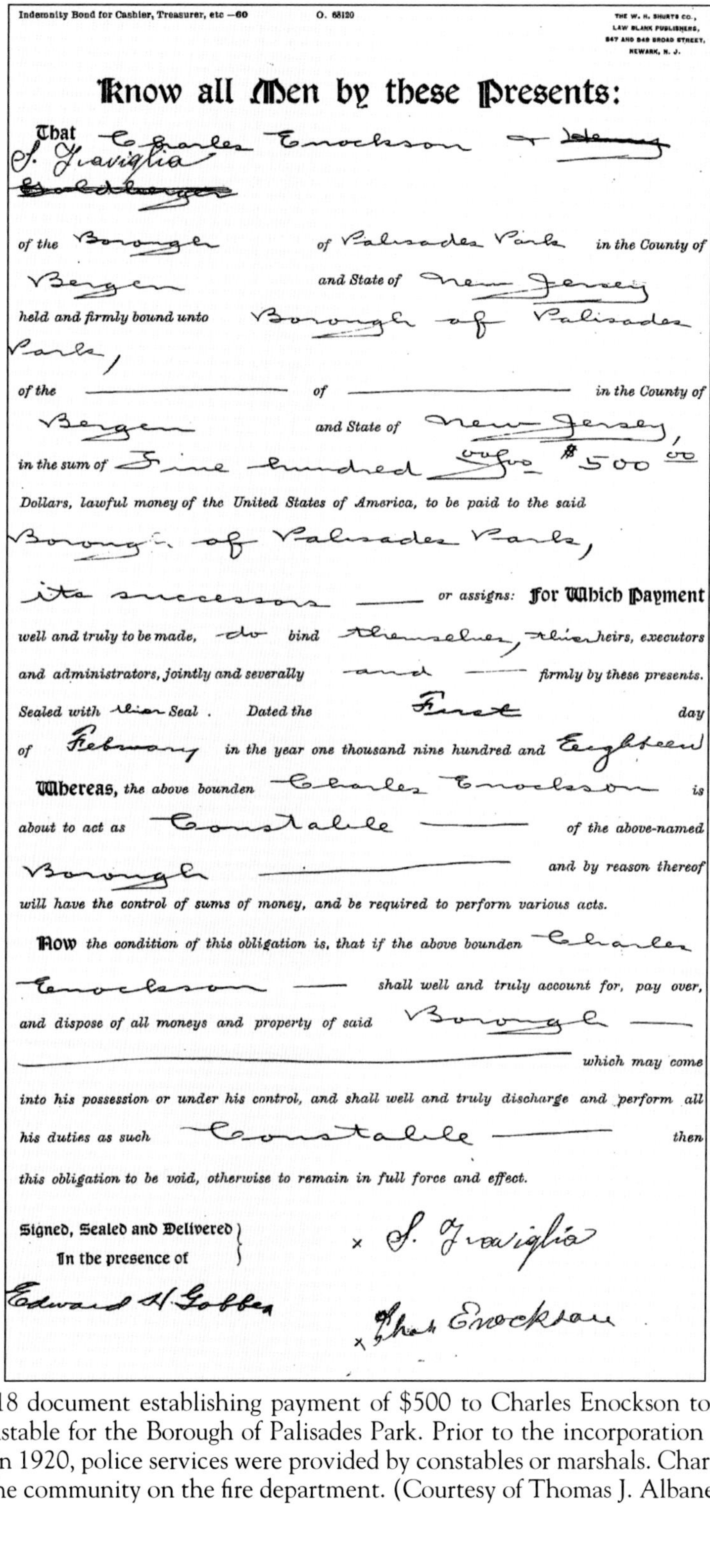

Indemnity Bond for Cashier, Treasurer, etc —60 O. 68120 THE W. H. SHURTS CO., LAW BLANK PUBLISHERS, 847 AND 849 BROAD STREET, NEWARK, N. J.

Know all Men by these Presents:

That Charles Enockson & ~~Henry~~ S. Traviglia ~~Goldberger~~

of the Borough *of* Palisades Park *in the County of* Bergen *and State of* New Jersey *held and firmly bound unto* Borough of Palisades Park, *of the* ______ *of* ______ *in the County of* Bergen *and State of* New Jersey, *in the sum of* Five hundred $^{00}/_{100}$ $500.00 *Dollars, lawful money of the United States of America, to be paid to the said* Borough of Palisades Park, its successors ____ *or assigns:* **For Which Payment** *well and truly to be made,* do *bind* themselves, their *heirs, executors and administrators, jointly and severally* and ____ *firmly by these presents.*

Sealed with their *Seal. Dated the* First *day of* February *in the year one thousand nine hundred and* Eighteen

Whereas, *the above bounden* Charles Enockson *is about to act as* Constable ____ *of the above-named* Borough ____ *and by reason thereof will have the control of sums of money, and be required to perform various acts.*

Now *the condition of this obligation is, that if the above bounden* Charles Enockson ____ *shall well and truly account for, pay over, and dispose of all moneys and property of said* Borough ____ ____ *which may come into his possession or under his control, and shall well and truly discharge and perform all his duties as such* Constable ____ *then this obligation to be void, otherwise to remain in full force and effect.*

Signed, Sealed and Delivered In the presence of

x S. Traviglia

Edward H. Gobber

x Chas Enockson

This is a 1918 document establishing payment of $500 to Charles Enockson to perform the duties of constable for the Borough of Palisades Park. Prior to the incorporation of the police department in 1920, police services were provided by constables or marshals. Charles Enockson also served the community on the fire department. (Courtesy of Thomas J. Albanese.)

This current Palisade Park Police patch is worn on the Class A uniform. It was designed in 1998 by Chief John Genovese and Lt. Paul Romano. The patch was premeditated with a version of the State of New Jersey seal, where the supporting females Liberty and Crese are pictured and two American flags fly proudly from the shield with three plows, honoring the state of New Jersey.

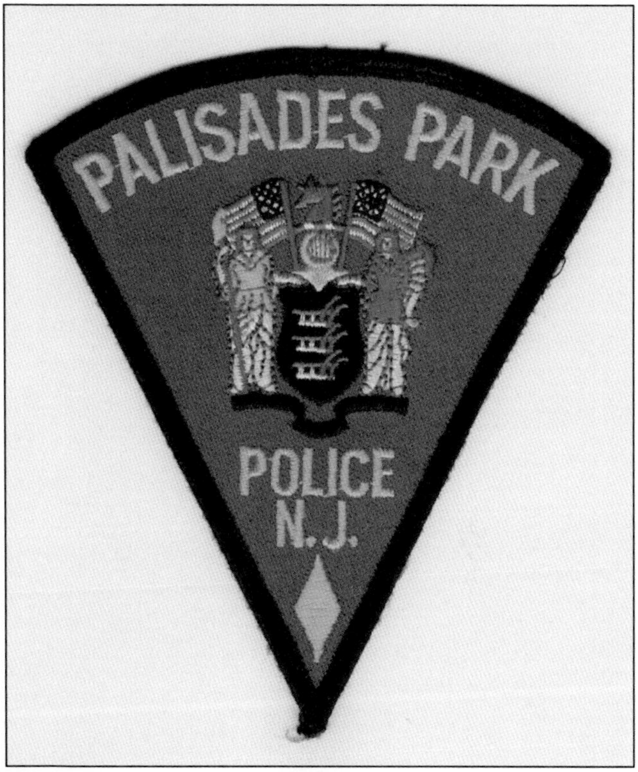

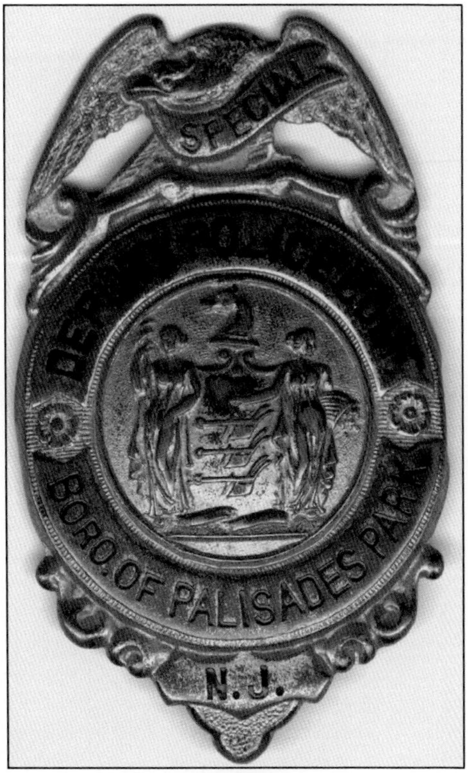

This is a *c*. 1931 deputy police commissioner badge. The first police commissioner of Palisades Park was councilman Albert King, who, on December 14, 1920, organized the police department with Mayor Robert Todd.

Whatever Our Aim, Safety Must Top Them All

ANNUAL DANCE

SPONSORED BY THE

PALISADES PARK POLICE DEPARTMENT

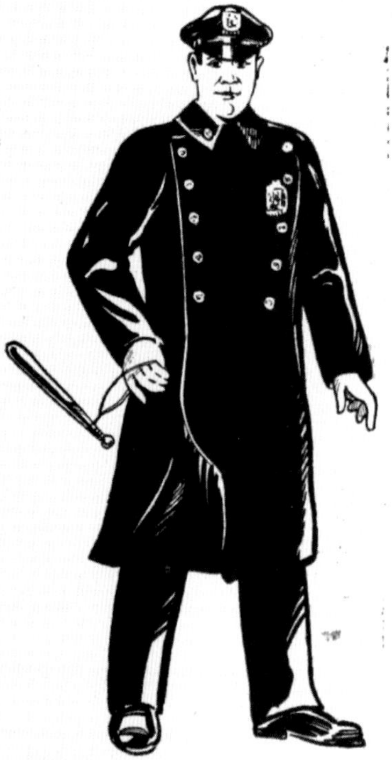

FOR THE BENEFIT OF THE

POLICE PENSION FUND

RECREATION HALL

410 BROAD AVENUE, PALISADES PARK, N. J.

SATURDAY EVENING, FEBRUARY 11TH, 1939

No wild night of winter is too bitter, or any blistering heat of summer intense enough to prevent the police from protecting your lives and property.

This is a 1939 program for the Palisade Park Police Department's annual dance to benefit the Police Pension Fund. Residents gathered at the recreation hall at 410 Broad Avenue for an evening of dancing. Chief David J. W. Bell opened the floor with "You Must Have Been a Beautiful Baby." The night began with each police officer leading an individual dance, followed by the mayor, council, and borough employees also leading a dance. The Palisades Park Fire Department led the dance to "Who Blew Out the Flame." Music was rendered by George Bayley and his orchestra. (Courtesy of Chief Michael P. Vietri.)

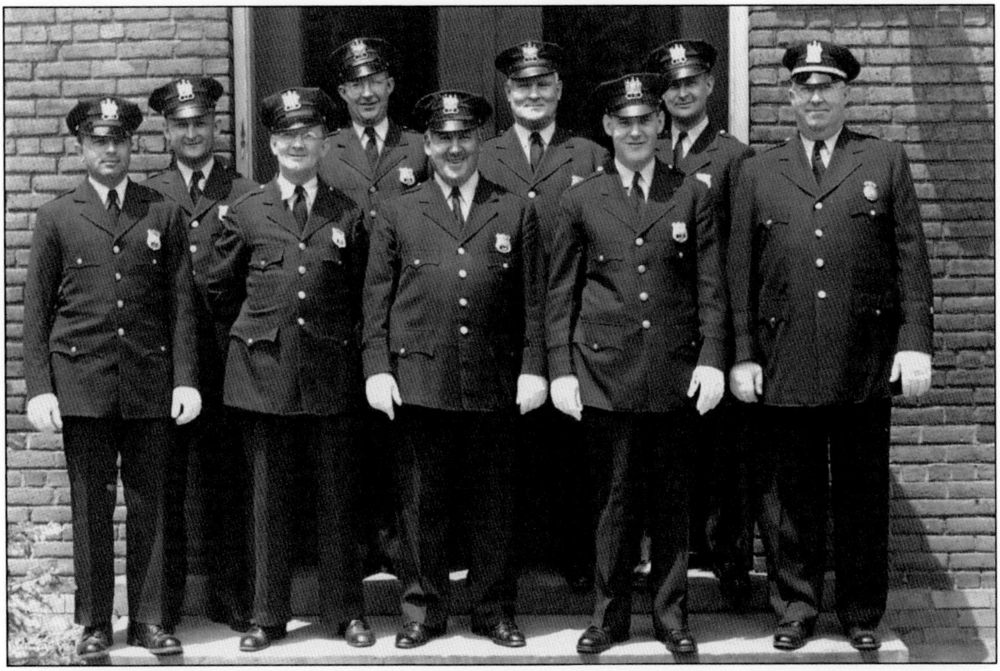

Members of the Palisades Park Police Department gather on the steps of the old borough hall in 1944. From left to right are officers Anthony Ribello, Walter Lewandowski, Robert Payton Sr., George Shokoff, George Farrell, Charles Simmons, Wallace Doremus, Leonard Cottrell, and Chief Joseph J. Shokoff. (Courtesy of Robert Payton.)

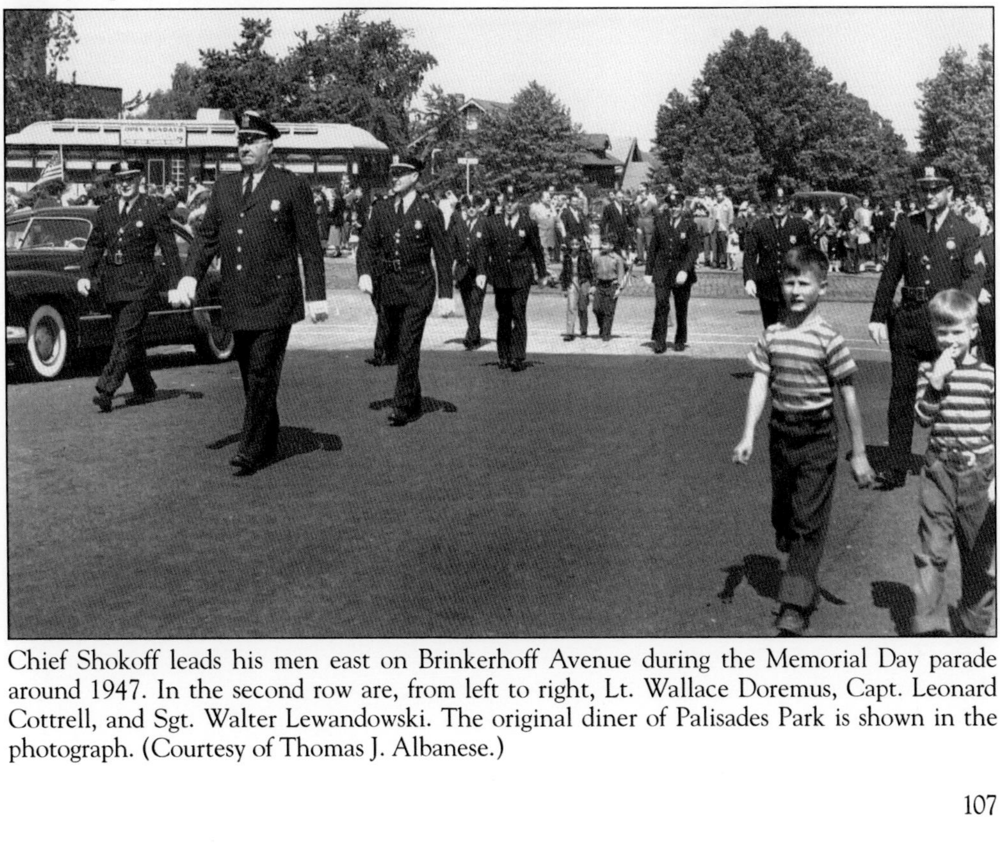

Chief Shokoff leads his men east on Brinkerhoff Avenue during the Memorial Day parade around 1947. In the second row are, from left to right, Lt. Wallace Doremus, Capt. Leonard Cottrell, and Sgt. Walter Lewandowski. The original diner of Palisades Park is shown in the photograph. (Courtesy of Thomas J. Albanese.)

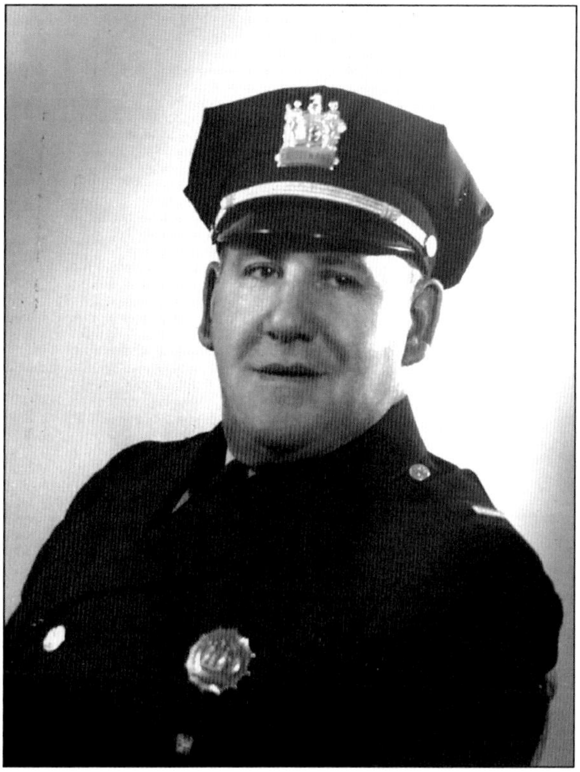

Lt. George Farrell was a distinguished member of the Palisades Park Police Department. He was appointed as a patrolman on June 9, 1925, by the police committee during Mayor Carl E. Heder's administration. He was promoted to lieutenant on January 1, 1945. (Courtesy of George J. Farrell.)

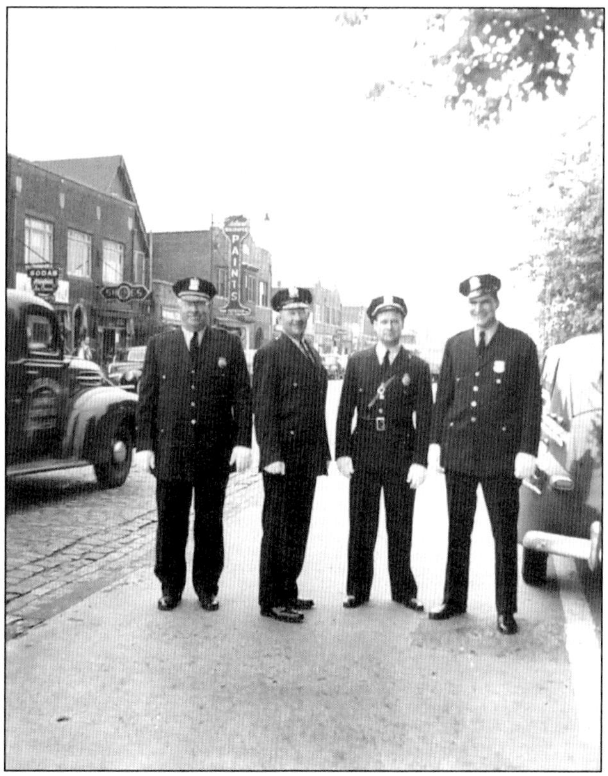

This photograph is of Memorial Day, May 30, 1948. Pictured here are, from left to right, Chief Joseph J. Shokoff, patrolman George Shokoff, Capt. Leonard Cottrell, and patrolman Louis Bellocchio. (Courtesy of Leonard R. Cottrell.)

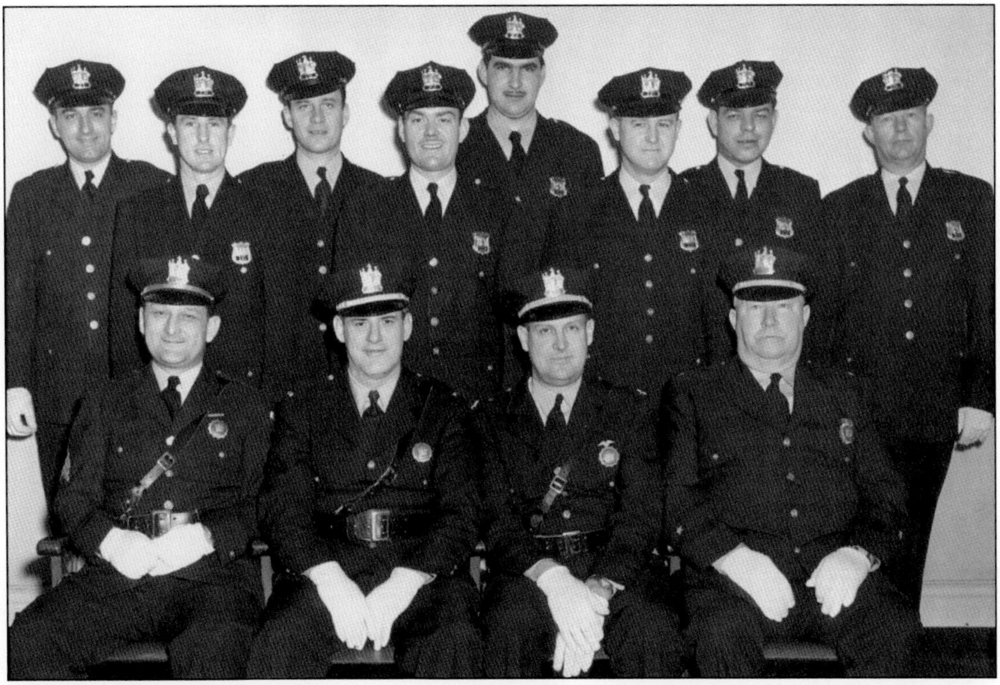

Seen in 1949 from left to right are (first row) Sgt. Walter Lewandowski, Lt. Wallace Doremus, Capt. Leonard Cottrell, and Chief Joseph Shokoff; (second row) patrolmen Anthony Pollut, John Moffatt, John Zenk, James Tenewitz, Louis Bellocchio, Martin Fay, George Wellinghorst, and George Shokoff. (Courtesy of *Golden Jubilee of 1949*.)

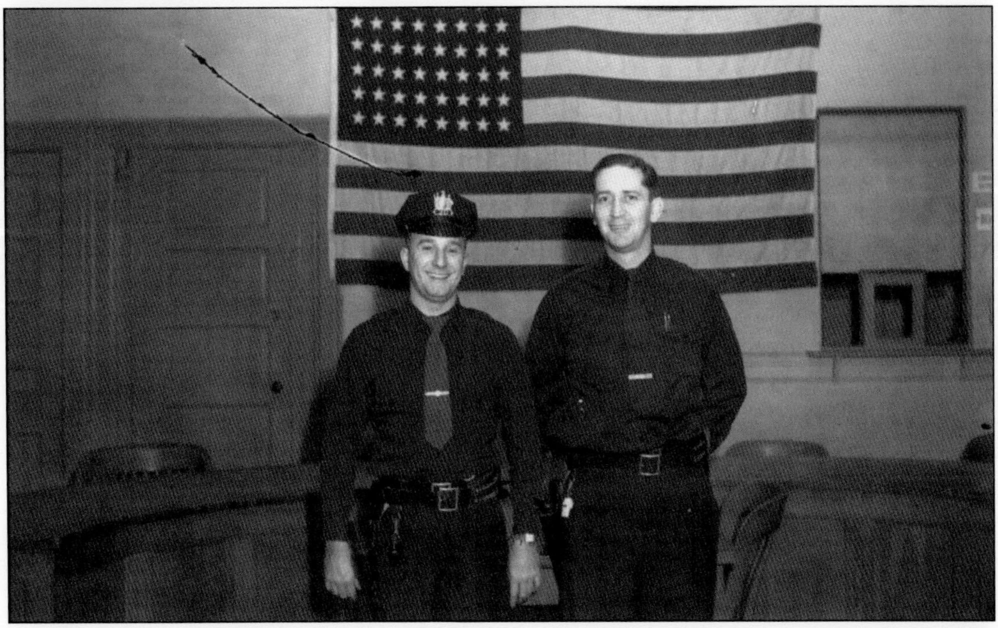

Patrolmen Alan Lustman and Robert Payton are pictured in the old borough hall in 1957. Lustman was appointed in 1955 and served as chief of police from 1985 to 1996. Patrolman Robert Payton was appointed in 1949 and served until 1984, when he retired as a captain. (Courtesy of Robert Payton.)

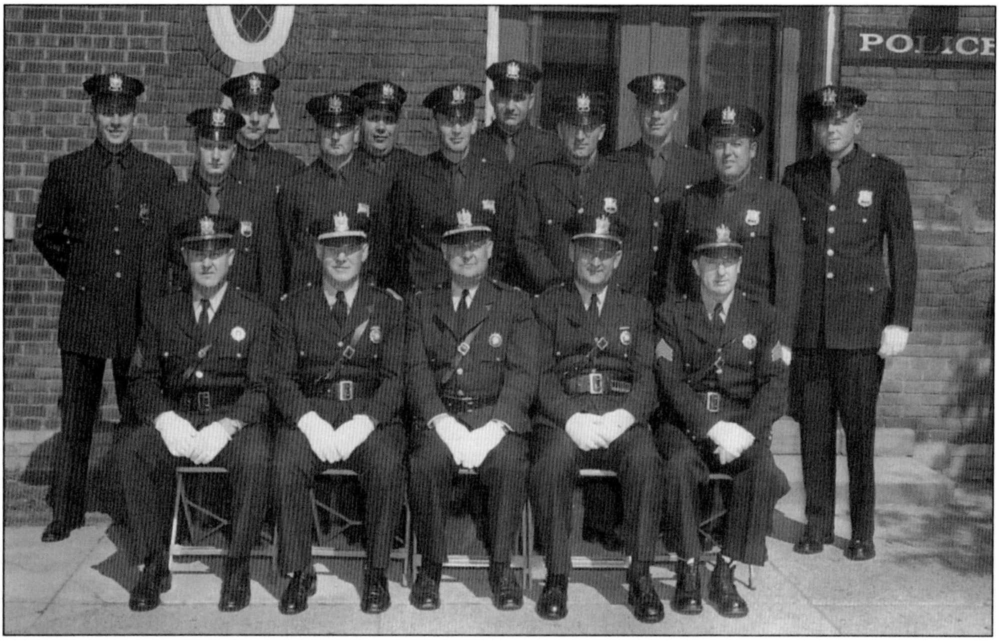

Seen in this May 31, 1958, photograph are, from left to right, (first row) Sgt. Martin Fay, Capt. Wallace Doremus, Chief Leonard Cottrell, Lt. Walter Lewandowski, and Sgt. John Moffatt; (second row) patrolmen Alan Lustman, Gerald Blessing, Robert Payton, Anthony Pollut, and Joseph Senft; (third row) patrolmen John Zenk, Ralph Grill, Daniel Germaine, Louis Bellocchio, Robert Moran, and William Jones. (Courtesy of Alan J. Lustman.)

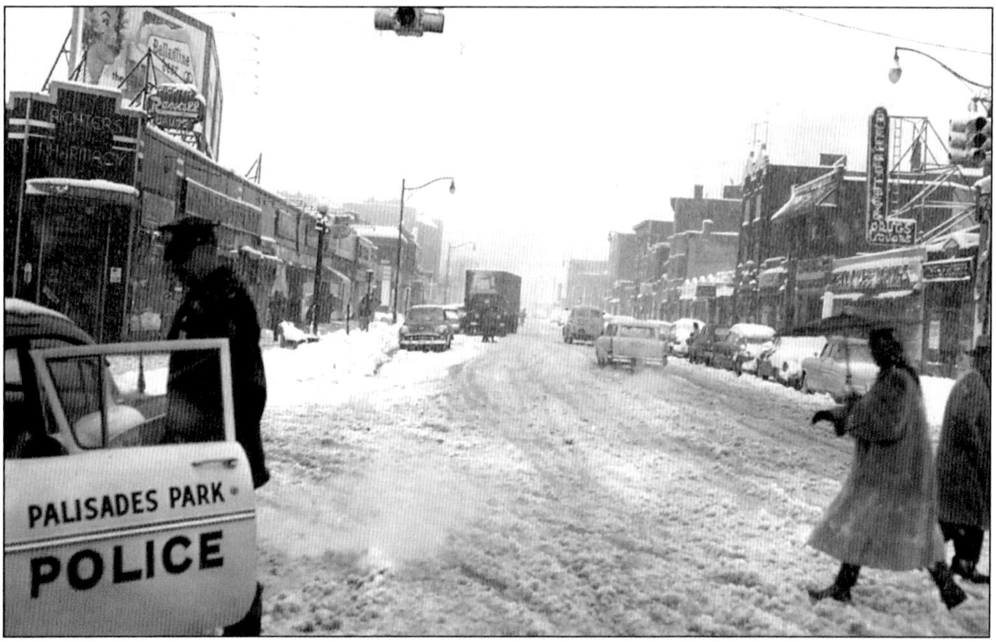

Patrolman Robert Moran is outside his vehicle at the snowy intersection of Broad Avenue and Central Boulevard in March 1958. Patrolman Moran and patrolman Joseph Senft were appointed to the police department on May 30, 1953. Both officers were graduates of the first class of the Bergen County Police Academy in 1955. (Courtesy of Florence Moran.)

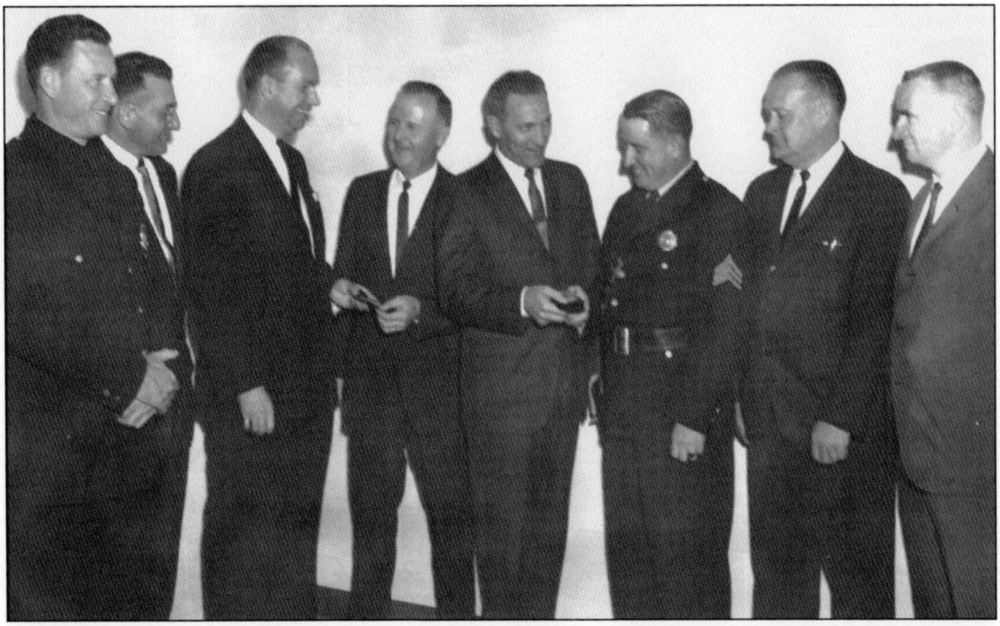

Promotional Night is pictured here on May 14, 1963. From left to right are John Zenk, Anthony Pollutt, chairman of the Police Committee Arthur Miller, Martin T. Fay, Mayor William J. Dorgan, John Moffatt, chief of police Leonard Cottrell, and Gerald Blessing. (Courtesy of Leonard R. Cottrell.)

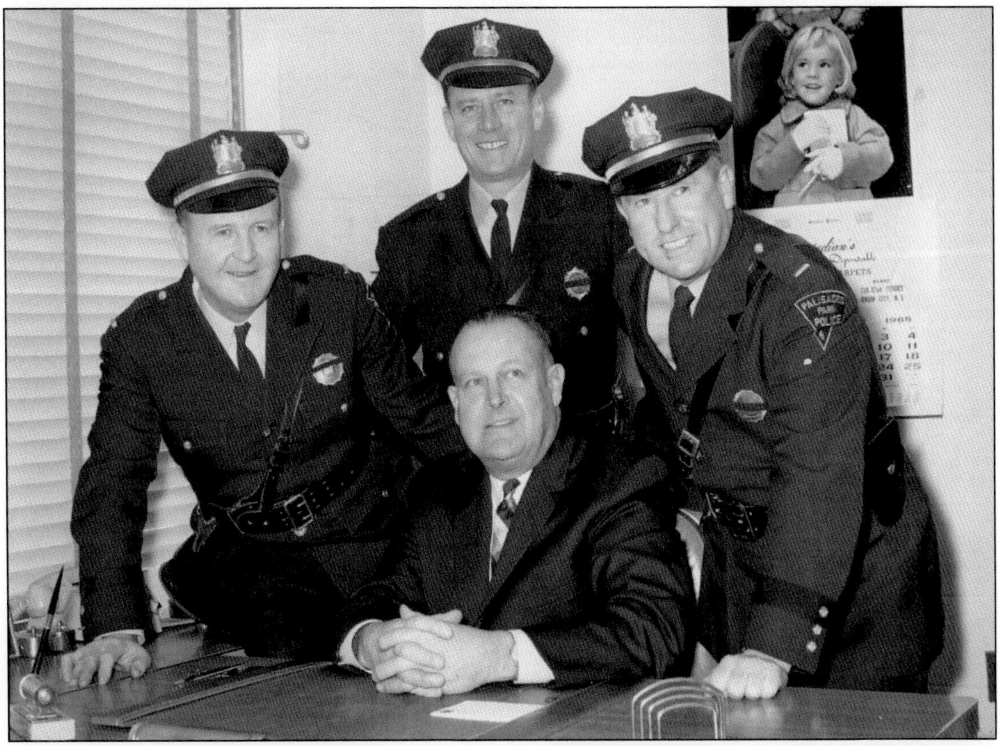

Pictured here in 1965 are Chief Leonard Cottrell (seated) with Lt. Martin Fay (left), Sgt. John Zenk (center) and Lt. John Moffatt (right). (Courtesy of Leonard R. Cottrell.)

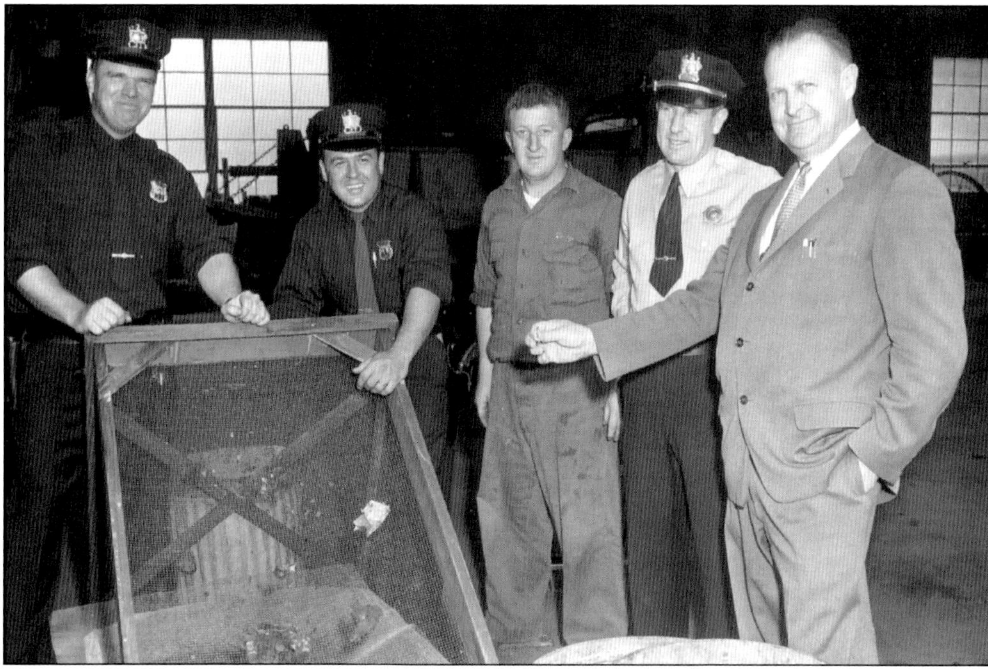

Chief Leonard Cottrell and his men along with members of the Department of Public Works located two diamond rings that were thrown accidentally into an apartment house incinerator. Mrs. Michael Hoffman, of Brooklyn, was pleased with the recovery efforts of her rings valued at $2,000. From left to right are patrolmen Robert Moran and Joseph Senft, superintendent of the Department of Public Works Anthony Casbar, Sgt. John Moffatt, and Chief Leonard Cottrell. (Courtesy of Florence Moran.)

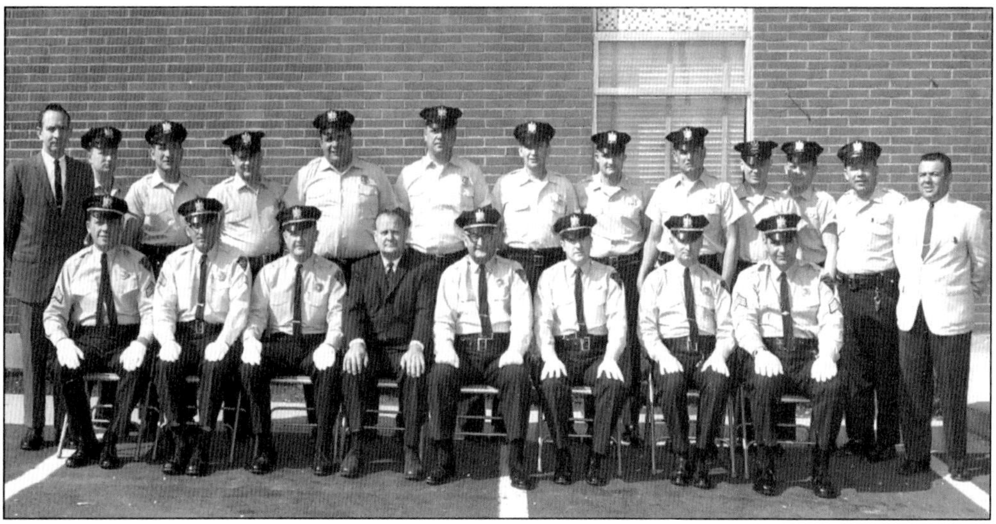

Memorial Day in 1965 is shown here. From left to right are (first row) Sgt. John Zenk, Sgt. Anthony Pollutt, Lt. Martin Fay, Chief Leonard Cottrell, Capt. Walter Lewandowski, Lt. John Moffatt, Capt. Gerald Blessing, and Sgt. Louis Bellocchio; (second row) patrolmen Ralph Grill, Alan Lustman, John Vanore, William Catona, Daniel Germaine, Robert Moran, Robert Payton, Ross English, Remo Framarin, Leonard R. Cottrell, Edward Shirley Sr., Frances Thorpe, and Joseph Senft. (Courtesy of Robert Payton.)

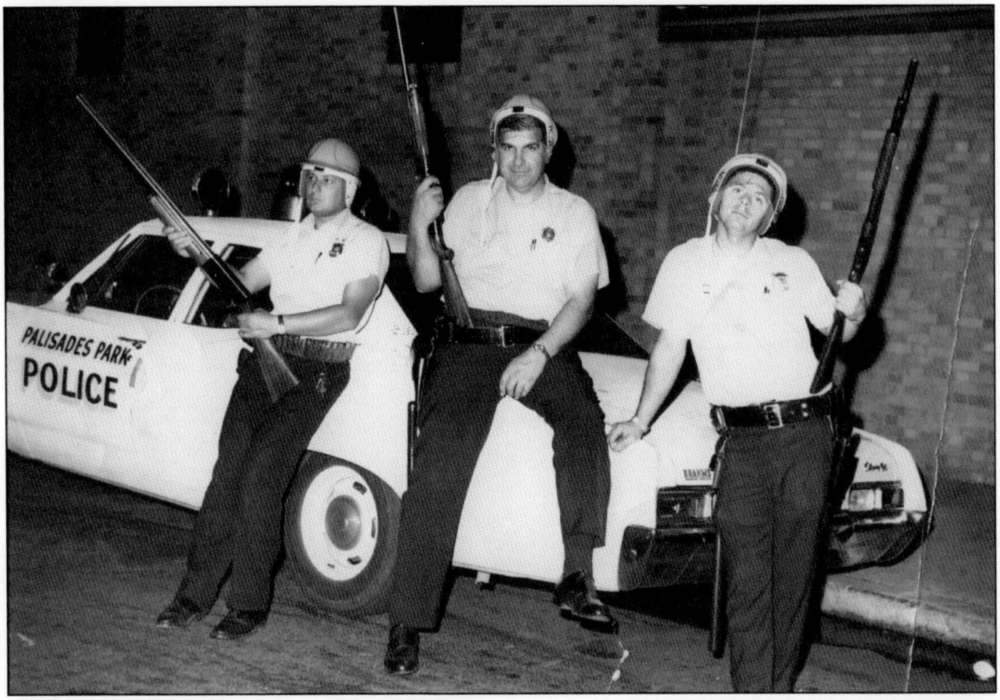

Police officers are dressed in riot gear in 1968. The men were deployed to the city of Englewood during a riot. From left to right are patrolman Remo Framarin, Sgt. Louis Bellocchio, and patrolman Michael Vietri. (Courtesy of Remo Framarin.)

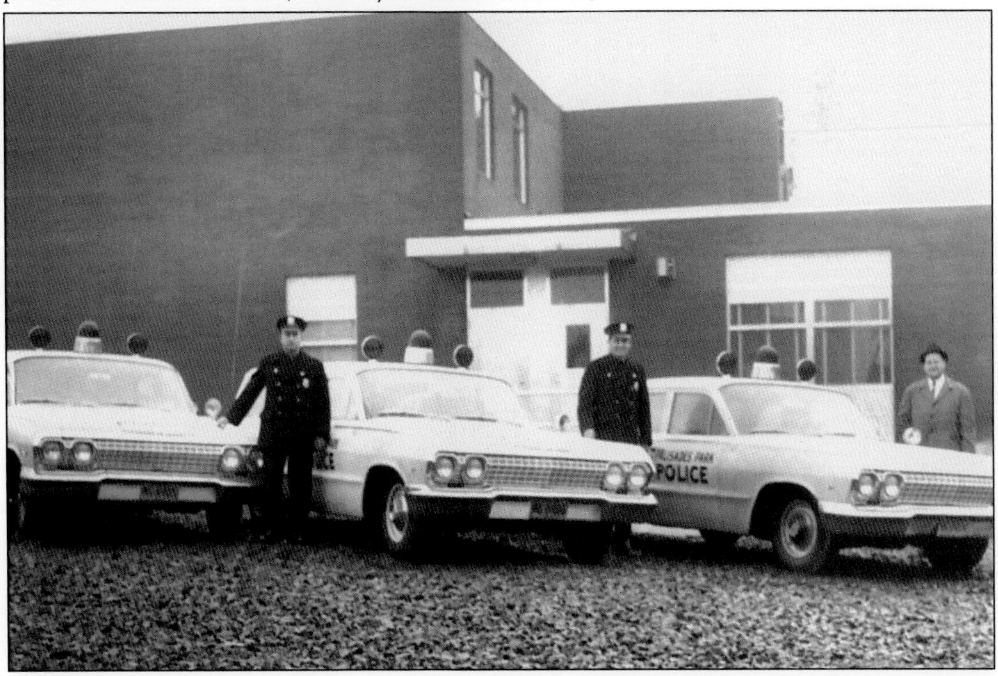

Patrolmen Alan Lustman (left) with patrolmen Remo Framarin (center) and Chief Leonard Cottrell are on the side of police headquarters with the patrol cars around 1965. (Courtesy of Leonard R. Cottrell.)

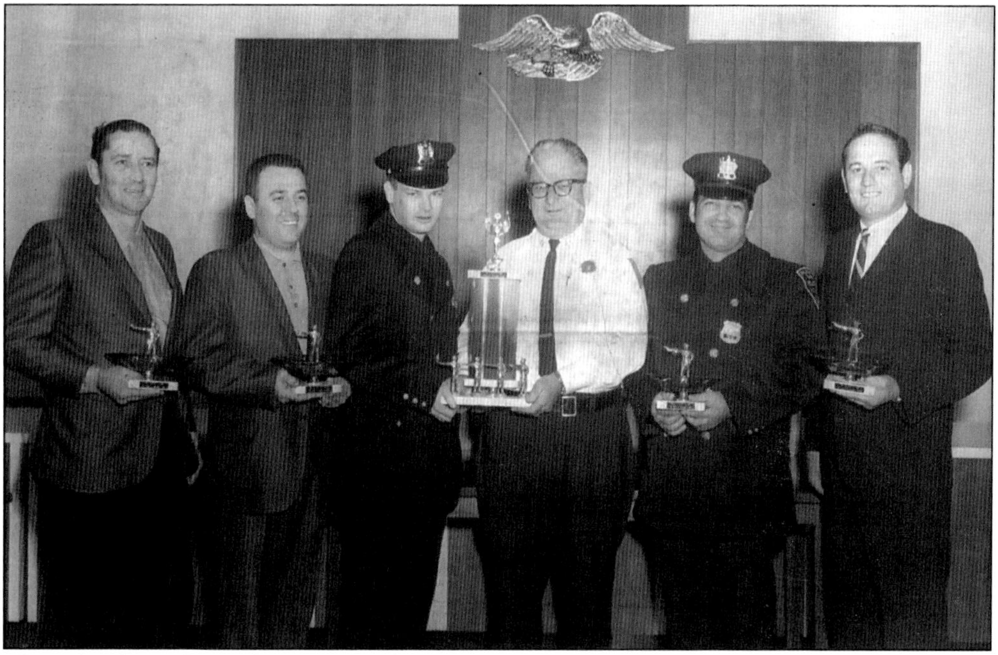

The Palisades Park Pistol Team proudly accepts their trophies on November 20, 1968. From left to right are detective Sgt. Robert Payton, detective Sgt. Joseph Senft, patrolman Leonard R. Cottrell, Capt. Walter Lewandowski, patrolman John Giannantonio, and detective Remo Framarin. (Courtesy of Robert Payton.)

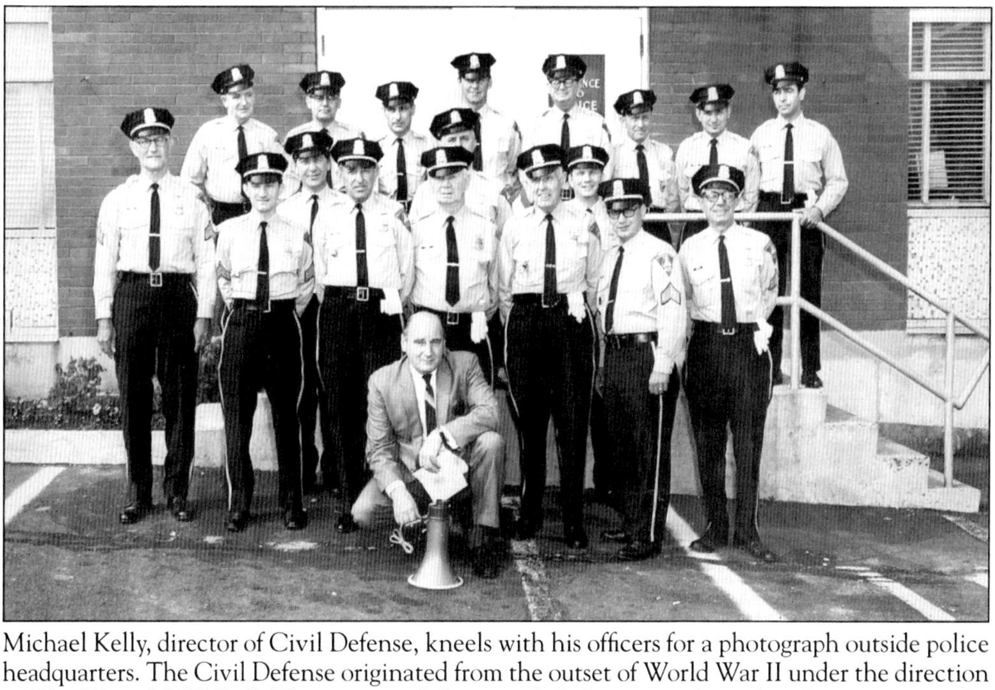

Michael Kelly, director of Civil Defense, kneels with his officers for a photograph outside police headquarters. The Civil Defense originated from the outset of World War II under the direction of Chief David J. W. Bell. Their responsibilities included assisting the police department in the event of an air attack, and they patrolled the streets with air raid wardens during tests and army alerts. (Courtesy of Remo Framarin.)

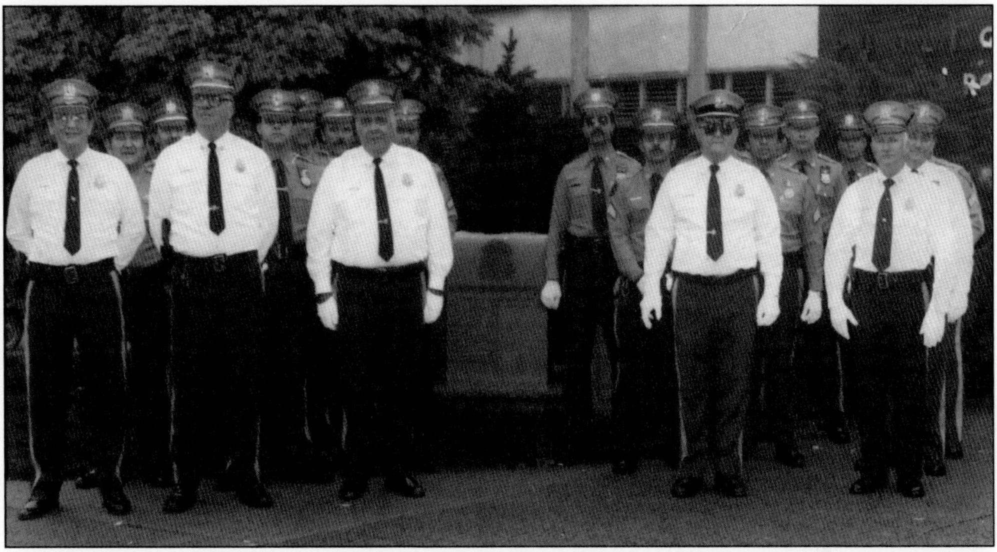

Police department members assemble outside the borough hall for Memorial Day in 1984. Seen here from left to right are (first row) Capt. Robert Payton, Capt. Robert Moran, Capt. Daniel Germaine, Chief Martin Fay, and Capt. Alan Lustman; (second row) Sgt. John Vanore, patrolman Steven Thompson, Sgt. Michael Paladino, Sgt. Henry Ruh, patrolman Charles Stark, Sgt. Frank Martini, patrolman Paul Romano, Sgt. Michael Vietri, Sgt. John Genovese, patrolman Fredrick Hanson, patrolman Scott Maresca, and Lt. Francis Thorpe. (Courtesy of Florence Moran.)

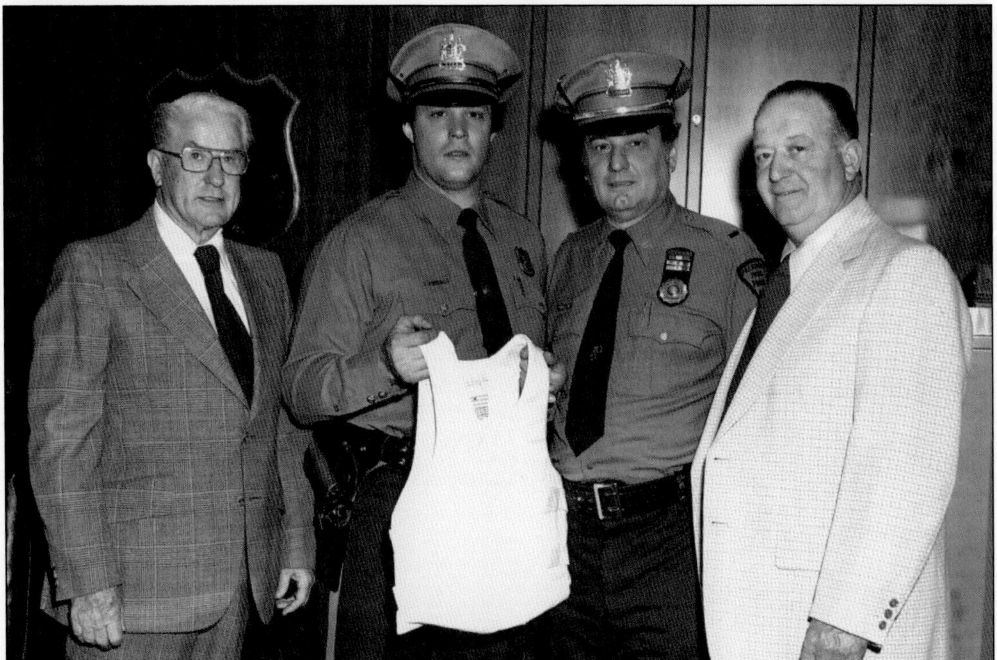

The first bullet-proof vests were issued to the police officers on May 5, 1980. From left to right are Chief John Moffatt, patrolman Richard Sopelsa, Lt. Remo Framarin, and Nicholas Martini, chairman of the Police Committee. (Courtesy of Remo Framarin.)

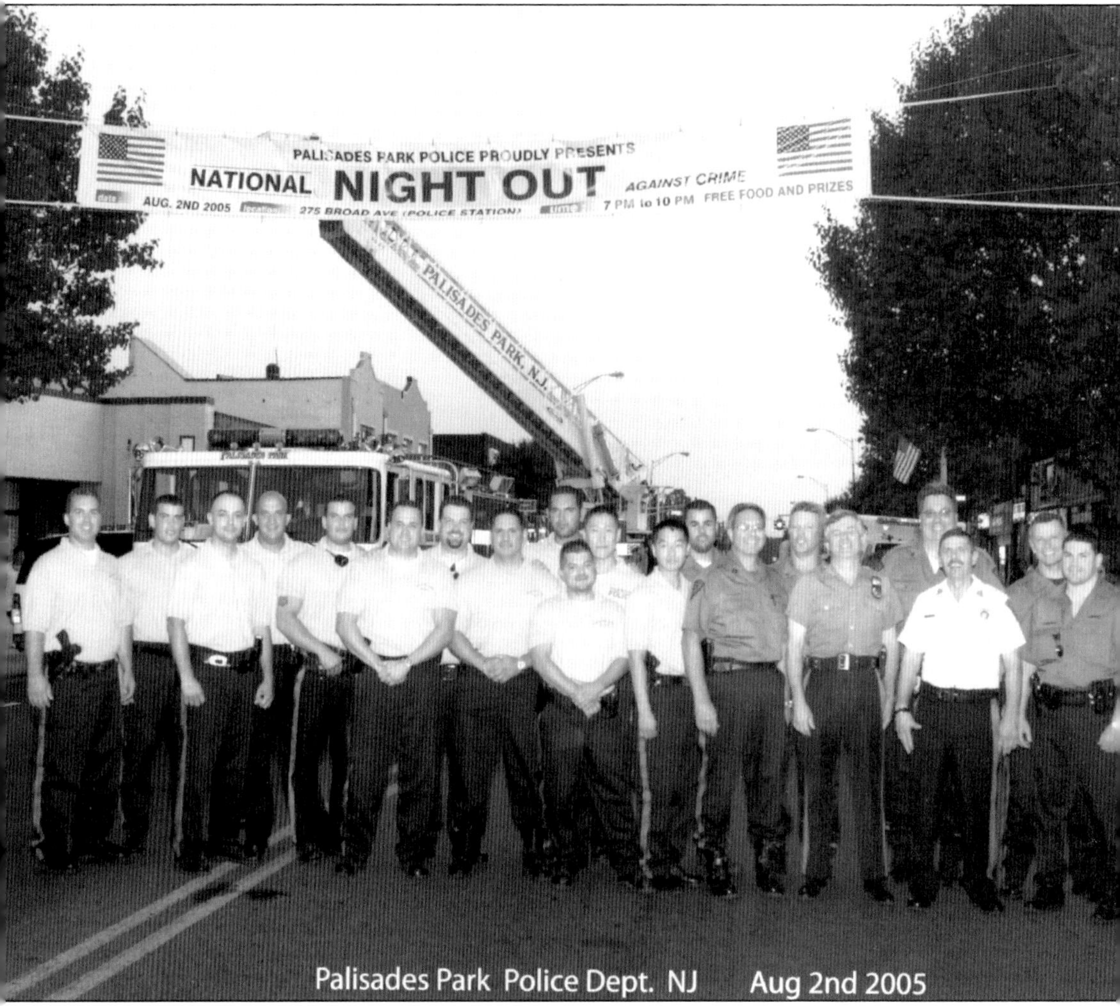

The second annual National Night Out, a police-community partnership program, was held on August 2, 2005. Standing, from left to right, are patrolmen Nicholas Giannantonio, George Beck Jr., Benjamin Ramos, Christopher Sambogna, Christopher Beck, Dennis Pavlik, Bruce Grasing, Anthony Espino, Michael DeBartolo, Mathew Aligo, Shawn Lee, Louis Lee, Marc Messing, Capt. Paul Romano, Sgt. Richard Sopelsa, Lt. Anthony Servis, Sgt. Anthony Muccio, Chief Michael Vietri, Sgt. Fredrick Hanson, and patrolman John Ferraioli.

Seven

Palisades Park's Bravest

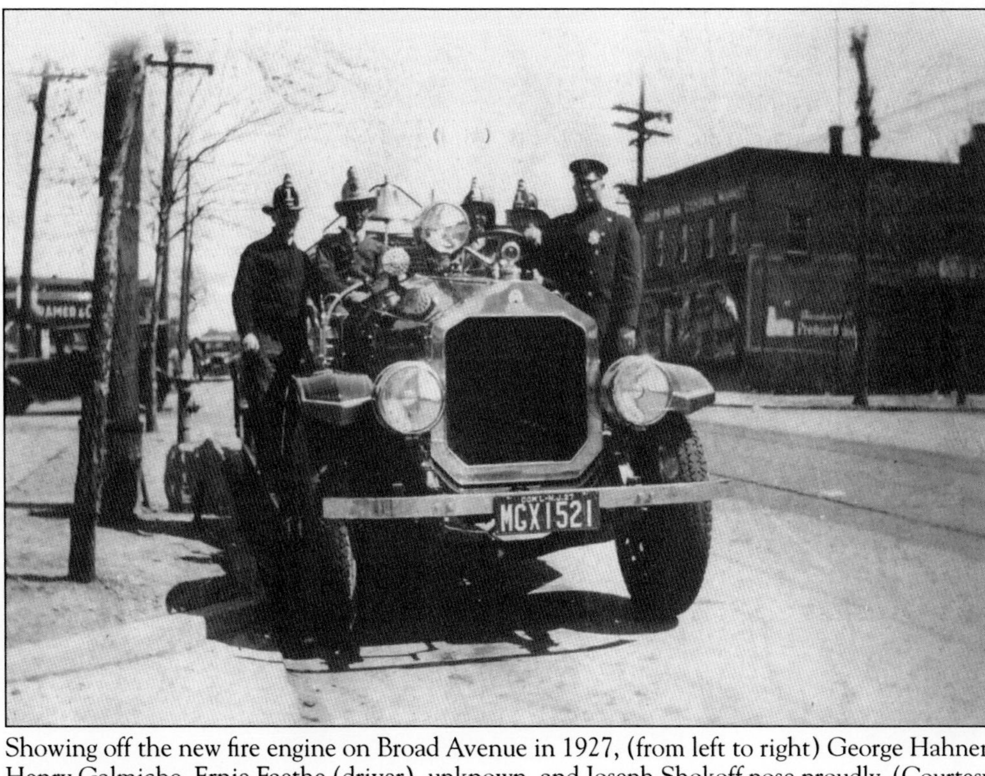

Showing off the new fire engine on Broad Avenue in 1927, (from left to right) George Hahner, Henry Galmiche, Ernie Faethe (driver), unknown, and Joseph Shokoff pose proudly. (Courtesy of Thomas J. Albanese.)

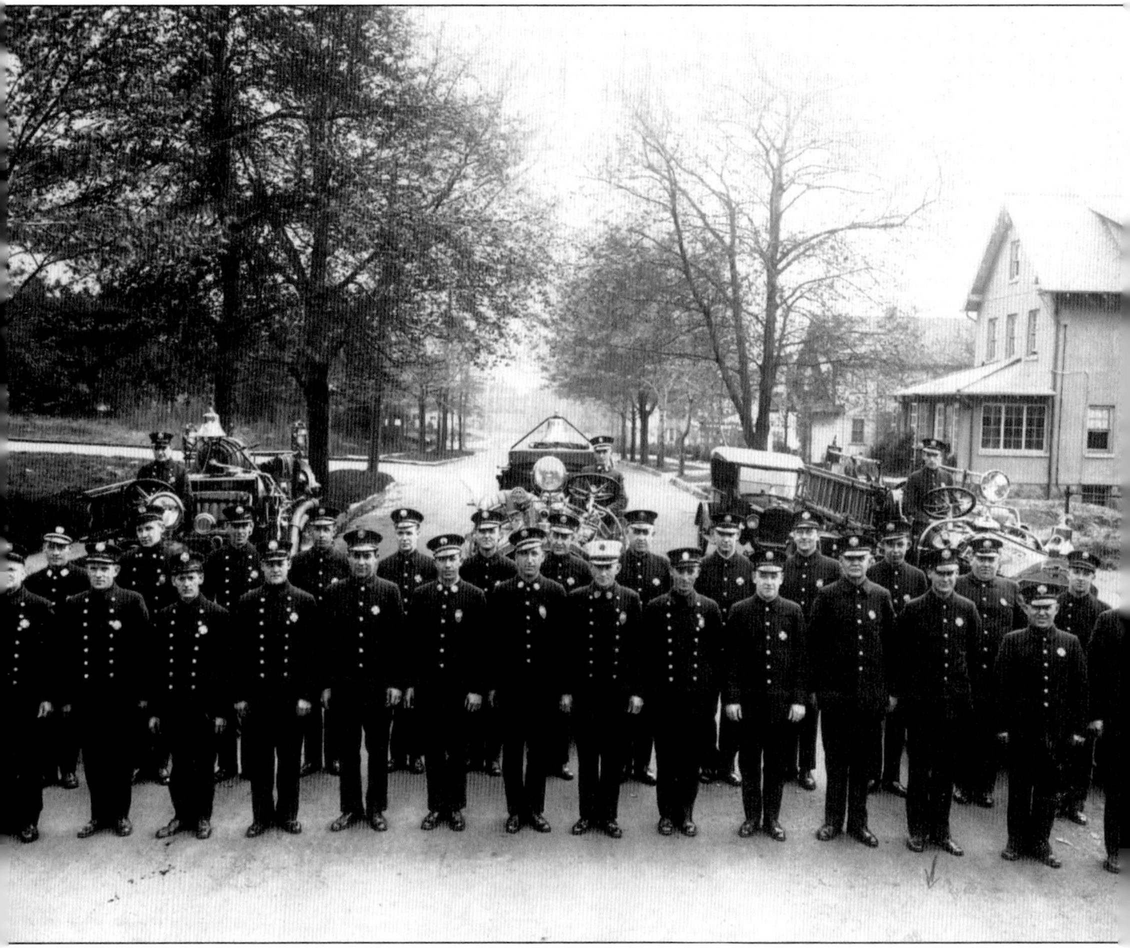

Members of the fire department gather in full dress uniform with their apparatus individually designed specifically for the fire service needs of each of the three fire companies. This photograph was taken on Highland Avenue near the Cleveland Place intersection. (Courtesy of Leonard R. Cottrell.)

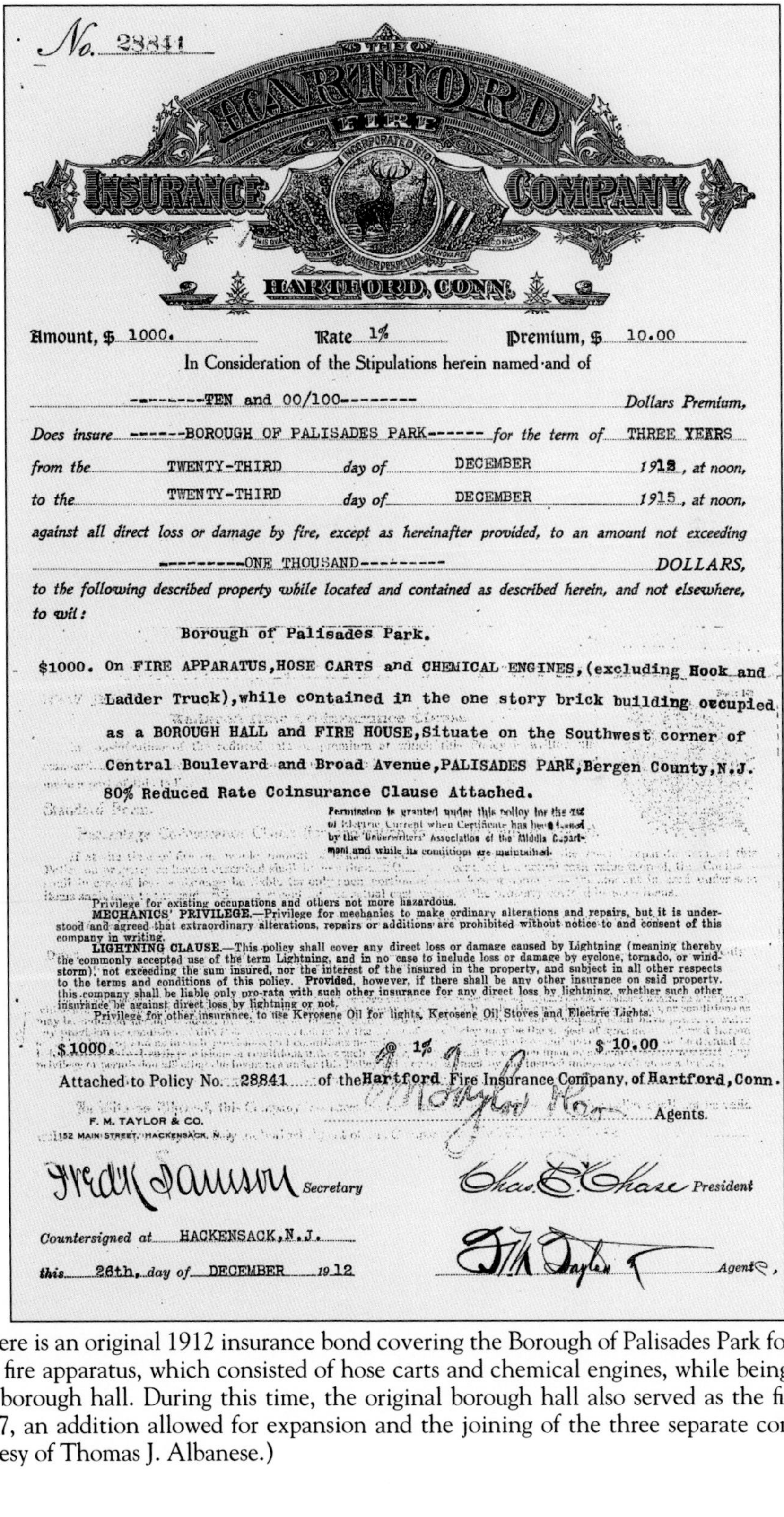

No. 28841

THE HARTFORD FIRE INSURANCE COMPANY

HARTFORD, CONN.

Amount, $ 1000. Rate 1% Premium, $ 10.00

In Consideration of the Stipulations herein named and of

--------TEN and 00/100-------- Dollars Premium,

Does insure ------BOROUGH OF PALISADES PARK------ for the term of THREE YEARS

from the TWENTY-THIRD day of DECEMBER 1912, at noon,

to the TWENTY-THIRD day of DECEMBER 1915, at noon,

against all direct loss or damage by fire, except as hereinafter provided, to an amount not exceeding

----------ONE THOUSAND---------- DOLLARS,

to the following described property while located and contained as described herein, and not elsewhere, to wit:

Borough of Palisades Park.

$1000. On FIRE APPARATUS, HOSE CARTS and CHEMICAL ENGINES, (excluding Hook and Ladder Truck), while contained in the one story brick building occupied as a BOROUGH HALL and FIRE HOUSE, Situate on the Southwest corner of Central Boulevard and Broad Avenue, PALISADES PARK, Bergen County, N.J.

80% Reduced Rate Coinsurance Clause Attached.

Permission is granted under this policy for the use of Electric Current when Certificate has been issued by the Underwriters' Association of the Middle Department and while its conditions are maintained.

Privilege for existing occupations and others not more hazardous.

MECHANICS' PRIVILEGE.—Privilege for mechanics to make ordinary alterations and repairs, but it is understood and agreed that extraordinary alterations, repairs or additions are prohibited without notice to and consent of this company in writing.

LIGHTNING CLAUSE.—This policy shall cover any direct loss or damage caused by Lightning (meaning thereby the commonly accepted use of the term Lightning, and in no case to include loss or damage by cyclone, tornado, or windstorm), not exceeding the sum insured, nor the interest of the insured in the property, and subject in all other respects to the terms and conditions of this policy. **Provided**, however, if there shall be any other insurance on said property, this company shall be liable only pro-rata with such other insurance for any direct loss by lightning, whether such other insurance be against direct loss by lightning or not.

Privilege for other insurance, to use Kerosene Oil for lights, Kerosene Oil Stoves and Electric Lights.

$1000. @ 1% $ 10.00

Attached to Policy No. 28841 of the Hartford Fire Insurance Company, of Hartford, Conn.

F. M. TAYLOR & CO.
152 MAIN STREET, HACKENSACK, N.J. Agents.

Secretary President

Countersigned at HACKENSACK, N.J.

this 26th day of DECEMBER 1912 Agents.

Seen here is an original 1912 insurance bond covering the Borough of Palisades Park for $1,000 for the fire apparatus, which consisted of hose carts and chemical engines, while being housed in the borough hall. During this time, the original borough hall also served as the firehouse. In 1927, an addition allowed for expansion and the joining of the three separate companies. (Courtesy of Thomas J. Albanese.)

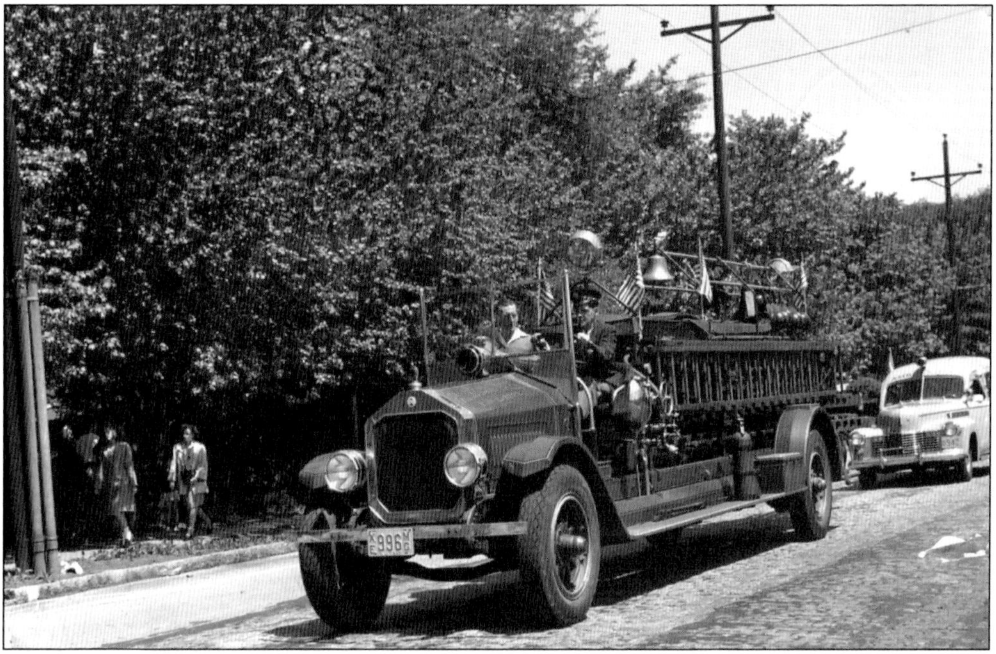

The hook and ladder truck is driving along Broad Avenue around 1942. In 1949, this ladder truck was replaced with a 100-foot aerial hook and ladder truck. The department also had two 1,000-gallon pumpers and a chief's car. (Courtesy of Thomas J. Albanese.)

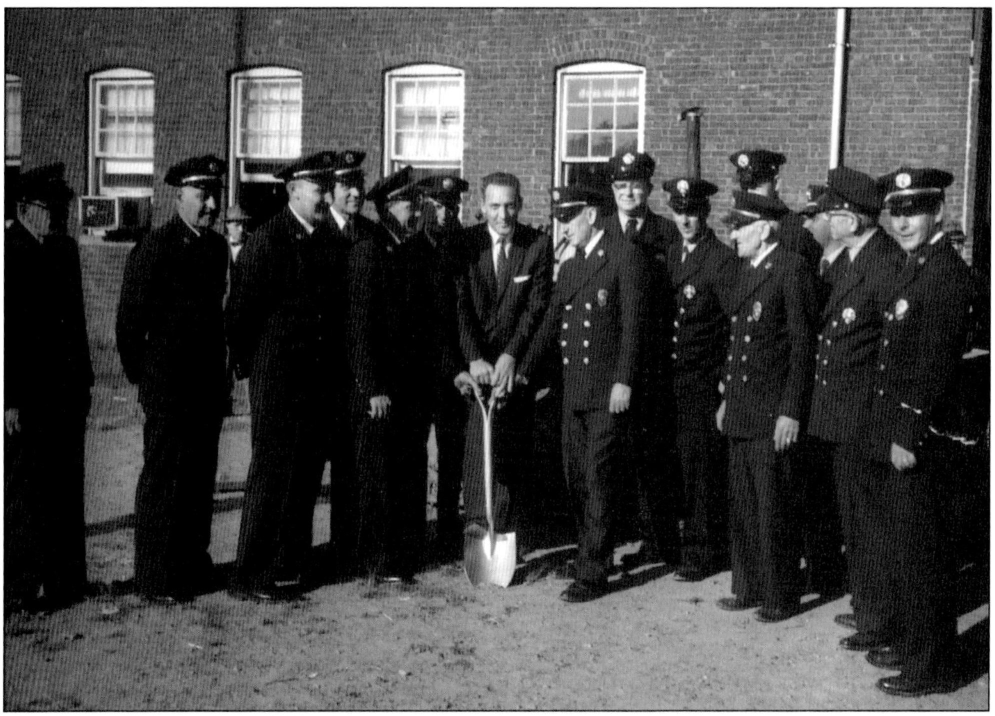

A groundbreaking ceremony was held on October 29, 1961. Mayor William J. Dorgan (center) is joined by the Palisades Park Volunteer Fire Department to celebrate the groundbreaking ceremony for the new borough hall. (Courtesy of Thomas J. Albanese.)

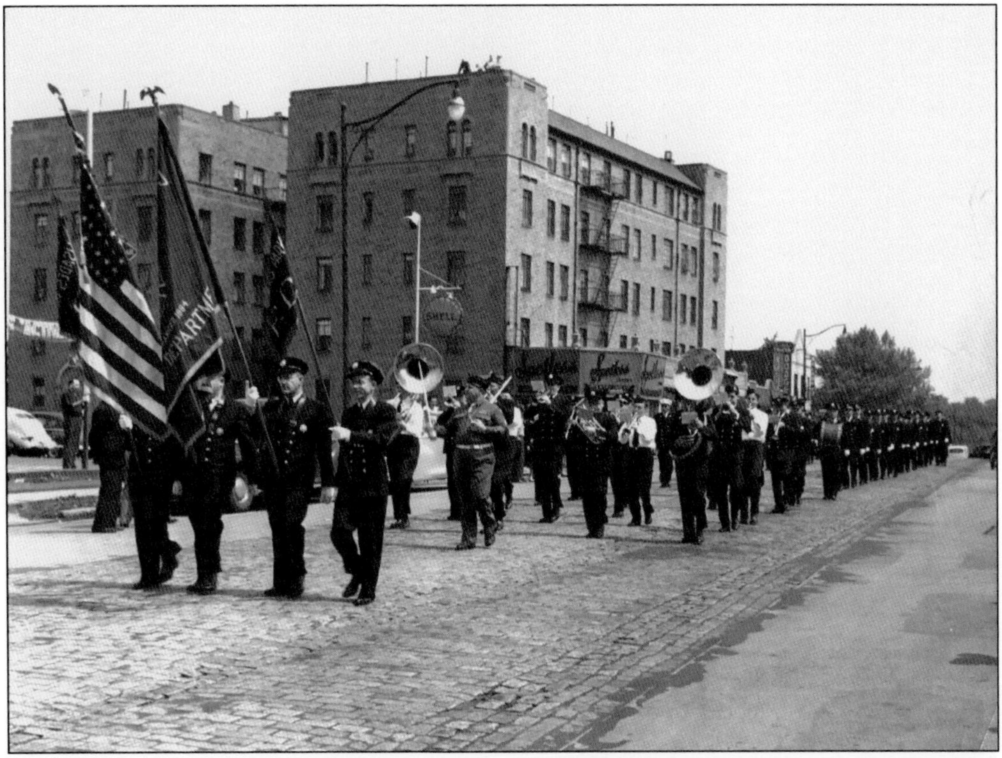

Above, firefighters and the fire department band march along Broad Avenue during the 1950 Memorial Day parade. Below, members of the fire department band pose for a photograph outside the firehouse. This band was founded in 1950 and has grown from an organization consisting of only firefighters to now including talented adult, college, and high school northern New Jersey musicians. The band has also become a highly esteemed regional concert and marching band. (Above, courtesy of George J. Farrell.)

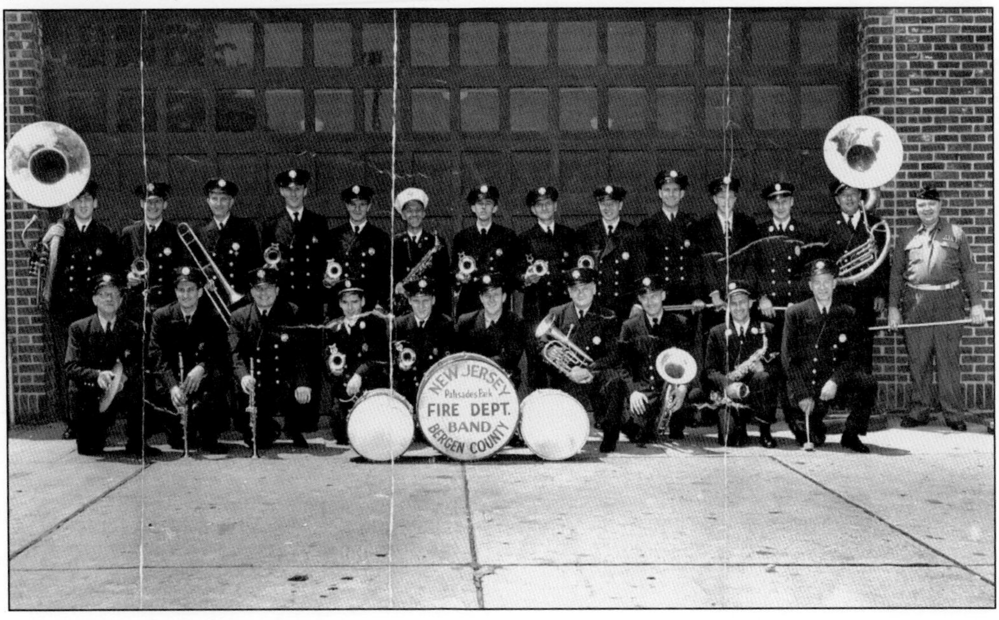

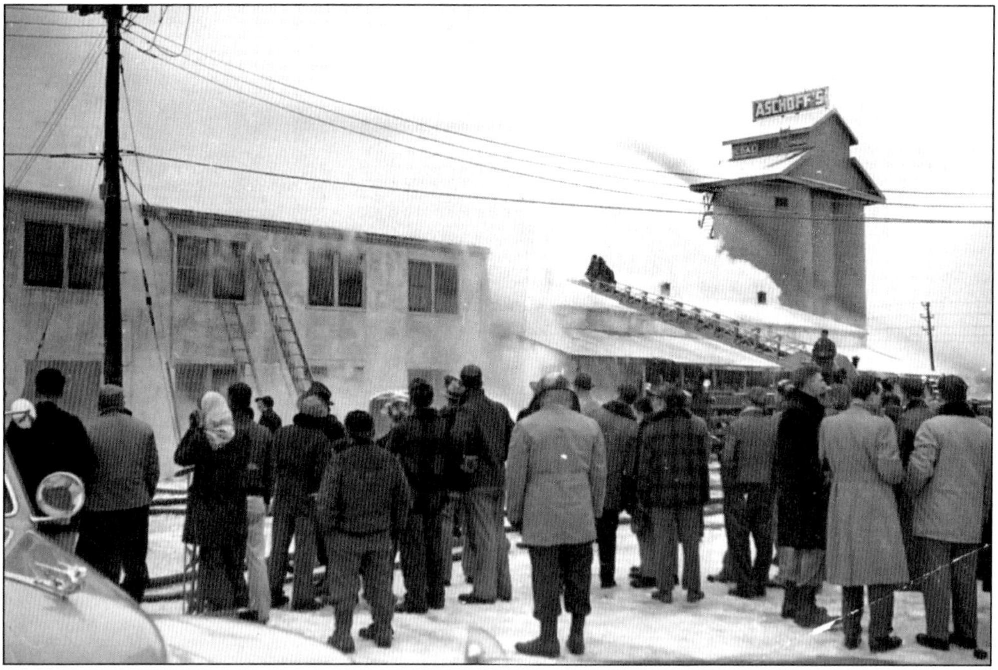

Above, members of the Palisades Park Fire Department bravely fight a fire at the Aschoff's Coal Factory located along the Erie Railway. Below, the Palisades Park Lumber Yard fire occurred on October 30, 1965. This fire was alleged to have been started by young boys playing with matches. It was so large, with tall flames and shifting winds, that it spread to neighboring homes. Over 300 firefighters and 25 fire trucks fought the blaze. During the fire, two trucks were lost, a 1950 pumper and a 1949 aerial truck. Firefighter Harold Farrar was bravely fighting the fire from the top of the ladder when he was alerted that the truck was on fire. Fortunately, he escaped without harm. Monetary damages exceeded $400,000. (Above, courtesy of George J. Farrell; below, courtesy of Arthur Anderson.)

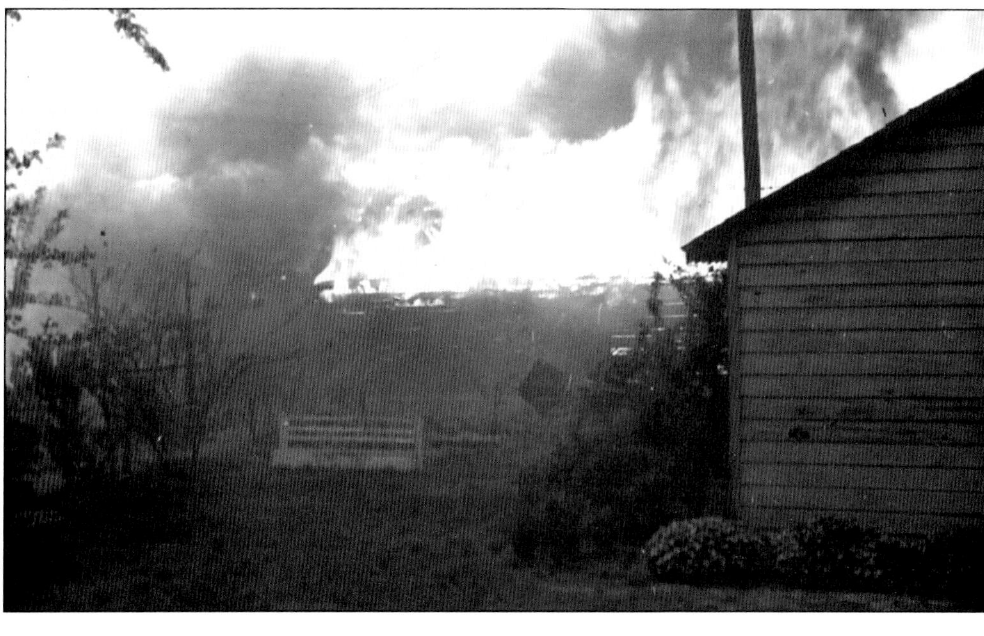

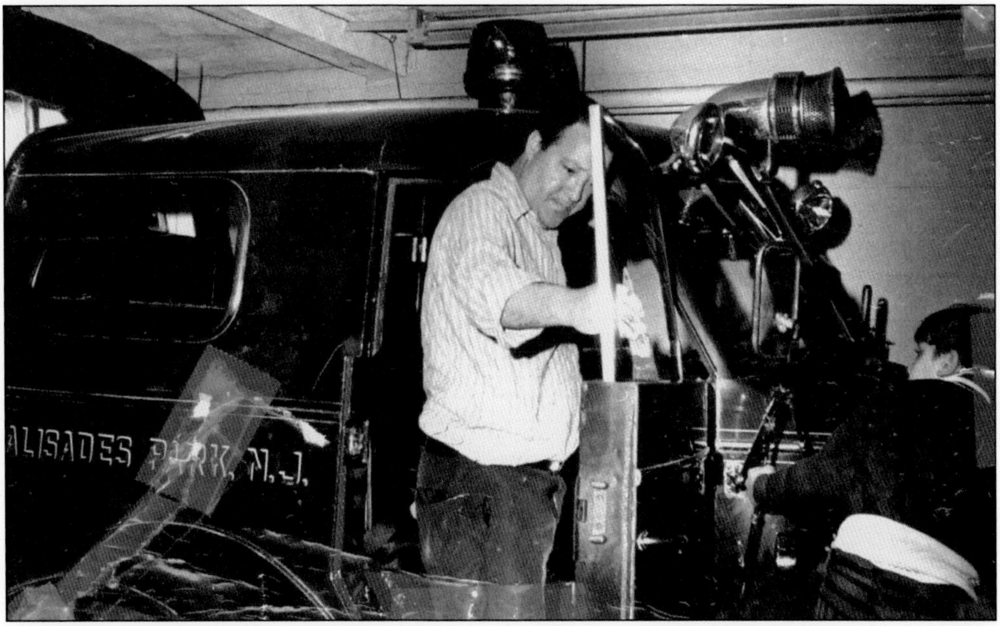

Firefighter Gerald Beck is painting the window frames of the 1954 American La France fire truck in 1972. This fire truck was the original squad truck. While fighting a heavy fire in 1973 at the Hunters Inn, firefighter Gerald Beck heroically rescued brave firefighter Louis Cannizzaro as the ceiling was collapsing on him. Both men escaped without injury. (Courtesy of Greggory K. Beck.)

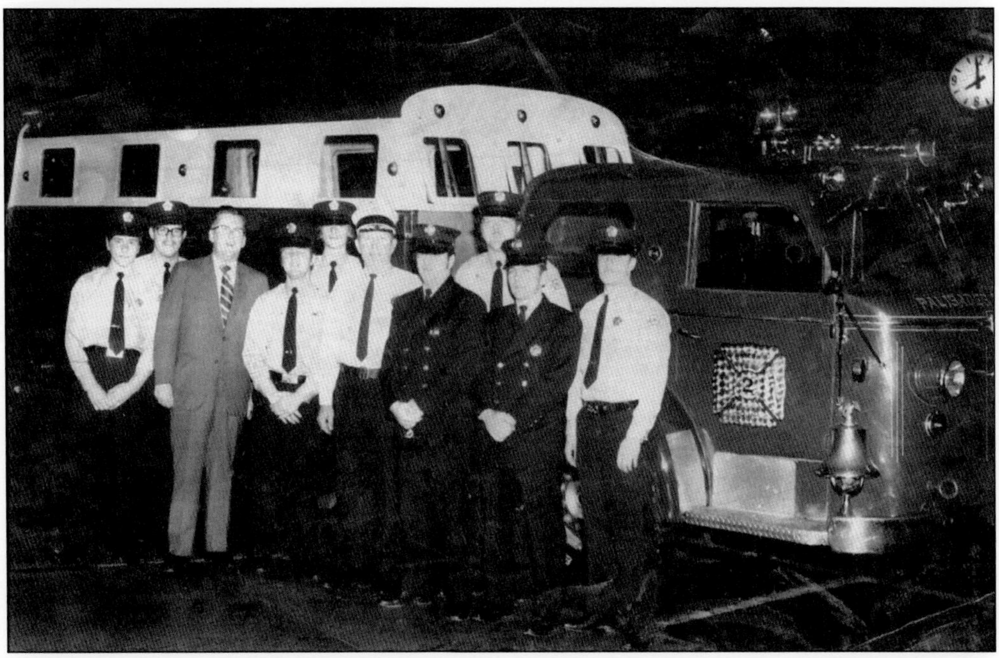

The Junior Firefighter's Association is shown here in 1973. From left to right are Jeffrey Spagnolo, George Ochsie, councilman Robert Monaghan, Richard Kappler, Guy Moore, Chief Henry Kappler, firefighter Thomas Lorentz, Paul Mistarka, firefighter Edward Lange, and George Beck. (Courtesy of George M. Beck Sr.)

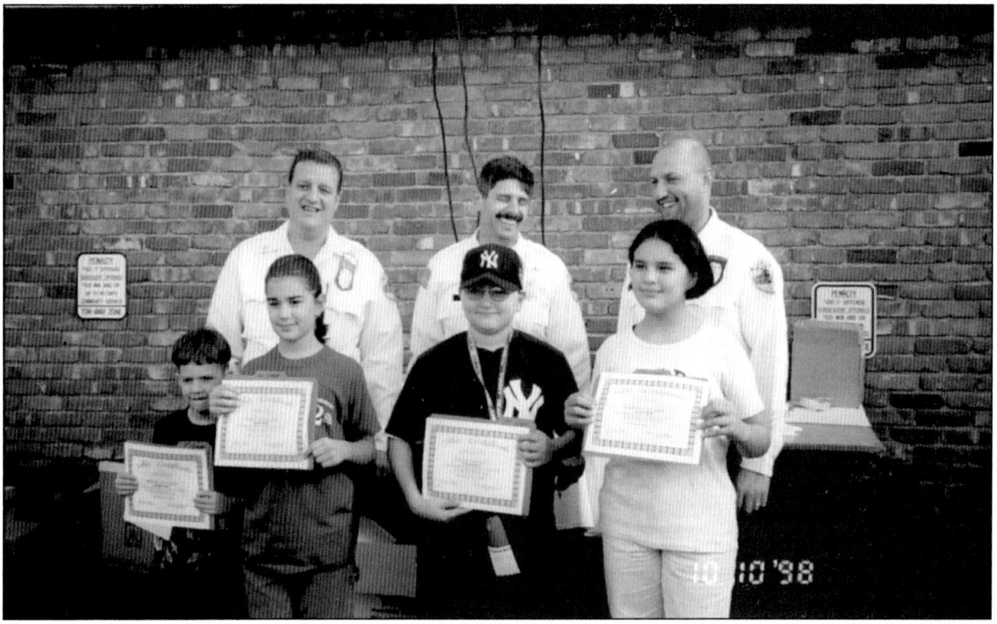

The first annual Fireman's Day was held on October 10, 1998. Chief George Beck (left), Deputy Chief Michael Vietri (center), and Battalion Chief Andrew Chiurazzi (right) present awards to children. Members of the fire department gather annually for Fireman's Day, a community outreach program designed to teach residents and their families about fire safety and to promote awareness. (Courtesy of Steven Killion.)

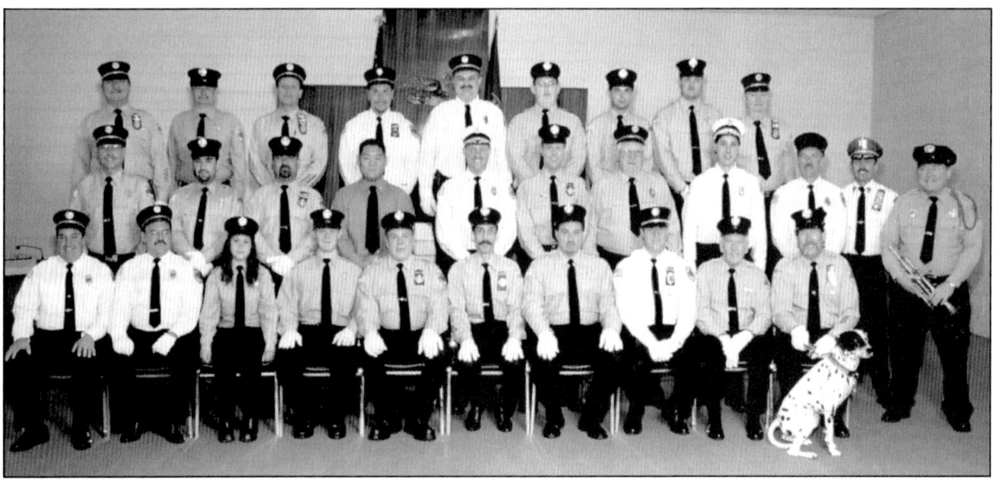

Chief Andrew Chiurazzi (center) and his men are in the borough hall after the Memorial Day parade in 2004. Seen here from left to right are (first row) Capt. Steven Killion; Capt. Ross Bruno; firefighters Sara Midgley, William Raimondo, Carmelo Raimondo, Jose Castro, and Raymond Laux; Lt. Joseph Kurz; and firefighters Christopher Byrnes and Michael Duffy with Peety; (second row) firefighters Donald Spohn, Charles Ost, David Colon, and Michael Chang; Chief Andrew Chiurazzi; firefighters Kevin Thomas and John Prisendorf; Battalion Chief Michael Valente; Capt. James Roper; and firefighters Michael Vietri and William Lockwood; (third row) firefighters Louis Cannizarro, Steven Guardino, and George Beck Sr.; Lt. Jeffery Boyce; Lt. John Mantone; and firefighters Luke Midgley, Frank Lofaro, John Morin, and Thomas Cusker. (Courtesy of Joseph Kurz.)

Eight

The Ambulance Corps

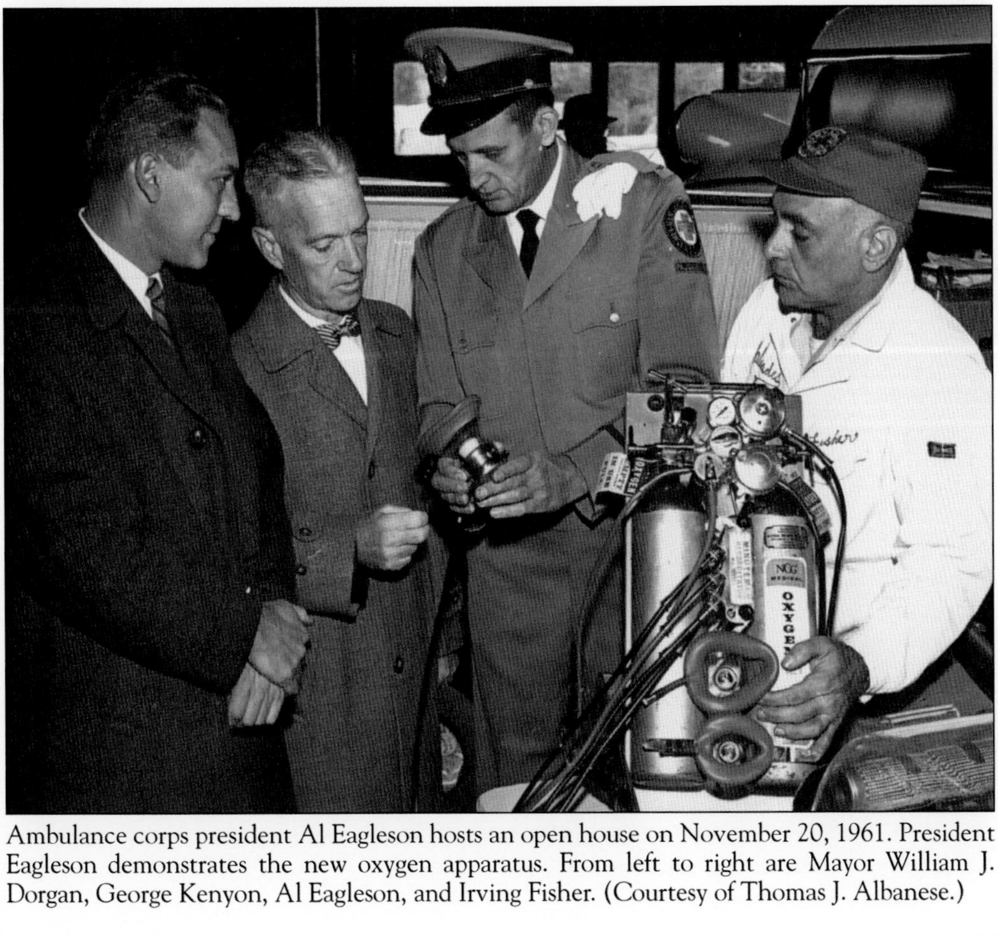

Ambulance corps president Al Eagleson hosts an open house on November 20, 1961. President Eagleson demonstrates the new oxygen apparatus. From left to right are Mayor William J. Dorgan, George Kenyon, Al Eagleson, and Irving Fisher. (Courtesy of Thomas J. Albanese.)

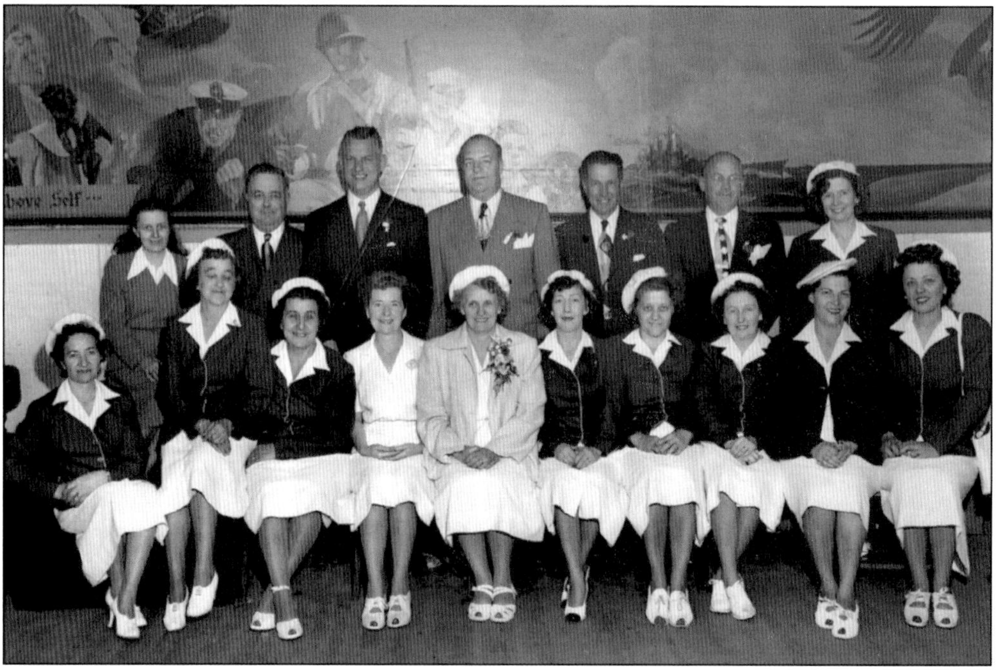

The Palisades Park Volunteer Ambulance Corp of the 1940s is shown here. These volunteers proudly served the emergency medical needs of the community. (Courtesy of Evelyn P. Meier.)

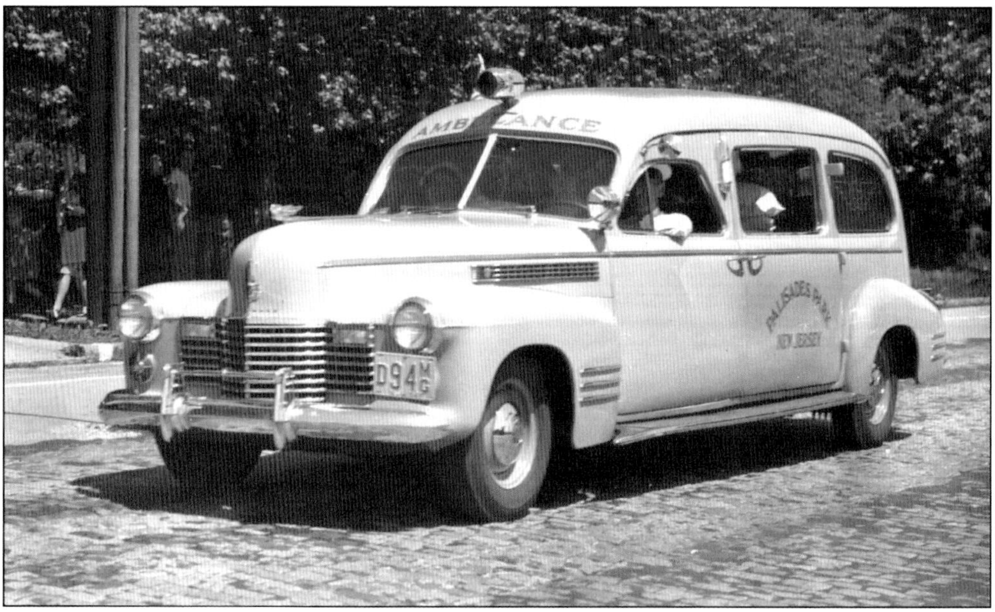

Members of the ambulance corps are driving their ambulance along Broad Avenue around 1942. It was in December 1940 when this ambulance and its attendants Harold Taylor and Verner Cottrell received their first serious call. The call came in through word of mouth, since at that time no ambulance system siren existed. They responded to East Brinkerhoff Avenue at Seventh Street, where 14-year-old Peter Casbar had a sledding accident, running into an exhaust pipe on a parked car. Harold Taylor and Verner Cottrell rushed the boy to Englewood Hospital, where he recovered. (Courtesy of George J. Farrell.)

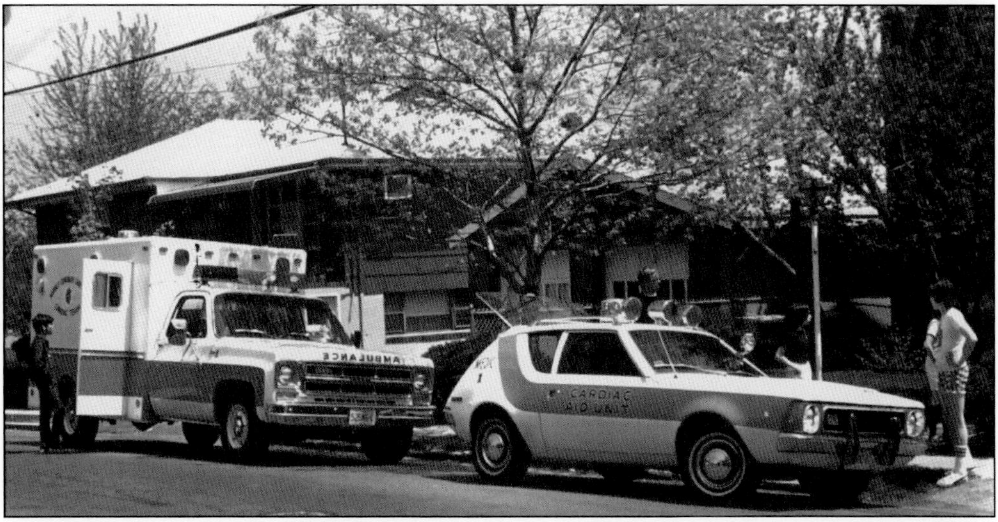

To accommodate the rise and seriousness of heart attacks, Palisades Park Ambulance Corps president Robert Stanton and Capt. Michael Evans formed the Cardiac Care Unit, which consisted of the pictured 1976 Gremlin automobile. The Medic 1 Gremlin was purchased with funds donated by the residents of Palisades Park. It provided a quick first response, while secondary apparatus responded a few short minutes after. In addition to other duties and training, cardiac team members received 200 hours of instruction each year. (Courtesy of Thomas J. Albanese.)

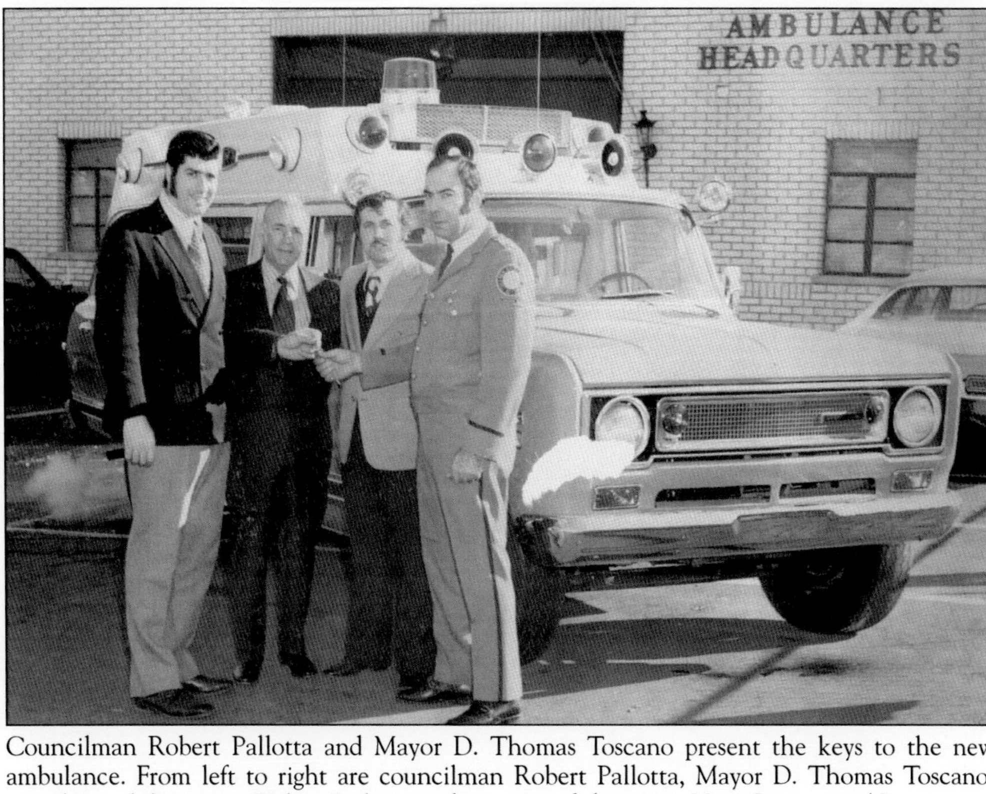

Councilman Robert Pallotta and Mayor D. Thomas Toscano present the keys to the new ambulance. From left to right are councilman Robert Pallotta, Mayor D. Thomas Toscano, president of the corps Walter Parkyn, and captain of the corps Vito Giannani. (Courtesy of Robert Pallotta.)

ACROSS AMERICA, PEOPLE ARE DISCOVERING SOMETHING WONDERFUL. *THEIR HERITAGE.*

Arcadia Publishing is the leading local history publisher in the United States. With more than 3,000 titles in print and hundreds of new titles released every year, Arcadia has extensive specialized experience chronicling the history of communities and celebrating America's hidden stories, bringing to life the people, places, and events from the past. To discover the history of other communities across the nation, please visit:

www.arcadiapublishing.com

Customized search tools allow you to find regional history books about the town where you grew up, the cities where your friends and family live, the town where your parents met, or even that retirement spot you've been dreaming about.

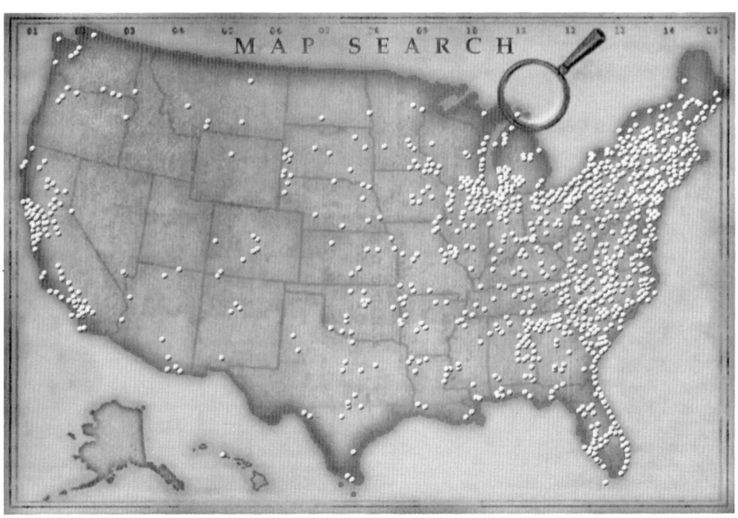